Women at the Top

Women at the Top

Challenges, Choices and Change

Marianne Coleman

First published 2011 by
PALGRAVE MACMILLAN

Palgrave Macmillan in the UK is an imprint of Macmillan Publishers Limited, registered in England, company number 785998, of Houndmills, Basingstoke, Hampshire RG21 6XS.

Palgrave Macmillan in the US is a division of St Martin's Press LLC, 175 Fifth Avenue, New York, NY 10010.

Palgrave Macmillan is the global academic imprint of the above companies and has companies and representatives throughout the world.

Palgrave® and Macmillan® are registered trademarks in the United States, the United Kingdom, Europe and other countries.

ISBN: 978–0–230–25220–2 hardback

This book is printed on paper suitable for recycling and made from fully managed and sustained forest sources. Logging, pulping and manufacturing processes are expected to conform to the environmental regulations of the country of origin.

A catalogue record for this book is available from the British Library.

Library of Congress Cataloging-in-Publication Data

Coleman, Marianne.
    Women at the top : challenges, choices and change / by Marianne Coleman.
        p. cm.
        Includes index.
        ISBN 978–0–230–25220–2 (alk. paper)
        1. Women executives. 2. Leadership in women. 3. Success in business. 4. Work and family. I. Title.

HD6054.3.C646 2011
658.40082—dc22   2011006606

10 9 8 7 6 5 4 3 2 1
20 19 18 17 16 15 14 13 12 11

Printed and bound in Great Britain by
CPI Antony Rowe, Chippenham and Eastbourne

Contents

Acknowledgements   vi

1   The Context: Women Leading at Work   1
2   The Challenges   18
3   Success Factors   45
4   Meeting the Challenges through Networking   68
5   Women and Choices   92
6   Individual Voices on Challenges, Choices and Change   115
7   Change for Women at Work   147

References   176
Annotated Bibliography: Women Senior Leaders at Work   185
Index   219

Acknowledgements

This book contains the voices of women who were generous enough to allow me to interview them and to whom I am more than grateful. Among these women are: Tess Alps, Fiona Anderson, Barbara Bagilhole, Kate Barker, Lynn Barlow, Penny Berry, Helen Boaden, Ruth Cairnie, Helen Calcraft, Diana Chambers, Lorri Currie, Elaine Dixon, Elizabeth de Bergh Sidley, Marisa Drew, Caroline Elliot, Elisabeth Fagan, Helen Fernandes, Clara Freeman, Sally Freestone, Rosalind Gilmore, Kate Grussing, Tiffany Hall, Pat Hanage, Judith Hanratty, Noel Harwerth, Jill Hill, Nicki Hill, Liz Jones, Christine King, Brenda Klug, Kimberley Littlemore, Susan Lynch, Liz Macann, Elizabeth Marx, Carolyn McCall, Barbara McGuiness, Scarlett McNally, Mei Sim Lei, Anne Minto, Gillian Mobb, Carol Peace, Ruth Peacock, Judith Pilkington, Ros Rees, Jan Renou, Emma Robins, Muriel Robinson, Cilla Snowball, Stevie Spring, Elaine Thomas, Herta von Stiegel, Siobahn Wheston, Marti Wikstrom, and others who preferred not to be named.

I also owe a particular debt of gratitude to Ken New, Kay Ellen Consolver, Clare Wynn-Mackenzie, Kate Grussing and Carol Peace who helped me access many of those I interviewed.

The research on which the book is based was funded by WLE (Work-based Learning for Education Professionals), a Centre for Excellence in Teaching and Learning at the Institute of Education, University of London, and I am grateful to Caroline Daly, Karen Evans, Norbert Pachler and Manos Agianniotakis for their support.

I am deeply grateful to Ann Briggs and Eileen Carnell, good friends who were kind enough to read and comment on a first draft of this book, and to friends and family who have always supported and encouraged me.

1
The Context: Women Leading at Work

> The glass ceiling that women encounter refers to a subtle and almost invisible but strong barrier that prevents women from moving up to senior management.
>
> (Burke, 2005, p. 13)

This book contains the authentic voices of 60 women concerning the career challenges they have faced and how they have overcome them. It is set in the context of change for women and the first chapter sets the scene for the views of these 60 successful women, the challenges they have faced, the choices they have made particularly with regard to having children, and the changes they have seen and expect to see.

Introduction

Women's participation in paid work is a subject of interest to feminists, historians, sociologists, politicians, demographers and economists. It is a topic that is at the heart of many of the changes that took place in the latter half of the twentieth century and continue to affect us all in the twenty-first. The past hundred years have brought enormous changes for women at work in the UK and the rest of the Western world. One of the biggest changes has been the gradual encroachment of women on the previously almost exclusive male world of leadership and management. However, a decade into the twenty-first century, women still face particular challenges if they wish to be leaders at work. First, the image of a leader or manager remains resolutely male (Schein, 2001, 2007; Embry et al., 2008) and, despite equal opportunities legislation in the UK and elsewhere, this image influences those who are responsible for making appointments to senior roles. The persistence of the image is a barrier to women who aspire to seniority at work since women generally are not expected to be leaders. The second major challenge for women who aspire to a senior role at work is likely to be the decision whether or not to have children. It is no coincidence that many women who are successful as managers and leaders are childfree. For a woman, having both children and a demanding leadership role involves some difficult and constrained choices forcing her to prioritize one or the other.

This book is based on the views and perceptions of 60 women who hold leadership and management positions in work. It looks at some of the ways in which they have handled the challenges that women face in building a career and how they have found opportunities for support and development. I am extremely grateful to the women for allowing me time to interview them and permission to use their words in the public arena. Having researched and written on women in leadership in education for the past 15 years I welcome the opportunity to broaden my work to include women from a range of professions in both the public and private sectors, not only education (secondary and tertiary) but also medicine, finance, retail, oil and gas, property development, law, broadcasting, publishing and advertising. The women interviewed represent an age range from late 30s to early 70s, with the largest group being in their 50s. Most of them are married and about half have a child or children. Many of them are London-based, but others are situated in the North and Midlands of England. Although all are working in England at present, a number have lived and worked internationally. Several originate from the USA, two from other European countries, one from New Zealand and one from Malaysia. The title of the book indicates that the women interviewed are 'top' women. Most are at the apex of their organizations, including chief executive officers, board members, head teachers and heads of tertiary educational institutions. The surgeons are consultants. Those who are not heading up their business or institution have discrete responsibilities within them, are important as specialists, or may lead on specific projects. It is the views of all the interviewed women that dominate this book.

To put the views of these women into perspective, the next section sets out the general context for women leaders, specifically in relation to the UK, but the picture presented is fairly typical of the context in comparable developed economies (see, for example, Vinnicombe et al., 2008).

Women in top jobs

Although women now represent nearly half of the labour force in the UK (ONS, 2007), they are still poorly represented at the top levels. In politics in the UK, women account for 19.3 per cent of MPs and 14.3 per cent of local authority council leaders. The parliaments of Scotland and Wales are more equitable, with 34.1 per cent of members of the Scottish Parliament being women and 46.7 per cent of the National Assembly for Wales. However, women only make up 25.6 per cent of the UK members of the European Parliament (EHRC, 2009).

In the legal system, 18.7 per cent of judges are women (Judiciary of England and Wales, 2007). In education, 16 per cent of vice-chancellors are women (University UK, 2007) and approximately 39 per cent of secondary school head teachers are women, although women make up 60 per cent of all secondary school teachers (DCSF, 2010).

In the private sector women leaders are also very much in a minority. A quantitative analysis of the number of women directors undertaken by Martin et al. (2008) showed that although one in four directors of UK companies is female, most are in the smaller firms, and only one in 226 of the larger firms have a majority of female directors. Also women directors are mainly found in the service sector. The annual Female FTSE report (Sealy et al., 2008) indicates that women hold a total of 11.7 per cent of FTSE 100 board directorships but that at the time of the report there were still 22 companies in the FTSE 100 that had all-male boards. Of chief executives of media companies in the FTSE 350, only 10.5 per cent are women (EHRC, 2009). The imbalance of men and women in board positions is well recognized. In 2009, a full scale Parliamentary Treasury Committee held an inquiry into Women in the City, taking evidence on the proportion of women in senior positions in finance, and the extent of the glass ceiling, inequalities in pay, the extent of flexible working and whether the culture of the City was sexist (House of Commons Treasury Committee, 2009). Even in the creative and cultural sectors where women predominate, they are relatively rare in positions of power (Holden and McCarthy, 2007).

These inequities are remarkably persistent. There is a very slow rate of change with regard to women accessing the top positions. In the 2009 edition of the 'Sex and Power' index published by the Equality and Human Rights Commission (EHRC), in six categories there were fewer women than there had been five years previously. The estimate is that at current rates of change it will be 55 years before women will be equal in numbers to men in the judiciary and 73 years before there are equal numbers of women on the boards of FTSE 100 companies. In addition, there is still an average pay gap of 18 per cent between the earnings of women and men in the UK.

Despite this slow progress, there are economic factors that have favoured the progress of women at work in the late twentieth and early twenty-first centuries. Drawing on the 1980 Women and Employment Survey, Scott et al. (2008) note two features particularly affecting women which have shaped the economy. One was the reduction in heavy industry, leading to male unemployment, and the other the development of women's employment in part-time jobs. These factors, among others, have meant that women have had a steadily growing participation in the workforce, even those with children, so that by 2004, 70 per cent of mothers with dependent children (those under 16 and 16 to 18-year-olds in full-time education) were working. The latter part of the twentieth century also saw a big increase in the proportion of women gaining high-level qualifications (Scott et al., 2008).

Despite the changes benefiting women in the workplace there remains the particular challenge of combining work and family life: 'it would be foolish to deny that women will remain disadvantaged in the labour force for as long as the share of family care between men and women remains so uneven' (ibid., pp. 13–14). Family responsibilities are thus identified as one of the main reasons for women's subordinate positions in the labour force. The other remains the continued stereotyping of women as supportive and subordinate rather than as being in charge. Media presentations of women at work can both highlight inequity and reinforce unhelpful stereotypes.

Women in the news

The media have an ongoing influence on attitudes and there is regular media coverage of issues which highlight the major challenges faced by women at work: the poor representation of women in top jobs; discrimination; stereotyping and the difficulties for women of combining a career and a family. Dunn-Jensen and Stroh (2007) point out that media portrayal of women in the workforce tends to be based on 'myth' rather than scholarly research and that the news media offer a 'negatively skewed portrayal of women in the workplace' (p. 30).

A trawl of newspaper stories in English newspapers of 2008–2010 produced a number of themes including important challenges for women: the continuing pay gap between men and women; particularly in the financial sector (for example, Davies, 2009); the slow rate of change in the proportion of women in top jobs (for example, Boseley, 2008); and the particular resistance to getting women onto the boards of FTSE 350 companies (for example, Sunderland, 2009). There is also an ongoing discussion about ageism towards women, particularly those who are in the media (Brooks, 2010) and there are reports of the challenge of sexism and discrimination, particularly in the financial services of the City of London (for example, Pidd, 2009) and stories of senior women in the BBC who appear to receive more censure for their expenses claims than their male equivalents simply because they are women, and as senior executives are more noticeable than their male colleagues (Brick, 2009).

Strong emotions are often connected to women's issues and feminism. During August 2009 four people, three men and one woman, stood in for the UK prime minister, each for a week. While the three men garnered very little press coverage and kept a low profile, Harriet Harman, then Deputy leader of the Labour Party, used the week to launch several initiatives relating to women, resulting in a great deal of coverage. Commenting on this in *The Guardian*, Perkins (2009) stated: 'The spluttering ire she provokes reflects the capacity of both Harman and the feminist agenda to polarise opinion.' Strong emotions tend to come into play in relation to 'the feminist agenda', particularly where affirmative action is concerned, for example the press coverage of women-only shortlists for vacant parliamentary seats (Elliott, 2009). This initiative is welcomed by some as being the only way to speed up change but abhorred by others who see it as both disadvantaging men and leading to the appointment of women just on the basis of being women rather than merit.

The absence of large numbers of women at the top level in the business world provides another media focus: the features that cover the experience of truly exceptional women. These stories of spectacularly successful women seem to imply that there is actually no problem, as, since these women have made it, others should be able to do the same. Among these exceptional women are Martha Lane Fox, co-founder of lastminute.com, who was a non-executive director of blue-chip companies while only 36 years old (Spanier, 2009). Another example, this time in the US, is the appointment of a Latina woman, Sonia Sotomayor, to the Supreme Court, normally the preserve of white middle-class men (Younge, 2009). Further examples are Clara Furse, who headed the London Stock Exchange for eight years (Davidson, 2009) and Helen Alexander who, prior to being appointed the first female president of the CBI (Confederation of British Industry), was head of the Economist group (Wray, 2009). There is also press coverage of those women who manage to have a very prestigious and well-paid job while having large families (Carvel, 2008), including Helena Morrissey who has had nine children and runs a £40 billion investment firm (Chittenden, 2009).

The issue of family and career is another major challenge for women documented in the press. The stories here relate to the choice to be childfree in order to have a career (for example, Ford, 2009), the difficulty in going back to a career after a break for childcare (Groskop, 2008) or criticism for taking too much maternity leave (Chittenden, 2009). There is also coverage of work/family balance and the choice of a small minority of men to take an active part in childcare (for example, Gentleman, 2009) and there is ongoing debate about whether mothers damage their children by returning to work when they are very young (McVeigh and Asthana, 2010).

Finally there are a number of media stories that highlight the successes of women in work, particularly the positive contributions that they make to the boardroom and to company profits (for example, Ward and Carvel, 2007). A sub-set of these stories relates to women running hedge funds with the hint that, as women tend to be more risk averse than men, having more women in decision-making roles might have averted the worst excesses associated with the financial disasters of 2008 (Walsh and Hastings, 2009).

Apart from this minority of stories stressing the positives that women might bring to the boardroom, media coverage of women at work generally focuses either on examples of high-level discrimination or on women as mothers, including examples of extraordinary women who combine motherhood and career success and the debate about the rights and wrongs of young mothers working. Just as with the academic literature on the subject, the two main challenges for aspiring women leaders who wish to break through the glass ceiling remain: discrimination based on gender stereotypes and the difficulties of combining motherhood with a career. The 'subtle' barrier of the glass ceiling described by Burke (2005) in the opening quotation continues to be a force in the lives of women.

Changing attitudes to women

The statistics quoted earlier in the chapter indicate the extent to which women are still a minority in positions of importance at work and alert us to the slow pace of change regarding women and leadership. However, it is now at least accepted that women may compete for and obtain senior roles in most walks of life, despite a lingering resistance to women occupying certain positions, for example as bishops in the Church of England. In the UK the Equal Pay Act (1970) and the Sex Discrimination Act (1975) have recently been strengthened by the duty on public organizations to promote gender equality. Legislation has established the rights of women in the workplace, including the right to maternity leave.

It is easy to forget the attitudes to women at work that were still the norm in the middle years of the twentieth century. For example, in respect of women head teachers:

> In the mid twentieth century a leader of a teachers' union in Britain claimed that 'only a nation heading for a madhouse would force upon men – many married with families – such a position as serving under a spinster headmistress'. (Partington, 1976, p. 37)

In respect of women more generally, Jane Miller, writing in 1996 about her life in education, recalls as a young teacher being introduced to the renowned Arthur Koestler, who was

> genuinely surprised and dismayed to hear that I taught boys as well as girls between the ages of eleven and eighteen... he did not at all fear for my safety, but for the safety of the boys I taught. How could more or less fully grown and possibly even intelligent young men expect to learn from a youngish woman they could only relate to sexually and who could not conceivably be equipped intellectually to prepare them for university, let alone for adult life? (p. 6)

We have moved a long way from those views, although they still have influence, particularly with older generations. The advances that have been made in the last century have been tremendous and have been supported by the two major waves of feminism. Progress for women at work during the twentieth century was considerable but hardly smooth, requiring women to change like 'chameleons' (Adam, 2000, p. 306). In particular the history of women during the twentieth century was coloured by the impact of two world wars, the economic depression and two waves of feminism:

> A woman born at the turn of the [twentieth] century could have lived through two periods when it was her moral duty to devote herself, obsessively, to her children; three when it was her duty to society to neglect them; two when it was right to be seductively 'feminine' and three when it was a pressing social obligation to be the reverse; three separate periods in which she was a bad wife, mother and citizen for wanting to go out and earn her own living, and three others, when

she was an even worse wife, mother and citizen for not being eager to do so. (Adam, 2000, pp. 306–307)

Social expectations about the place of women in the world have therefore been altered by wars, the economy and the impact of waves of feminism. The following section offers, through the lens of feminism, a theoretical and historical context for the views of women as expressed in this book.

The impact of feminism

First-wave feminism aiming for equal rights for women in the early years of the twentieth century is equated with the suffragette movement and women gaining occupational rights. Once women had achieved the vote, activism for reform relating to women's rights went into abeyance. The rise of second-wave feminism in the 1960s initiated a change in the status of women, but as it developed many different viewpoints emerged: 'there is no unchanging feminist orthodoxy, no settled feminist conventions, no static feminist analyses. Feminism is diverse and it is dynamic' (Kemp and Squires, 1997, p. 12).

Second-wave feminism emerging in the 1960s had roots in the prevailing culture after the Second World War when there had been a reversion to the idea of a woman's place being in the home. This is a period Adam (above) refers to as being when a woman was a: 'bad wife, mother and citizen for wanting to go out and earn her own living'. In the years following the Second World War, the workplace was seen as a mainly male environment with an assumption that managers were men, and women, if not in the home, were in a generally subordinate position. Leadership and organization theories developed in the post-war years were based on gendered assumptions and did not take into account the possibility that women might behave somewhat differently from men at work. Runte and Milles (2006) argue that the absence of gender from theories of leadership arose from the separate discourses of work and family that were endorsed throughout the Cold War period following the Second World War. It was the research and writing of academic feminists such as Rosabeth Kanter (Connell, 2002) that first presented a gendered analysis of corporations and business organizations and of Charol Shakeshaft (1986) that pioneered a gendered analysis of educational leadership and management.

Although the second wave of feminism included diverse views, there were two major strands. One aimed to achieve equal opportunities for women and men while the other stressed the differences between men and women and in its most extreme form rejected men and considered women's ways to be superior.

The equal opportunities strand included two differing stances. The first is what Evans (1995, p. 31) calls 'weak equality of opportunity'. This is likened to a race which is: 'correctly conducted, and monitored carefully throughout'. However, in the weak equality of opportunity argument, no thought is given to the conditions under which the race is run or to the preparation and training leading to the race. In contrast, the second stance which might be called 'strong equality of opportunity' (ibid.) gives attention to preparation and context and might involve 'women being given a head start' in the race, in other words involve some sort of positive discrimination for women. Whether the equal opportunities stance is 'weak' or 'strong', it broadly assumes that women and men are similar and equal.

The other major strand of second-wave feminism saw men and women as very different, with different types of knowledge and skills. For example, standpoint theory holds that women have a particular view of the world and of life because of their experience as women, which is bound to differ from that of men. Cultural feminists believe that there are essential qualities in being a woman that apply to all women. These qualities include those of caring and nurturing. Just as she identifies the idea of 'strong' and 'weak' equality of opportunity, Evans (1995) distinguishes between 'weak' and 'strong' cultural feminism, with strong cultural feminism emphasizing the differences between men and women and inherently valuing the ways of women as superior to those of men. On the other hand, weak cultural feminism, which is somewhat identified with the work of Gilligan and the ethic of care (1982), identifies qualities that might be stereotypically feminine, but does not exclude men from sharing these qualities. In this stance, androgyny may be seen as ideal, with good leaders sharing qualities that are both stereotypically feminine and masculine.

Second-wave feminism has been critiqued on many grounds, for example, that it does not take account of class or ethnicity and that it was derived by and for white middle-class women. A strong criticism is that it cannot necessarily be applied to women in the developing world. Post-modern and post-structuralist critiques of second-wave feminism emphasize the importance of the individual and their multiple identities, rejecting what might be seen as essentialist and universalist assumptions and the narrative of patriarchy. The rejection of second-wave feminism is part of the third wave of feminism.

Third-wave feminists identify as a different generation to second-wave feminists and their focus is on the individual and their personal empowerment. Third-wave feminists react against the concept of victimhood that they see as implicit in second-wave feminism, and they place more emphasis on individual agency. There appear to be two aspects to third-wave feminism: one is the academic theorizing of post-structural feminism which is unlikely to directly touch the ideas and lives of most women (Connell, 2002); the other includes fresh activity on, for example, reclaiming the night, and recognition that second-wave feminism did not eliminate all the challenges that women face as well as being identified with more controversial views. Examples of the more controversial elements of third-wave feminism include the sometimes 'laddish' behaviour of young women and the idea that women can be empowered through stripping and lap dancing (Walter, 2010).

Feminism continues to change and evolve, but there are persisting strands which underpin the gendered experience of women and men. Connell (2002) identifies these as: power relations; production relations; emotional relations; and symbolic relations. The analysis of power as patriarchy was a key concept of second-wave feminism. In work situations, power was and mainly continues to be held by 'gatekeepers' who are male and unthinkingly continue to exercise their power in a way that favours other men but disadvantages women. Post-structuralist feminists see power in the discourse. For example, women are constrained by a discourse of beauty which presents an unrealistic image of ultra-slim women in the media as a powerful ideal for women.

Production is gendered in society, with occupations identified as 'male', for example engineering, or 'female', for example nursing. This vertical segregation of men's from women's jobs compounds the difficulties inherent in the horizontal barriers to career progress known as the glass ceiling. Overall, women are identified with the private domestic world of care and support of others, while men are seen as having a rightful place in the public arena of work, and are distanced from the domestic.

Emotional relations likewise are gendered, within the family and within the workplace, with women often expected to take the supportive roles. Finally Connell (2002, p. 65) identifies the symbolic aspects of gender in society:

> Whenever we speak of a 'woman' or a 'man', we call into play a tremendous system of understandings, implications, overtones and allusions that have accumulated through our cultural history. The

'meanings' of these words are enormously greater than the biological categories of male and female.

The historical identification of feminism with Women's Lib in the 1970s means that it is seen as old-fashioned in the twenty-first century. Difficulties in pinning down a clear definition of feminism may mean that it is misunderstood. There are now no undergraduate programmes in women's studies in the UK (Oxford, 2008); it had come to be seen as a soft option, or as no longer relevant. Alternatively, a more positive view of the disappearance of women's studies may be that: 'feminist-inspired ideas have been absorbed and are now debated within mainstream subjects' (Oxford, 2008, p. 31). However, there appears to be a backlash against feminism and particularly against positive discrimination or affirmative action for women. The academic focus on social justice has shifted from gender to other aspects of diversity, particularly ethnicity. Gaskell and Taylor (2003), analysing the ways in which the women's movement affected change in Australia and Canada from 1970 to 2000, showed how there had been a shift in the social justice discourse away from women and towards boys as a problem and towards justice for ethnic minorities. Important cultural figures like Fay Weldon and Margaret Atwood, who were previously identified as iconic feminist writers, are now questioning whether or not they are feminist and turning their attention elsewhere (*The Guardian*, 2009). There is a general feeling that the gender battles have been won, although important voices like that of the Fawcett Society make a clear argument that this is not the case (Banyard, 2010). In research carried out for the Equal Opportunities Commission (EOC), Howard and Tibballs (2003, p. 7) concluded that young women generally rejected the idea that women are unequal. Paradoxically they felt that they had experienced discrimination in relation to work, but 'see this as a result of individual choice and natural gender differences, rather than bias in society as a whole'. The tendency for women to ascribe responsibility for career problems to the individual woman, rather than to the ways in which society and culture operate to disadvantage women is discussed further in Chapter 3.

In writing this book, my feminist stance is one of strong equal opportunities, recognizing that there are skewed differentials deeply embedded in our culture, with societies tending to favour men over women, and that, in the interests of social justice, positive action on behalf of women might be needed. There is continuing change towards a more equal society for women and men but the change is slow. Although I resist essentialist ideas stereotyping women and men, I recognize that their experiences and socialization are different and are therefore likely to influence their views and attitudes. To some extent it may then be possible to generalize about the ways in which women and men differ while always remembering that there are bigger differences of attitudes and behaviour within each sex than between them.

Despite the many positive changes in recent history that have improved the domestic and public lives of women, there remains a huge discrepancy in the proportion of women and men in positions of authority in most areas of work. It seems not only inequitable but positively bizarre that only around 11 per cent of the directors of boards of the top FTSE companies in the UK are women and that without legislation to change the situation, as in Norway, there is little to indicate a major change in the near future.

Why are there so few women in 'top jobs'?

In addressing the situation of women in top jobs, it is necessary to consider both the possible barriers to career progress for women and factors that have helped their career success. Much has been written on these topics, and the bibliography at the end of this book indicates recent reviews (for example, Burke and Mattis, 2005; McTavish and Miller, 2006). The section below offers an overview of key factors identified in the literature which are of particular relevance to the analysis of women's lives presented in this book.

Barriers to career progress

In relation to barriers, Miller (2006, p. 5) stresses the: 'masculine organizational culture in UK and European organizations' which frustrates women's ambitions and tends to promote 'masculine' ways of working, including long hours. Secondly, she identifies the continuing stereotypes which permeate our culture, leading to the identification of men with more agentic behaviour and with leadership and women with the more nurturing and supporting 'communal' roles. Thirdly, she points to the perception of employers that women will have children and as a result become 'an organizational liability' (p. 7). In an article reviewing the persistence of the glass ceiling over the past 20 years, Weyer (2007, p. 488) draws attention to the social roles of men and women: 'most leaders are men because leadership is described as a task that requires behaviours deemed masculine', and goes on to say that a 'greater significance and general competence [is] attributed to men over women' (p. 494). Major structural and social changes are likely to be needed to fully overcome such barriers. The difficulties of combining parent-hood with a demanding work role have already been mentioned. Many authors (for example, Tharenou, 2005; Gatrell, 2006) found that women reported difficulties with childcare, and with the handling of multiple roles and that this limits their managerial aspirations.

A further potential barrier for women wanting to access senior roles was seen to be their exclusion from male networks which limits their social capital (Tharenou, 2005). The combination of factors form-ing barriers to women's progress is summed up by Miller (2006) as: 'Institutional sexism, masculine organizational culture and practices [which] compound to frustrate women's progress in careers and profes-sions' (p. 8). In a wide review of recent literature on women leading at work (Coleman, 2008a), the themes that emerged were: the continuing importance of the glass ceiling; gender stereotypes relating to leader-ship; and the resulting gendered leadership discourses. Assumptions about family responsibilities were an integral component of the stere-otypes relating to gender and leadership.

Barriers to career progress for women can then be summarized as:

- a masculine work culture, particularly at senior levels;
- gender stereotypes which cast men as leaders, women as supporters and nurturers and therefore 'outsiders' as leaders;
- the actual and perceived impact of family responsibilities on wom-en's ability to work.

These factors are then translated into everyday actions or inactions which serve to some extent to frustrate the career progress of women. Although these factors are generally thought to explain the relative absence of women from senior roles, they are challenged by Hakim (2004), who presents her alternative view, termed 'preference theory'. She believes that theories explaining the subordinate position of women in the labour market are plausible and will have elements of truth, but that the theories have not been tested rigorously. Instead she considers that most women simply prefer not to make their career the main focus of their lives. Preference theory explains the lack of women from the top of the career ladder; the theory goes that most women choose to be 'adaptive', combining employment and family work, or 'home-centred' rather than 'work-centred' (pp. 14–15). She considers that work-centred women are, and will continue to be, in a minority, with prioritization of work by only about 20 per cent of women as opposed to 50 per cent of men. Qualitative research, such as that presented in this book, can neither prove nor disprove any stance on barriers to women's progress. Indeed, within Hakim's preference theory, the women interviewed for the book would all belong to the 20 per cent who are work-centred. However, the qualitative research of Kumra (2010) and Broadbridge (2010) has questioned the applicability of preference theory to women and the in-depth interviews on which this book is based also indicate the perceived importance of structural barriers in the career progress of successful women. Insights arising from these interviews give glimpses of rich and complicated lives and cast doubt on the idea that women have a completely 'free' choice in respect of career. The women interviewed identify in detail the elements that act as barriers and facilitators for women who are ambitious.

Factors that help women progress in their careers

Studies of factors that help the career success of women have been analysed by Tharenou (2005) in terms of social and human capital. Broadly, social capital includes the women's social contacts, and human capital is based on their knowledge, skills and abilities. These types of capital indicate ways in which careers might be promoted. For example, social capital can be increased through networking and mentoring while human capital is increased through qualifications, professional development and relevant on-the-job experience. The review of factors that help and support women at work (Coleman, 2008a) similarly identifies the particular importance of networking, of mentoring and coaching as well as organizational initiatives including affirmative action.

The development of human capital is determined to a large extent through education prior to work and while working, but personality factors play a part. Research in this area is limited but, as gender stereotypes might predict, qualities of leadership include 'masculine' qualities, such as 'dominance, forcefulness, independence, aggressiveness' as well as 'an instrumental task orientation focusing on getting the job done, or the problem solved' (Tharenou, 2005, p. 43), and women who have a successful career might be expected to display these qualities. The data from interviews indicates the role played by the determination and agency of successful women, although many of them also recognize and aspire to more feminine qualities in their leadership.

Challenges, choices and change: the origins of the book

The data from the in-depth interviews with 60 high-flying women have been analysed for emerging themes, and linked to prior research and theory to offer an informed view from women who are at or near the top of their professions. The sub-title of this book, *Challenges, Choices and Change*, arose from the issues that dominate the relevant literature, and media coverage, and then arise again through the interviews of the women featured in the book. The issues are: the challenges that women face in getting to the top of their chosen career ladder; the difficulties in breaking through the glass ceiling; and the somewhat constrained choices they make relating to combining a career with motherhood in the context of a changing culture.

It is artificial to separate out the three elements of challenge, choice and change. For example, the decision on whether to have a family and a career, and how to combine the two, is both a choice and a challenge. Changes in society are impacting on how the choices may be made, with men more likely to take some responsibility for their children and a growing general awareness of a need for balance between work and family.

This chapter has established that men outnumber women in leadership in virtually every walk of life. It provides an introduction to theories that underpin the changing views about women leading and managing at work in the twentieth and twenty-first centuries, and a snapshot of the issues relating to women that attract the attention of the media.

The remaining chapters open with particularly apposite quotations from the interviews. Chapter 2 focuses on the challenges faced by women who aspire to the male-dominated areas of leadership and management. The stereotype of the male leader remains strong. Although there are differences between types of work, and there are some definitely 'gendered' occupations, all the women interviewed are clear that it is harder for women to obtain leadership positions than men. This is changing over time, but they perceive a bedrock of stereotypes. In some cases the prejudice against women remains almost as strong as it ever was. In the world of surgery, for example, women report isolated cases of bullying from mature and well-established men, although these are in contrast to the supportive attitudes of the younger men who are more used to seeing women in the stereotypically male role of surgeon. Bullying also featured in comments about the world of finance, particularly the City of London. The ways in which leadership is stereotyped also creates a challenge for women and indeed for many men who do not want to lead in stereotypically masculine ways. Consideration is given to leadership styles and examples are drawn from the interviews of the ways in which the women have challenged existing ways of working.

One of the most important potential challenges for women is that of managing to combine family and career, and this is considered separately in Chapter 5.

What are the factors that have helped these women to overcome the challenges and to succeed in their career? Chapter 3 focuses first on the individual, their own agency and determination, their love of their chosen career and their hard work and ability. However, the women also give credit to those who have helped them, as mentors, as role models and through coaching. Often it is a former boss who continues to guide and act as a sounding board, offering advice or commenting on proposed options. Mentoring and coaching combine and are not confined to the early years of the career, and formal coaching has been used by some of the women to help them over a particular difficulty such as a poor relationship with a superior.

The support available through networking is a factor picked out by many of the women interviewed, and the focus in Chapter 4 is on networks as means of support and development. As well as belonging to mixed networks of men and women, many of those interviewed belong to one or more women-only networks, all of which offer emotional and informational support to members, provide role models to younger women and offer some sort of training. Networks solely for women can play an important role in providing emotional and instrumental support, and the latter part of this chapter analyses the support of these networks, focusing on five examples.

Girls and women make gendered choices about which subjects to take at school and university, and about their career. There is no doubt that the decision whether or not to have a family considerably affects the career progress of women, and Chapter 5 focuses on these choices, particularly those relating to family and work. Some of the women interviewed have either chosen not to have children or been aware that they could not have children and so have concentrated their efforts on their work. Those who have children have been faced with a society which has not taken on fully the implications of women having a career as well as a family, so that:

> almost each and every woman, no matter her initial optimism, will reach a point when she realises that as long as she squeezes her needs into the male mould that has prevailed for decades, equality of sorts is hers. (Roberts, 2005, p. 326)

The interviewed women who were mothers had used various approaches to planning their children, including waiting until their career was well established, or having their children early, before they had started to build a career. The difficulties of taking maternity leave in one's late 20s or early 30s are well recognized, as this is a time when a woman can fall behind even by taking a minimum maternity break (Scott et al., 2008). One of the benefits of having children late is that financial security means that women can afford to pick and choose the best childcare or employ what one interviewee termed 'a raft of nannies'.

Chapter 6 presents the individual 'stories' of six named interviewees from different work areas, to contrast their experiences over time with regard to challenges and how they overcame them, their choices about family and career, and the changes that they see affecting women at work. The stories provide rich illustration of many of the issues discussed throughout the book and illustrate the progress that women have made in the past 50 years. What will change in the future? Chapter 7 focuses on the changes that the women note at present and envisage for the future. There are changes in attitudes to families and children, with evidence in some sectors of a more family-friendly attitude for both women and men. These changes do not seem to be universal, with some industries retaining the 24/7 culture.

On the positive side, many of the women recognized changes in work practice with new and flexible ways of working, including the use of technology to allow working at home, and the emergence of agencies that specialize in the employment of women and men who want to work more flexible hours. Large-scale change for women leading at work requires a radical shift in cultural expectations about women, men and families. The women interviewed have been successful in the current context and the chapter ends with a review of factors derived from the interviewees that an individual woman should consider if she wants to make it to the top of her chosen profession, and recommendations for employers who are working towards gender equity.

The annotated bibliography includes the literature that I have found useful and relevant in writing this book and provides a rich source of recommended further reading.

2
The Challenges

> There are two types of women: ones who perceive there is not
> a problem – they are wearing blinkers; they tend to pull up the
> drawbridge – then there are women who admit there are issues
> but also see that there are lots of things that can be done.
>
> (interviewed woman)

The quotation above sums up the views of the successful women whose
voices are heard in this book. This chapter focuses on what they perceive
to be 'the problem' – the career challenges and difficulties that have been
barriers to their progress. We will look at 'the things that can be done' –
the ways in which they feel that they have been able to counteract and
handle the challenges they identify. Although there are references to
relevant literature, the voices of the women dominate the chapter.

The main challenges for women wanting to progress in their
careers were identified in Chapter 1 through the existing literature
and media as:

finding their place within a masculine work culture that tends to reinforce the glass ceiling;
encountering gender stereotypes which cast men as leaders and women
as supporters and nurturers and therefore 'outsiders' in terms of leadership; and
the impact of family responsibilities on women's ability to work.

In this chapter we look at the perceptions of the successful women,
focusing particularly on their views of the masculine work culture, the
glass ceiling and gender stereotypes, unpicking the elements of work
culture that the women describe, examining their experiences and how

18

stereotypes affect them. Discussion of the major challenge of the impact of family responsibilities will be the focus of Chapter 5.

The women interviewed were keen to recognize the positive in their past and present experiences. However, they were all aware to some extent of male domination in aspects of work, particularly leadership and management. A very small number of the women thought that they personally had not met gender barriers, but still recognized that there were very few women in senior roles and thought that this should change. There were differences between the younger and older women, since older women had experienced more overt discrimination. A fairly typical reflection on her experiences from an older woman was:

> I think there is no question that we are all prone to prejudice. We are shaped by our history and environment. I remember in my early days that one of the leading partners I worked for was more interested in having an affair with me than giving me some of the work to do, so I left the firm. The management style of certain people is very dictatorial and trying to find a constructive way of handling this can be an obstacle. Discrimination is built into society.

One of the younger women, though happy and secure in her work, still commented on her perceptions of inequality: 'I imagine a world where if completely supported I think I would have been running something by now. I would be in a much more senior position. My ideas are regularly taken forward as those of others.' The idea that women's comments are first ignored and then taken up when suggested by men is found elsewhere, for example Roberts (*c.* 1995). In general, linguistic analysis shows that there are many differences in male and female communication styles which cause problems for women at work. For example, women are shown to use indirect speech, make use of tags such as 'you know', or 'isn't it?', interrupt to reinforce a comment made by another, use inclusive communications and encourage collaborative talk, while men speak more directly, take long turns and are less collaborative, and interrupt to change the flow of the discussion (Schick-Case, 1994; Peck, 2006). These differences may affect the recognition of women's ideas. It is not just a matter of recognizing that there are differences, but of the value that is put on those differences. Barrett and Davidson (2006, p. 14) support the idea that the differences can be seen as inferiority with the implication that women need to change and adapt to male patterns of communication rather than that the culture might change to be more amenable to different ways of working.

A masculine work culture

The tendency to identify men with the public domain of work and women with the private domain of the domestic is now clearly out of date, as women are almost equally likely to work outside the home as men (Scott et al., 2008). However, the work that women do in the public domain is often compromised by the fact that they tend to carry the main burden of responsibilities in the home and as a result are less likely to prioritize their career and may work part-time. In addition, there is a lag in our perceptions and expectations about women and work, with older people remembering a time when fewer women worked and were more restricted in the work that they did.

Despite increasing feminization of the workforce, women are more likely to be found in certain professions and in occupations at middle and lower levels in the workplace, so that women who aspire to management and leadership are more likely to encounter a male culture. This is particularly true at the highest level, for example serving at board level. Women make-up only 11 per cent of directors of UK FTSE 100 companies, and accounted for 14.6 per cent of the US Fortune 500 in 2006 (Burke and Vinnicombe, 2008). It is only in countries such as Norway, where by law 40 per cent of board members have to be women, that things are different and where the culture of a board is as likely to be influenced by women as men. Women interviewed for this book confirmed the feeling of being the only woman at a board meeting. For example, one CEO who is in the media commented on the isolation, the need to be totally prepared and in command and the danger of being taken for a 'token' woman:

> Today at lunch there were 18 men and me. It was quite striking. I spoke early in the lunch, and some of the men who were older, I could see them thinking, is she going to do a classic female waffle? Men will give each other more latitude. Sometimes it is imperceptible, but it is there. I think that women have to be better than most men round the table. There only has to be one time when you are mistaken and a woman will not be given the benefit of the doubt. Women are in such a minority in leadership in work that they stand out more. Everything that they do is taken more notice of. It [the male attitude to women] is a bit like the hidden curriculum in schools; it is quite dormant, under the surface. There is a generational thing on boards. They see a younger woman and they think, I bet she is only there because she is a woman.

In response to a question about barriers for women, the same woman referred to misogyny and the need for women at the top to be tough:

> When I first sat on a group board there were two or three on the board who were misogynists. You would be quite shocked. It did exist, but it never stopped me. There were enough other people to balance it out. It was shocking though. It was not as if we were in manufacturing, or in a sector where you might expect it... You are either tough and stand your ground or you are undermined if you are not confident. I have seen it happen to some of my friends.

Such treatment of women may be more likely to occur in male-dominated industries.

Masculine industries

Women like the CEO quoted above were surprised to find misogyny in an area like the media, but in other sectors, such as engineering, power generation or mining, women in management and leadership are particularly scarce, and in the past male discrimination was taken for granted. One woman recalled: 'Sure, I worked for a couple of bosses who were real sexists, numerous ones. I had a boss who was an Italian man in the mining industry. He could not comprehend a successful woman.'

Women in management positions in masculine industries are isolated and have to be able to call on reserves of strength and confidence to survive and win through. One woman commented:

> I'm in a very female orientated world now, but in the jewellery and watch sector it is a completely male industry. You got there but just earned it. You started ten rungs down from any man, but just had to work harder, and then if you deliver people respect you.

Broadbridge (2008), who studied senior executives in retailing, concluded that women tend to have to adopt a male cultural norm in order to succeed, putting career before family. Difficulties for women of reaching the top levels of management are compounded in more masculine industries. A woman who had recently retired from a career in engineering commented on this:

> There were barriers but they did not stop me, they were for breaking down. Most of the barriers have gone now, but the one at the top hasn't.

When asked 'Do you think it will go?' she replied:

> I don't know. There are more women now in directorships in retail
> and the consumer led sectors. Maybe as that growth happens some
> of the other sectors will change. You just don't get them [women]
> in macho industries. Whether things will creep across I don't know.
> There isn't a lot of sector transfer.

One in four of the companies in the FTSE 100 have no women board
directors (Vinnicombe et al., 2009). Occupations and industries remain
gendered. At least some of the roots of this can be traced to decisions
about subject choice at school and university. Girls are more likely to
choose social sciences and humanities and boys to choose science and
mathematics-based subjects. This leads to gendered career choices; for
example, engineering, construction, manufacturing and information
technology are largely dominated by men, and education and other
public services are dominated by women (Purcell and Elias, 2008). (See
also Chapter 5 of this book.) Vertical segregation into types of industry
is enhanced by horizontal segregation as women are generally clustered
in the middle and lower ranks and men are disproportionately found
in the upper levels of status and pay in all sectors. Even in an area like
education, which is numerically dominated by women, men tend to
hold the majority of the leadership roles of the more prestigious secondary and tertiary levels, with the less prestigious early years institutions
led by women. Interviewees from higher education were aware of the
challenging male culture which in some cases had been re-invigorated
by managerialist, neo-liberal ideas (Isaac et al., 2009; Tomas et al., 2010;
Wilson et al., 2010) in which they operated once they had reached the
top management level:

> As Dean I was in a truly male world. ... at university level it was a
> world of men in suits. It was daunting and I felt marginalised both
> as a woman and as an art and design person. The men were conde-
> scending, there was sexist language, it was like the dark ages but it
> was the early 1990s.

Meeting with men whose subject area was very 'masculine' proved a particular challenge when the concept of equal opportunities was introduced:

> When I was Chair of the Equal Opportunities Committee I was
> asked to go round each School in the University to introduce the

Equal Opportunities policy. When I went to the School of Maths and Computing they were all men. I felt really on the spot and isolated. I think that they thought it had been invented by Social Sciences just to annoy them.

Although about half of the employees in advertising are women, they account for only about 15 per cent of advertising board directors (Klein, 2000). A CEO in advertising explained how 'the one bit of the industry that remains resolutely male is the creative side'. The creative aspect of advertising is generally seen as the most glamorous part of the industry. The reasons for its continuing domination by men were thought by the CEO to be the perpetuation of the idea that advertising is 'aggressive and macho' by the colleges of art, and also that the culture surrounding the creative side of advertising is still the 'pool table thing'. In addition she was aware of the gender role stereotype (Tharenou, 2005; Vinkenburg and van Engen, 2005) held by some that:

> the female brain means that creativity in the purest form is less likely to be present, that creativity is less suited to the female brain. They think they are OK at planning and account handling but not creative work.

Gender stereotypes are considered later in the chapter (see p. 35).

In all types of industry, access to networks helps in acquiring social capital (Tharenou, 2005) and networks have tended to be male-dominated.

Male networking

Networks may be formal and informal, and are discussed fully in Chapter 4. Here they are considered for their contribution to a male work culture. Women from every field commented on the existence of a male culture at work which is underpinned by informal male networking and bonding through sport. A woman secondary school head teacher stated:

> I'm not a member of a golf club. I don't follow a football team or go to a pub. It is always difficult in having a conversation with men. Men immediately have something in common. Football, cricket and rugby are major items.

While a woman in advertising commented on:

> The male ways of getting things done, playing golf, long lunches with too much alcohol, leering at women, all those kinds of male behaviours are isolating for women.

A woman in broadcasting similarly referred to the 'clubbability' of men who 'talk together and make decisions'. Another said: 'It was a club environment. The top management team were men. At social events the men clubbed together and then there were us girls. They were nice blokes, but it was male dominated.'

A woman who is a board member of a public company commented that:

> the times I have been most uncomfortable I have been in an environment that is too male, old boys together. In those circumstances, when it is like a club, excluding you, I don't do well.

In work sectors like engineering, where women were and are still extremely rare, men might not have to take women into account at all. One woman engineer recalled:

> I was told that I don't network enough. There are social networks all to do with golf and playing sport. Maybe if a woman is an incredibly extrovert, particular character who takes on the persona of a man, maybe she could join, but it would be extraordinarily difficult. One of the men I knew who was a mentor to me once said that when he was appointing managers he would always look for involvement in a team sport, because it would mean the person would be a team player. I pointed out that would exclude me and asked: 'would you not appoint me because I can't hit a ball with a bat?' He realised that he needed to think about what he had just said.

Women in such male industries as engineering are still breaking fresh ground and establishing new ways of working for both women and the men around them, although their minority status appears to make it difficult to challenge the almost overwhelmingly male culture (Powell et al., 2009).

Women pioneers

In work areas which women have only entered fairly recently it had been necessary to take a stand, make a breakthrough and set new precedents:

There was one incident early in my career when I was leading a large multi-disciplinary team on an off-shore tendering exercise. My functional boss said I could not go off-shore as a woman. I was floored. It was the first time someone had said I could not do something because I was a woman. I went to my line manager and explained that I thought this was somewhat unfair. He agreed and made it happen. He was the least likely man to champion a woman's cause – 30 years an oil man and I was the first woman in his team. I was the first woman to stay overnight on an offshore platform and the business didn't grind to a halt!

Rather than being daunted by being the first in the field several women had taken the view that it was their duty to 'educate' the men around them into realizing that women could actually do most of the things that men had thought they could not.

In relation to barriers, I remember when I was a senior engineer there was a job that required work to be done on the shop floor. There was a feeling that I should not do it in case I was treated badly. It was a load of rubbish. As long as you are competent and nice, there is no problem with the shop floor. It is important to get the men around you to adjust to what is possible.

Another woman talked about being prepared to 'coach' men to deal with women in senior roles in the workplace. Nevertheless, women who are very much in a minority have to be prepared to feel somewhat exposed in an all-male gathering and rally reserves of confidence and experience:

I am not intimidated. It is not uncommon that I will give a presentation to 40–50 engineers who are all men. I suppose I was prepared for that by having brothers and for a term being a girl in the sixth form of an all boys' school.

Macho culture

Women who are working in a very masculine environment have to find ways of fitting in, and there were a small number of references to women who have become 'one of the boys' in order to succeed. One of the interviewees referred to them as women who 'have taken on the male attitudes and are successful by assimilation to the male world'. She went on to comment on 'the parties, the drinking and the excessive travel' which she would have found hard to adapt to. Powell et al. (2008) found that women engineers did not challenge male hegemony, often endorsing it through adopting a masculine identity. Women who adopt such masculine discourses and ways of being are recognized by Olsson and Walker (2004) who also identify an alternative stance taken by women in very male environments, who differentiate themselves by asserting female difference.

Traditionally men have not been expected to take part in running the home, but have been cast in the role of breadwinner, so it is not surprising that male ways of behaving include spending long hours at work. Even in schools where women are in the majority, there can be a rather macho culture of long hours, particularly in schools that embrace a business model of management. However, a long-hours culture is more the norm in types of work where women tend to do less well and where it is particularly difficult to achieve career success alongside a family life (see Chapter 5).

A job necessitating long hours may be difficult for some women, particularly those with children, but another stumbling block, and an incidental barrier to promotion is international travel, particularly where the expectation was, or remains, that a man travelling abroad might be accompanied by his wife. Under these circumstances, new rules had to be developed for a woman in a senior role travelling with her husband. A woman engineer commented:

> The only thing I never did was have experience of working abroad, which was seen as very valuable. There was an assumption that if you were married you were not offered the opportunity to work abroad because it was too complicated to work out what to do with your husband. People know now not to do that. That lack of experience abroad then is a barrier.

Women who did travel in their work might find that, as women, they encountered barriers in certain cultures. One woman in a power industry noted:

> I recall one incident in South Korea. We had a trip planned for a week to Seoul with a series of meetings facilitated by the British Council. On my visit to Samsung they said my counterpart was not available although the meeting had been set up weeks before. I was really disappointed after all the preparation. I was then met by three of his direct reports, a woman and two men and after an hour of good discussion they excused themselves for a few minutes. Later they came back and said that he could see me now. I had got through the

internal test. They were intrigued by a woman travelling on her own and having a very senior role. It was a new experience for them.

In the context of barriers to women's career progress, women from every work sector represented in the interviews commented on some aspect of male culture, present or past, including male networking, 'clubbability', long hours or going to places women had not been before. Among many, there was also a tendency to recognize some form of discrimination, sometimes overt, for example bullying and sometimes more subtle micro-political manoeuvres.

Discrimination and the glass ceiling

Eagly and Carli (2007, p. 1) choose to reject the concept of the glass ceiling in favour of the alternative metaphor of the 'labyrinth'. Their view is that 'barriers to women's advancement are now more permeable' than the 'rigid, impenetrable barrier' of the glass ceiling, and that the idea of the labyrinth is closer to the varying but still difficult career paths that women take. A further alternative metaphor is that of the 'firewall' (Bendl and Schmidt, 2010), also seen as more permeable than the glass ceiling, but more complex. Whatever the metaphor employed, the conclusion is still that discrimination against women continues and that woman's traditional role in the family is an impediment to career success. Reflecting on the interview data, the concept of the glass ceiling still seems relevant as the women recognize that there is a barrier at a certain level that is hard to break through. They recognize that the glass ceiling may have moved upwards and also may be higher or lower in different types of work. Although some women do make it to the other side of the ceiling or firewall, or through the labyrinth, the general feeling was that such women were the exceptions:

> I think there is a glass ceiling. If you look at broadcasting, you've got some high-profile women, but a real body of male influence, then women in the next layer down. There are women at the top, but at the bottom end of the senior grade there are not many women.

There is some evidence that the glass ceiling has been shifted to a higher level (Altman et al., 2005) and this was the perception of some of the senior women interviewed:

> [I did not meet barriers] in the sector I was in, not until I was getting near to the glass ceiling, which was real. I was the youngest person,

man or woman, to make it to the senior management of a company [within the larger company]. I had to be better as a woman to get anywhere. The glass ceiling does not start until the level of the main board of a FTSE company.

Very few women reach the main board of a FTSE company, so it may be more realistic to place the glass ceiling at a lower level than that.

The younger women interviewed tended to be more optimistic about the progress of women but those reaching middle age began to realize that there might be something impeding their progress as women. One stated:

I have been thinking about this in relation to changing roles. It never occurred to me before. Consultancy is relatively 'flat' in terms of hierarchy, but when I look at management, how many women are there? I have never seen an active barrier, but there are serious difficulties like men not wanting to have a woman in teams, or being extremely hierarchical.

In broadcasting, one woman commented about reporters: 'I still think women on the road have to be much better than men. There is sexism. I can see it now. Managers will appoint people who look like them. They don't understand women. Look at the top table and who is there?'

In the relatively 'feminine' world of education, some of the women head teachers interviewed felt that there was a recently renewed preference for men in the role of head, one stating:

Until recently I would have said 'no' [about discrimination]. I think I was quite naïve. I found it difficult to believe there could be discrimination because I was a woman. My background never let me believe it was possible. Recently, over the last five years I have met blatant prejudice.

Another agreed: 'We worry that it's lurching back again. There are less women appointed now, they are appointing young men in grey suits.'

A woman working in a particularly male environment relating to surveying commented on how things had changed for women but in a negative way:

I was positively discriminated for by this guy I worked for, but no one is doing that now. In a few years there won't be any equity partners who are women. They don't seem to care. They don't seem to worry about how that will look. I don't think it will put the firm in a good light at all.

It may be that the assumption that gender is no longer an issue is affecting current recruitment practice. in contrast to a time of greater gender awareness ten or more years ago (see the discussion of feminism in Chapters 1 and 7).

The role of 'gatekeepers', those who appoint to senior roles, is particularly important. It has long been known that there is a tendency for people to appoint in their own image (Morgan et al., 1983). One woman in broadcasting commented on the implications:

> There is a lack of transparency in how people are selected in the higher levels. Below that it is very open and transparent, but this does not happen with the top ranks. With the very senior ones it is transparent, but not just below. It is still that 'hand on shoulder' approach which is not helpful for gender and diversity. There is definitely hypocrisy there.

Many of the women interviewed, particularly the younger ones, were clear that they had not met gender barriers in their actual place of work, but that in the wider world they were aware of gender barriers, for example with their firm's clients. One woman in advertising explained:

> I have been supported throughout my career by the men I have worked with, but there are barriers with male clients. As a young woman I found there is quite a lot of resistance from men to working in a senior relationship with a woman, but this has receded as I got older. One man said that he had been more comfortable working with so and so at the previous agency, by which he clearly meant that he preferred to work with a man. The difficulty comes with men who are not comfortable with being marked by a female. I think that is something of a generational thing and for women ten years younger than me it may be quite different.

It remains to be seen whether younger men will always be comfortable working in partnership with a woman or taking direction from a woman. However, the work of Schein has shown and continues to show (2007) that men of all ages are prone to identify the manager as male and to resist the idea of a woman as leader.

Bullying and manipulation

Change may be coming in some sectors, but there were still examples of unreconstructed misogyny, and even bullying recounted by a small number of those interviewed. For example, a women surgeon commented: 'I only had difficulties after becoming a consultant. There was bullying from other consultants, questioning my performance and undermining my confidence.' Another stated: 'I worked for two disagreeable men who were totally unsupportive. At the end of the job one said: "I was never going to support you to get a senior registrar post".' However, the culture in surgery was felt to be changing rapidly with more transparent procedures for advancement and younger members of the profession having very different views on the place of women. There were references to the bullying nature of life in financial institutions in the City, for example:

> the culture around the trading floors is very aggressive, almost animalistically aggressive. If you go into that you have to realise you are in a zoo.

Bullying is an overt form of gender harassment, but women reported more subtle forms of sexist behaviour. For example, a woman recalled:

> there were a lot of senior business men who did not like having a woman economist at all and they did not take the trouble to conceal it. For the first six months I was not sure I would survive. I was continually told by people how much they liked my predecessor. It was my first management job and I still remember now how awful it was. My number two thought he should have had the job so he made my life difficult. He did not tell me things. For example there was a press conference and it was the norm for the chair to come in to be briefed an hour before. When that happened, the number two was all briefed and ready but I wasn't, as he had not told me that this was what normally happened.

A similar set of circumstances was reported by a woman who was in higher education:

> There were certainly barriers when I went into an Associate Dean position, from men who found me intimidating and a threat. I subsequently found out that there had been things going on behind my

back…It was on moving into a senior management position when the barriers came up. I have found the same with other women, for example I was talking to one who was a Pro Vice-Chancellor and had gone back to being an 'ordinary' professor because of this.

The micro-politics of academic life and its relationship to gender have been analysed by Morley (2000) who comments (p. 232) that it 'involves rumour, gossip, sarcasm, humour, denial, "throwaway remarks", alliance building, to the detriment of women leaders'.

There was also evidence of women experiencing the 'glass cliff' (Ryan and Haslam, 2005, 2006) the process whereby women are promoted to difficult leadership positions carrying with them a high possibility of failure. When the woman then fails, she is blamed because she is a woman. One head teacher mentioned that: 'If there is a difficult job that a man does not want, often a woman will get it. They are parachuted in to schools in difficulties but are they then appointed for permanent positions?'

In general, men were thought to be better at being 'political'. A woman in broadcasting summed this up, referring to the male 'rules of the game':

You do have to play the political game. When I see women who should have made it they have not had time to do it. They have had children or are concentrating on something else. Men are quietly political. If I try to be political I can be seen as being stroppy. Men do quiet self promotion, and men do better generally. I find it interesting to observe the behaviour of males around me. The senior women who have made it do it too and their skills are observable. The rules of the game are male and you have to take them on if you want to be successful.

The rules of the game include knowing how to ask for and get appropriate financial rewards.

Discrimination and pay

The gender pay gap is widely known and is somewhat due to structural factors. The first Triennial Review of the Equality and Human Rights Commission in 2010 commented that:

Women now do better than men in every aspect of educational qualification but the pay gap between men and women remains. After falling continuously for the past 30 years, progress seems to have halted. (EHRC, 2010, p. 27)

Purcell and Elias (2008) have analysed the gender pay gap among relatively young graduates and found that it appears even in the early career, and widens as the graduates' careers develop. An element of the explanation lies in differences in work sectors but it was decisions relating to family life in their 30s which tended to exacerbate the differential in earnings. For example, women with dependent children in the UK earn 43 per cent of male weekly pay compared with 75 per cent for women without dependent children (Harkness, 2008). In the USA, a study of women and men who took time out from work showed that women took a surprisingly short amount of time, an average of 2.2 years, but that taking out even one year led to a reduction of 11 per cent in salary, while three years or more led to a reduction of 37 per cent on return (Hewlett and Luce, 2005).

A recent study by Fernandez-Mateo (2009) showed that even in the contract employment market, where positions are short-term, men tend to have higher wages than women. One possible reason may be that men are simply better at negotiating pay. Those women who commented on pay differentials supported this hypothesis. Negotiating pay was seen to be part of the political game that women are bad at:

> I think that men are better at negotiating grades and salaries. Women tend to come across as needy and whiny. We find it hard to say: 'this is what we are worth.' We tend to go away and feel hard done by and it can fester. It still does happen. We have not learnt to ask for what we deserve. I ask myself what should I be doing about it? It is a dilemma we have.

Although women might blame themselves for being unable to negotiate, women and men are often perceived very differently in a negotiation situation. Stuhlmacher and Winkler (2006) reviewed relevant research findings which indicate that men are more task-oriented and women more relationship-oriented, that there are gender stereotypes that are helpful to men and unhelpful to women in negotiating, that men are generally seen as more powerful and that these factors might be cumulative so that a small bias in each could have a large implication over a lifetime.

Relatively few women talked about pay differentials, and those who did were mostly in the media or finance. Even then there was a reluctance to become involved in financial negotiation. One stated:

> I sometimes think I am not paid enough. I have never worried about this before because I love my job. At a recent appraisal, my boss told me I was one of the best series producers, and so I wondered if I was paid as one of the best. I am actually quite low on the pay scale. My boss says it is a very narrow pay scale and the differences are not that much, but I would like it to be more transparent. It is distasteful to me to be concerned with the money but the difference in pay between men and women has been discussed recently.

In the medical world one of the women consultants who had taken on an additional (unpaid) educational role commented about how different she was from the men in her attitude to earning:

> Getting on with the job and not getting recognition is a very female role. Also I don't do private practice and my colleagues just don't understand why I would not want to pick up another £100,000 a year. I make the choice because of time.

In the financial world, there were references to the testosterone-fuelled culture which tended to mean that, although everyone was well rewarded, it was normal for men to have higher salaries and bonuses:

> It comes down to reward mechanisms. If the thing to do is to roar down the street in a Ferrari in front of your mates, they will kill for that. A woman who is content with a bonus of £5 million not £15 million is not even playing the game on the same terms. There are terrible culture clashes. Probably women are good at analysing stuff but not the rest of it.

Although there may be exceptions, the perceptions of the women interviewed were that men were likely to be paid more than women for the same job mainly because men are intrinsically valued more than women and are also likely to demand more (see also Chapter 6 in this book).

Discrimination and age

As individuals age, they may be increasingly valued at work for their maturity and experience, or they may be written off and regarded as something of a liability. In most cases, the women interviewed did not comment on age and the older interviewees appeared to have been able to incorporate a work role such as serving as a non-executive director on a board into their retirement from a full-time role. The exception to this was the opinion held by women in the media that older women were not valued and were not listened to:

> There are elements who can be dismissive about you if you are a middle aged white woman. There is an age thing which does not seem to apply in quite the same way to men. There is a feeling that creativity comes from the young things. The opinions of older women aren't necessarily listened to.

It was definitely felt that women were disadvantaged by age more than men:

> At 53 I'm wondering is there a next career stop? If I was a man I would probably not think like that. Men assume they will be there till they are 65. Women I know who have left their jobs find it incredibly difficult to get jobs in their 50s. They are thought to be too set in their ways or too old. This applies to women more than men.

The dominance of men in the culture made this particularly relevant, as youthful attractiveness might benefit a woman in the workplace:

> I am beginning to feel I look my age, and – though I don't like to believe this – I think that has an effect. I have a fuller figure in a way that just does not shift, greying hair... it all plays into a subconscious way that people receive and perceive you. I'm falling into an older group now in people's eyes.

In the relatively glamorous world of news journalism an older woman might be less able to participate:

> There is a hell of a lot of attraction-frisson in this business that is rarely acted on. Those journalists who go out on the road, there is this sort of 'we have had a tough time, therefore we can play a bit harder.' There is a frisson that disappears when you get older. Probably it is the same wherever people work hard and do difficult things. This spirit bubbles up and helps them cope.

Paradoxically, women may also be disadvantaged by appearing too young, for example as consultant surgeons, or too attractive and therefore being written off or 'put down' and diminished, for example through derogatory stereotyping.

Stereotyping

All the women interviewed are clear that women and men are treated differently and that it is harder for women to obtain leadership positions than men. This is changing over time, but they perceive a bedrock of stereotypes. In the complexity of social relationships that exist in the workplace, stereotypes allow us to make quick and easy judgements of individuals based on the ways in which we categorize people. Fiske and Lee (2008, p. 14) refer to stereotypes as: 'the categorical associations – including traits, behaviours, and roles – perceivers make to group members based on their membership'. They go on to point out that such categorization leads to an emotional response of prejudice to which discrimination tends to be the behavioural outcome. One woman now at the end of her career in finance expressed this very clearly:

> It just isn't changing, it's ingrained. People are more conscious, more aware, but it is inevitable, you tend to gravitate to people who are like yourself. It takes a special person to reach out to work with someone different. It is not just a man/ woman thing. It is difficult for people to reach out to ethnic minorities. I've had plenty of experience of that too.

In the work situation in the Western world, the in-group is likely to be made up of white, middle-class males who unthinkingly apply categorizations and classify those not like themselves as outsiders (Lumby with Coleman, 2008). These stereotypes are shared by the vast majority of people, including other women (Schein, 2007). Recent research in the USA (Bligh and Kohles, 2008) indicates that even at the level of the Senate, women senators experience the negative effects of gender stereotypes and expectations.

A woman consultant surgeon interviewed stated that: 'Once I was in a consultant post I just had this feeling that you were viewed slightly differently, as slightly weaker, by everyone, patients and doctors.' Over time, definitions and categorizations may be subject to modification and change, but at the very top and in some circumstances these categorizations can be experienced as immutable. One senior woman in the world of finance stated:

> I went to an interview with a head hunter. He said there are some jobs you just have to be 6 ft tall for. He was saying he wanted a man.

There are some things where people still think they must have a man. People still worry about a physical look. I find when I go into meetings I have to brace myself as a 5 ft 1 woman. As a 6 ft man I would not do that.

In fact stereotypes derived from physical appearances are common both in excluding women from certain jobs and also in controlling or demeaning them. Women head teachers who are short are questioned on whether they can maintain discipline with boys and young men (Coleman, 2002). Being young and attractive carries with it a particular type of difficulty of being taken seriously. A woman in advertising commented: 'working with a senior management guy, when a bright young girl comes walking in, it can be difficult for her to be heard in those circumstances'. In another instance a woman working in the media illustrated an attempt to keep her in her place through drawing attention to her feminine appearance:

One of the partners was putting me down and nicknamed me 'Dolly', he put me in the slot of being a woman and a blonde. These things are always done in jest. When you confront sexist behaviours they say: 'I was just joking. What, don't you have a sense of humour?'

Fiske and Lee (2008) point out that a very modern type of sexism is doubting that sexism exists any more and then expressing disapproval of those who disagree, implying that they are old-fashioned and out of date. In their study of how women might access the boardroom, Thomson and Graham (2005, p. 31) comment on how gender bias is now politically unacceptable or 'dismissed as a figment of a paranoid imagination', even though the proportions of women directors remains so low. Another way of dismissing women's concerns is to adopt 'benevolent' attitudes which actually seek to control women as they remind everyone of women's traditional stereotypical roles in life and therefore their 'lack of fit' (Fiske and Lee, 2008, p. 29) in the work situation. However, women (and men) who are seen to perform differently to their gender stereotypes also encounter hostility. A senior woman in the energy industry commented:

I do think there is a barrier for me which is about style. I had a personal development one-to-one to discuss my development and opportunities. The feedback is always 'you are incredibly smart and good at delivering results, but you are stubborn'. I'm stubborn! I know I am interpreting this, but I experience the sense that the boundaries of behaviour that are acceptable for women are narrow. I tend to be upfront. I am considered stubborn and aggressive. Others behave the same way and it is fine.

Leadership is generally identified with male qualities, but where women adopt masculine-type leadership behaviour they are perceived as not being feminine and resented. This catch-22 perception of being too aggressive is a double bind referred to by Still (2006, p. 187) as the femininity/competence bind. Too feminine and you cannot be a leader, too competent and you are regarded as not feminine and therefore strange.

Perceptions about women's 'fit' in the workplace can be extremely damaging to potential women leaders. One woman working in the financial world, having met all the criteria for promotion and having been passed over persistently while her male peers were promoted, said:

> I was not a member of the boys' club. People who did not know me perceived me as assertive, people who knew me were fine. I was black-balled by people who had never met me. The promotion procedures allowed subjectivity. The most challenging task was managing perceptions and my reputation with senior managers where there had been zero interaction or direct exposure, yet their 'vote' was material in performance and compensation decisions.

The feeling of being an outsider extends to a perception of women having less support for promotion. A woman in broadcasting said:

> I work in a particularly 'boys' part of the organization. Some men executives are not individuals to encourage people. They don't have that generosity about them and that means that you are stuck. Maybe it will change.

Exclusion from support may be unthinking, but it occurs particularly where women are very rare. One of the surgeons commented that:

> I got negative comments from the surgeons I was working with on the way up but not the top ones. They did not mean to be negative

but some things just came out. When I was doing my rotation they assumed that I was in surgery just because I was doing my time there. When I said I wanted to go into surgery, they said things like: do you know how few women consultants there are in surgery? They did not say: what you need to do is this.

However, in another situation one woman felt that she had been picked for jobs where, although there were still stereotypes about women, they had worked to her advantage: 'I suspect I am seen as a team player. It encourages people to appoint. I am not seen as difficult.'

In education, women were aware of being pigeonholed as supportive and nurturing, being directed into pastoral jobs; for example, 'you get touchy feely jobs to do'. One head teacher reported that feedback from her interviews for headship included 'that I might be better in a smaller school, not dealing with difficult people'. Another head teacher talked about how:

> the PTA has different expectations of a woman head. If the male head I worked for missed a meeting, no one thought anything of it. As a woman it's a black mark if I don't help put up stalls and bake buns.

Another woman head teacher recalled: 'the men in the local group used to tease me about my filing system, saying: "Oh [she] will have a copy of that". It boosted my ego that I could produce these things, although I was also a bit irritated that they took it for granted'.

The women also speculated on how women and men were different in the ways that they work and lead (see below).

Internalizing stereotypes

It is not surprising that a mainly masculine work culture which depicts women as outsiders or as inferior to men in a senior role leads to some women in effect blaming themselves for the challenges that they face. One woman stated:

> Were they [barriers] put in front of me or did I stumble over them myself? Absolutely I was discriminated against, but some of the barriers have been my own also.

When asked to give examples, she added: 'Probably not understanding the intrinsic needs of a chairman, making the wrong call, not being aligned in the right way....' All of which might be at least partially due to differences in communication styles and resulting misunderstanding (Still, 2006).

A lack of female role models is not helpful to women who aspire to leadership. A woman now in a senior role in higher education recalled: 'The hurdle I faced was my perception of leadership jobs – there were just no role models. I did not have an expectation that I could do these jobs.' While a woman in advertising considered that the barriers she met were:

> largely self imposed. It was my own fear or lack of self belief. I never actually had anyone say to me 'don't apply for that job'. It was my own perceptions that got in the way although they were driven by the culture. As I have become older and older I have got braver. I started out as pretty conformist and scared to change from one sector to another. As I have got more senior, I have become braver.

Lack of self-efficacy, the belief that an individual has the ability to meet the demands of a task, is associated more with women than men (Stuhlmacher and Winkler, 2006) and may be a reason why women do less well than men in applying for and obtaining promotion and then in operating in a leadership role. In addition, a woman in a male-dominated area is more visible than her male colleagues and may be seen as out of place and more open to criticism. One woman in broadcasting identified that:

> I think women are open to self doubt more than men. I don't think men are beset by doubt much. I spent time planning ahead allowing for all the things that could go wrong. You knew you would be blamed for it. You dwell on things that go wrong more than the guys do.

Perceptions that women and men work differently

Stereotypes about women and men at work are culturally defined (Hofstede, 1980) and the qualities that are stereotypically identified as masculine or feminine remain fairly constant over time and between cultures (Schein, 2007; Bem, 1974). While sex differences are biological, gender differences relate to the ascribed and learnt social role (Eagly, 1987) identifying men with power and paid work and women primarily with a family role, so that women are found in supportive and nurturing roles and men in leadership at work. This differentiation generally includes beliefs about who is likely to be better at strategic thinking and who better at the more subordinate and detailed roles. A woman in broadcasting commented that: 'women are doing jobs where we use our skills. Women tend to do logistical organization. When I look round, people at the top taking decisions are men, and women are round the table doing the logistical stuff.' It may be that women are good at the lesser roles, but values in the workplace continue to favour the masculine style of work. O'Neill et al. (2006) identify the tension between current ideas of good leadership and management as participative where leaders have good interpersonal skills, and the reluctance of male leaders to adopt behaviour seen as feminine.

From the interviews there was a strong perception among the women that men were more competitive than women in the workplace and that women were more generous in giving support and more honest. A good example is that of one woman manager who recalled:

> I felt isolated at a senior level. When I became a general manager of xxx and in my next two jobs when I was on the executive board, for example, I really had to work hard to maintain my confidence at board meetings. I think it's a basic difference between men and women. I'll tell the truth, I won't fudge. Maybe I'm naïve. Men will bullshit. In meetings I was often put on the spot. In virtually all my jobs, men will try in meetings to deflect attention from themselves by putting you in a difficult spot. That was a huge problem. What they would do, is raise a problem for the first time in a meeting in front of the boss. If I was in that position I would pick up a phone and ask about it in advance and try and sort things out. When I did talk to some of them about this behaviour, they admitted they did it. They agreed they would not do it again, but they did.

She is now working as a leadership coach and consultant, and 'one reason for doing this was that I was frustrated with the patterns of behaviour from some senior men'.

A woman in broadcasting reported on an experience of meeting a young, particularly competitive man:

> With xxx I had a good position in his team. I thought I was doing a good job and so did he. Then an archetypal male arrives and he thought it was his divine right to come in and be next in command. He tried to undermine and land grab that role. With a different boss he might have been able to do that. My boss said: 'you tell me if there are any problems if he steps out of line'. I felt I had to win this myself.

I outed him by being better. He made a couple of mistakes and left. The boss did not intrude, but in the end I knew I had that support, but it was earned. The smartarse never saw it. With a different boss it might have been very different.

A senior woman in a retail organization commented on how the culture suddenly changed when there was competition for promotion:

> In one organisation I was in, it was going through a lot of change, change at the top and a lot of the males were vying on who would get the top job. When that was happening behaviours changed and personal agendas were driving the decision making. I found that uncomfortable.

In contrast to the intense competitiveness of some men, there was a perception that women tend to be more principled than men in their work:

> If you have some core principles, for example I am driven by satisfaction for this division to do well. Of course there are personal ambitions, but I would always balance my interests against those of the division. I don't have a coterie of people around me, but I do see a lot of chaps who do relishing their power. Once you start doing that, I can't stand that, although I am sure it gets you on.

Men are perceived to use their male networks to make life more comfortable rather than for the good of the organization:

> Women are not as good at networking as men. I find I have got too much integrity for it. People are not going to get anywhere by buttering me up. I see things happening with men like – 'I want to work with my mates, I have fun with them, it's easier to work with them'. Women also are ambitious, but they are more driven by the common good.

A number of the women talked about their key principles or values that underpin their approach to work, for example: 'Integrity is what I hold highest in life – a bit strange perhaps in the advertising industry, but being honest is the best policy, it drives trust.' A woman in finance commented more extensively on her style:

> I'm very consensus driven. I have ideas of where I want to end up. I would define myself as a consensus-moulder. It's a team effort.

Strong teams win: teams with complementary skills who are prepared to focus and bring out the best in each other. It is a consensus
oriented style. I don't run rough shod over people, but manage with
a soft touch, but if necessary I will let people know who is in charge,
but not in a way that is unnecessarily bruising.

The attitudes towards leadership expressed here and echoed in
Chapter 6 are reminiscent of the findings of Ruderman and Ohlott (2002)
who analysed their interviews and surveys with high-achieving women
to extract a number of key themes which were: authenticity, connection, controlling your destiny, wholeness and self-clarity. The executive
women interviewed by Olsson (2006, p. 207) were aware that there was
an alternative paradigm of leadership emerging. Olsson reflected that
the stories of the women she interviewed 'break through the constraints
of heroic masculinism to reconfigure a distinctive female archetype of
leadership for women in management'. Many of the women interviewed
for this book expressed the belief that they operated somewhat differently to their male peers. There has been some theorizing on this for
example, Ward et al. (2010) identify the concept of the 'Alpha Female',
who exhibits leadership strength, low introversion and high self-esteem
and emotional intelligence, and Ross-Smith and Huppatz (2010) pro-
pose that women in senior management establish 'gender capital' which
impacts on management and leadership discourse.

There is now some evidence of the presence of a 'critical mass', probably three women on a board to influence the nature of decision-taking.
Research undertaken by Erkut et al. (2008) indicated that women directors make three important contributions. First they represent the views
of a wider group of people than normal including employees and customers; secondly they are more likely to question things persistently
than are men, perhaps because they are less afraid of showing igno-
rance, and thirdly they tend to be more collaborative in their approach.
One woman interviewed commented that: 'If there are no other women
on the board it can be a little bit isolating although I have never com-
plained. It helps if you have more than one woman on the board; it
improves the dynamic.' Research on gender and teams (Gratton et al.,
2007) has indicated that the best performances come from teams which
are made up equally of men and women.

Although all the women interviewed referred to a greater or lesser
extent to the challenges they faced in a male-dominated world of work,
a number of them commented positively about the benefits they had
experienced as a woman in a man's world.

The advantage of being a woman

Although relatively rare there were examples of women being actively sought for membership of an organization in the public eye:

> I feel that to be fair I actually benefited from being a woman on two occasions. Xxx wanted a woman and looked to appoint one. Of course they had to be good, but at the margin if two people were equally good he would appoint a woman…Here, I replaced the only woman and it was the same thing [i.e. they wanted a woman for the job]. They have difficulty finding women and they are anxious about the difficulty of finding a replacement if I were to leave early.

Women may also be sought by other women: 'My current line manager is a Pro Vice Chancellor, a woman who I get on particularly well with. I feel she may have wanted a woman for the job. They interviewed two males and two females and I got a gut feeling that they wanted a woman. It may have helped me in this role.'

In other situations, the scarcity of women meant that a woman might make more of an impact. For example, a woman surgeon commented: 'At one stage it was an advantage being a woman just because people knew me.'

There were also those who felt that they might have benefited early in their career when women in leadership were even rarer than now. One woman recalled: 'I was exceedingly lucky to be a graduate in the 1970s when larger organisations were trying to get women into management jobs.' She was then moved as a production manager to Glasgow: 'I loved it. I was a complete surprise on the shop floor, a woman and a woman from the south. I liked being different and new.' However, she was able to call on her own resources in a way that not every woman might: 'I had a history of being a tomboy. I felt I was just as capable as the next person.'

There are undoubtedly women who are capable of fitting into a male environment very happily, usually because they and their male colleagues share the same technical expertise and interests: 'gender has never made any difference. Since I have moved into a technical world I find myself in meetings that are all men. When I mix with colleagues they are all men.' In some instances they may even feel more comfortable with men:

> I am surrounded by men and I am most comfortable with that, maybe because of the time I am working in a male dominated environment. A while ago I had to join in with a group of women on an

exercise. We were asked to make up groups and there were two men who I gravitated towards but they did not want to partner with me as a woman. I am so used to being in a male environment I found this strange. Women are not interested in talking technology and I don't know the language [of women] so the conversations are often short.

However, women in specialist technical areas are relatively rare and most women, although happy working with male colleagues, felt that there was something special and supportive about working with female colleagues (see Chapter 4 on networking).

The main issues

The perceptions of the women interviewed are that there is a male culture of work which, although changing, still hampers women's entry into and progress through their careers. Although there might be denial of gender discrimination, there is still evidence of some bullying, of manipulation, and of more subtle demeaning of women through language. In addition, women continue to be paid less than men. Gender stereotyping about women in work is deeply built into our society and is only slowly diminishing. In some instances, the women interviewed anticipate that things are becoming more, not less difficult for women with career ambitions. Without essentializing the differences between men and women leaders, many of the women ponder on whether they and other women operate somewhat differently to men. Finally, there are some occasions when women feel that their gender has advantaged them.

In the next chapter we focus on the reasons the interviewed women give for their success.

3
Success Factors

> I think opportunities are of your own making. I think you have to be proactive and go out and search for opportunities.

> You can win them over with passion and commitment. Being good is not enough. You have to be better and be seen to be better. People can then say: 'She is a woman, but she is very good.'

> I was lucky that I had mentors who gave counsel. You need to be able to talk to someone who can be a sounding board.
>
> (views of three interviewed women)

The factors identified by the women as contributing to their success were first and foremost their own agency: their determination and drive, their hard work and appropriate qualifications. Secondly they talked about support at work, particularly mentoring and coaching, as being important factors that had contributed to their career success. Finally, many of them mentioned networking. Mentoring and networking are clearly identified as being of prime importance in the support and development of women at work (Coleman, 2008a).

The focus of this chapter is first on the personal agency of the women in building their human capital to bring about their career success. The focus then moves to support in the workplace through mentoring and coaching. The other important factor in career development, the building of social capital through networking, is the focus of Chapter 4.

The women whose views are represented in this book are all successful in their careers. This does not mean that they necessarily see themselves as successful, however. For example, one woman commented: 'I don't perceive it as success at all when I compare myself with those who have climbed higher.' However, she added the important proviso: 'when I think about it they tend not to have children'; the undoubted impact that family has on career will be considered in Chapter 5.

Leaving the question of families to one side, women were still relatively modest about their success. One woman chief executive commented:

> I am not sure that I am that successful. I wish that I had started my own business. I am successful as an employee, but the way to be truly successful in advertising is to own your own company. The fact that I have not done so is probably partly due to being a woman who may be more likely to be scared of failure.

Even at the level of CEO, this fear of failure may be related to lack of a particular type of confidence, and to the fact that failure of a woman would be noticed more because women are relatively rare in running a company in the world of advertising. Women in such exposed positions are on the edge of a 'glass cliff' (Ryan and Haslam, 2005, 2006).

The successes that they have achieved do not blind them to the difficulties and frustrations that they have experienced along the way that were discussed in Chapter 2. Those who were the most successful relished their position, since being at the very top meant that their life became simpler in some ways: for example, they could set the pace and handle their own childcare issues, and other people's diaries had to fit round theirs. They were also quite likely to qualify any claims to success they might make, and to include 'being in the right place at the right time' as a factor in their individual successes. For example, a woman in the media commented:

> I have a wonderful job, I work in a fantastic company and we have worked very hard to make it a success. Success is a combination of luck and choosing the right place to work. I've been lucky with the job and the place and lucky to work for and with great people.

In a few cases, being 'in the right place at the right time' was allied to a specific change at their place of work which was beneficial to them. For example, one woman mentioned that a strategic decision to get more women involved in broadcasting was helpful to her. A woman in property development mentioned some specific experience which had aided her career: 'I used to sell off a lot of land for local authorities and suddenly there was a demand for that and not many people were doing it. That helped [my career]'.

However, the factors most often identified as helping them to be successful were, on the one hand, their own agency, including their determination and hard work, and, on the other, the support they received at work and at home. Their view of their own agency predominated and, although they were aware of difficulties for women and were supportive towards other women, they were generally indifferent to feminist ideas. This area will be discussed further in Chapter 7. Despite the apparently general indifference to or rejection of feminism, the women were basically very supportive of other women, offering constructive help, within the work context. The support they offer is considered further towards the end of this chapter, which focuses first on the personal agency of the women and then on the importance of mentoring and coaching.

Personal agency and success

Discussion of the paucity of women in leadership and management tends to focus on the barriers that deter women from climbing the career ladder (see the many references in the Bibliography) rather than the factors that have helped women rise to the top. These factors might be organizational, social, as in networking, or personal, including personality factors and family support (Tharenou, 2005). The women spoke extensively about the ways in which they had been proactive in shaping their own careers. They referred to their hard work and determination, their love of their work, their own personal strengths and the valuable qualities that they brought to their roles, including qualities instilled in them from childhood. They also commented on factors relating to their families, including the support of husband or partner or good childcare arrangements, and these factors will be discussed along with other issues relating to families and children in Chapter 5.

Determination, confidence and clarity

Many of the women from all work sectors identified the importance of their own high levels of determination in helping them build their careers. Key words and phrases that emerged from the interviews were 'drive', 'determination', 'ambition', 'single-minded', 'persistent', 'dogged', 'proactive' and having a 'positive mindset'. One woman expressed this attitude as her:

Dogged determination. The ability to always believe there is a solution to something, or else a way round it. I can get stressed, but for me the way to solve it is to do something about it. I like challenging environments. I'll find a route and lead people through it and people trust you then.

The determination and challenge were echoed elsewhere, for example a secondary school head teacher reflected: 'I've not been afraid to take risks. I've taken them in everything that I have done. I don't do ordinary things because I get bored. I take calculated risks.' When asked why some women make it to the very top, one responded: 'Fearlessness is what the women have who do break through...They are afraid of nothing.'

The level of determination and development of human capital was sometimes linked to general levels of confidence gained from their early experiences:

Confidence comes from my educational background which was an all-girls' school. We did not make way for men. My upbringing helped, my mother was a practising doctor. I felt I had a right to be here as much as the blokes.

Another woman referred to the role played by her 'Presbyterian background, where you are expected to do your best. My parents had high expectations of me and this affects your character for life.' A woman in finance referred to her own level of determination allied to that of her family:

I was determined to succeed. I left Malaysia to come to the UK when I was 18 to train as a chartered accountant and there was pressure to do well. Also I personally wanted to be successful and very good at what I was doing.

Although confidence was seen to be an important factor in success, and lack of confidence is sometimes seen as a factor contributing to women's career difficulties, it was thought that women who are too confident risk being seen as not conforming to the gender stereotypes identified in Chapter 2 and may suffer as a result. For example, a woman in broadcasting commented:

I am happy to speak up and not backward in coming forward. Sometimes this may be to my disadvantage. It depends where you are, in news it is important. It got me to a certain level then it becomes a disadvantage.

Determination was also linked to being clear about what they wanted. One woman saw this in relation to her work as a producer:

> I had absolute clarity about what I wanted to do. When I first started I stood behind and watched and I thought that it was the most wonderful job in the world. I actively pursued it.

Another, working in consultancy, knew that:

> what has helped is that I am clear I wanted to do interesting, intellectually stimulating things. Once I decide on an interest I am very determined and have high energy to put into the work. The main thing for me was not about role or hierarchy, but about work content.

Perhaps such clarity is relatively rare and these successful women are career-centred in a way that, as Hakim (2004) suggests, is only ever going to be true of a minority of women. A woman working in the media summed this up:

> I think you have to be driven to succeed. Some people want to achieve and some don't. I don't know what makes that difference. I think I have been successful because I am someone who goes into any situation, whether school, university or job to become a leader in whatever I did. I always want to do the best I can. I don't feel limited. If I can access the opportunity I try to be as engaged as I can and do the best I can.

Personal responsibility for making her own way in the world was expressed particularly clearly by one woman in broadcasting:

> If I want something, I think it is my responsibility to get it. I believe that everything is in my power. I paid my way through university. I gave up a job when I was passed over for promotion for a man with no experience of the job. I told my boss I was going to go and get qualifications and come back and do to him what he had done to me. Since then my hard work has given me recognition. I now have insights about how to deal with people when they are starting to bully. I now have the skills to say: 'I don't have to put up with it'. I have confidence.

The conviction that: 'it is my responsibility to get it' typifies the attitude of the women interviewed, who, in tune with current thinking

(Howard and Tibballs, 2003; Moreau et al., 2005), tend to take individual responsibility for their career success although they do see that women face contextual, cultural and social challenges in making it to the top.

Enthusiasm, passion and commitment

'Enthusiasm', 'passion', 'enjoyment' and 'love of work' were allied to their determination and seen as reasons for success by many of the women. A woman working in broadcasting commented on the centrality of her work to her life: 'When I have appraisals, the thing they like is my enthusiasm. Also I try never to let things get in the way of work.' One who was in the field of higher education stated: 'In terms of personal factors I have always enjoyed the job and got a lot of job satisfaction. I like research, teaching students and I like people.' Intense enthusiasm was expressed by a woman in advertising:

> There is a lot to be said for falling into the right profession. I have been in the business for 30 years and I still love it. It charms me, and intrigues me. If you have a passion for what you do it shines through. It makes you want to give more.

Another woman working in property development commented that:

> I have incredible interest and enthusiasm for my work... I enjoy people. I am having such fun, and I have gone on being enthusiastic about my work and this is what has helped me to get on well.

While another in the same field commented that: 'the fact that I enjoy the job is another thing. That comes across with people, you can always tell.'

The high level of commitment to their work seems to support the commonly held belief that women managers 'must over-perform to demonstrate their abilities in a male-dominated environment' (Burke, 2005, p. 15).

Work harder: be better

As we could see from the views expressed in the previous chapter, the women accepted that, to some extent, things were different, and usually more difficult, for women who wanted to progress in their careers. There was an assumption that women would probably have to work harder than their male colleagues to be accepted and to achieve. One woman in finance stated:

> I think that I always knew that to get on you had to work harder than a man. I had a passion for what I was doing and I had a couple of lucky breaks.

A woman in media thought that 'another thing that helps is seriously hard work of the old-fashioned kind. I have a strong work ethic. There is no substitute for hard work.'

This attitude was particularly apparent in the field of surgery, where women are still relatively rare at consultant level. One felt that her success had been due to 'determination, and probably a bit of luck. Not really believing the negative stuff. Probably working really hard and being able to manage without sleep.' Another commented:

> I remember thinking if I want to be a surgeon, I've got to do the same as the boys. As a woman you bring a different attitude, a different way of looking at things but you've got to be able to do all the things. Orthopaedics can be a bit heavy weight, but I always managed.

In other fields too, women commented on their perceived need to work harder. One said she was successful:

> because I have a work ethic. I have a panic ethic too. I wake up in the middle of the night and write notes, or log on and send emails. I can be over-committed in an anxiety to not leave anything undone or incorrect.

Another commented on her tendency to: 'run myself ragged and get ill', adding: 'they will let me do that', exhibiting a belief that organizations are not necessarily going to exercise care for their employees and again that the individual woman is responsible for managing her own work and career.

As well as working harder, some believed that they had to be better, particularly in the very male industries like engineering or power generation: 'The fundamental thing was a level of ability that was higher than that of my male peers. It had to be higher then, and engineering is a male world.' However, the feeling of having to be better was common in all work areas. One woman working in retailing commented that: 'I outperformed everybody. Also I have a demon work ethic. In some of those early days I had to outperform; you have to do better.'

The importance of acquiring human capital through qualifications and relevant work experience is recognized as particularly vital for women in building their career. Some of the women interviewed referred to the importance of having the necessary paper qualification and technical skills, as well as the baseline importance of being bright and clever. A woman in finance commented that: 'An advanced degree is important for feeling confident, standing out, sharpening skill sets.' Women in higher education recognized the importance of their having academic credibility and therefore the need to keep up their research and publications. Those rare women who are successful in technical areas referred to the importance of being able to 'pick up technical things quickly'. In worlds as different as secondary education, finance and advertising women commented on the importance of getting an MBA, and the credibility and confidence that it gave them. A woman in advertising explained:

> When I was 30, and on the Board, I did an MBA. I did it part-time and it meant working till four in the morning and at the weekends. It nearly killed me. It gave me a level of confidence which women may lack; that particular intellectual confidence. Women tend to be less assertive, more collaborative and that does not play well if you are senior in the room. When I started the MBA I did a four hour test involving numeracy and working things out. There was a lot of multiple choice, a very masculine approach. I came out with the bottom score of my group in that, but at the end of the course I came out top. It taught me to recognise what I knew.
>
> I think that there is a perception that women, particularly women who are attractive in some way, can't be both attractive and smart. There were people [women] in advertising agencies who were visibly clever, no make-up and so on, then there were pretty girls and there was nothing in between. When I started you had your photograph on the job application and what you looked like was an important part of getting a job in advertising. After I got the MBA I stopped apologising for a lack of intellectual confidence.

This woman had achieved board membership at the early age of 30, indicating a high level of ability, but she felt that she was still judged on her looks and attractiveness. She needed to hold the formal recognition of her ability in the shape of the MBA in order to fully occupy the place on the board that she had already won.

Many of the women also put down their success to skills that are particularly associated with women.

Qualities of women

Although there is conflicting evidence about whether women and men actually lead and manage in different ways (Collins and Singh, 2006; Pounder and Coleman, 2002), there are common stereotypes about male and female leadership, and certainly the ways in which women and men manage and lead are perceived differently. For example, a woman may be seen as aggressive whereas the same attitude from a man is seen as characteristically firm and fair. The experiences of women and men are different and likely to feed through into the ways in which they exercise their leadership. One of the women interviewed commented that:

> Intuition and empathy are stronger traits in women, women are better at it. They have had different experiences and built up different skill sets and have different role models. They have been used to listening to people and have had to work in a collaborative rather than a command and control environment.

My research with women and men head teachers (Coleman, 2002, 2007) has led me to the conclusion that women and men have different experiences of leadership, with women always having to overcome the stereotype that identifies men with leadership (Schein, 2007). However, although they may be judged differently, the majority of male and female head teachers aspired to similar styles of leadership that might be described as 'feminine', with the majority of both sexes valuing the qualities of caring, nurturing and tolerance and working in a collaborative and people-centred way (Hofstede, 1980).

Most of the qualities identified by the interviewed women fell into the more 'feminine' style of leadership. The personal leadership qualities most frequently referred to were those relating to teams, including the building and leading of teams. One head teacher commented: 'I am good at building teams around me. It's the teams I've created round me that have been successful and achieved major things.' A woman in the media felt that:

> I never considered myself to be a high achiever or very clever. I put my success down to being organised and committed. However, I have been, and am, a good man-manager and have brought on many

others who've worked on teams with me over twenty years. I consider myself to be good at this.

Allied to teambuilding, and again a 'feminine' quality, individuals picked out the importance of communications. Women in the media commented that:

> My communication skills have definitely helped me with my career progression. Women generally tend to be better in the area but I happen to have the skills.

> Being a woman, my role has quite often involved corralling the views of a number of stakeholders. These are also areas where women tend to have more skills.

Communication skills associated with women were understandably seen as particularly important in the media:

> It's not really about being a woman or despite being a woman. Women can compete relatively well in this business. The skills that you need are to do with communication, empathy and emotional intelligence in all areas of advertising: in creative work and in planning even in media sales these qualities are important.

Other 'feminine' skills were seen as being advantageous in advertising:

> As a woman, key qualities are relationship building, energy and positivity. Like most women I like to please and try hard, and these are qualities that are valued in this industry. Humility is something that is not often found in this industry and women tend to have that quality.

Working successfully with others is a skill that is particularly important in client relationships. A woman in property development commented:

> Personality is important, the ability to get on well with people. It is particularly important in my area as a consultant. I am advising people. A lot is about what you know, but a lot is also how well you get the message across. If they respect and like you as a person it is better.

Generally, research indicates that women tend to have a communication style which is 'more other-directed, warm and mitigated than men's, and men's communications are more dominant, status-asserting, and task-oriented than women's' (Carli, 2006, p. 76). However, findings also indicate that where women are in more powerful positions their communication style is more like that of men. In a minority of cases some of the personal qualities that were identified by the women interviewed included those more stereotypically identified with men, for example being decisive. A woman in the media stated:

> I am a data rational type of person. I find solutions not problems. I am a quick learner. I can assess things quickly and come to a decision. I need information to feel comfortable, but make decisions quickly.

Another similarly commented: 'As a consultant I'm reasonably smart and quite fast in finding solutions to situations. I am pragmatic but academic in background. Also clients like me because I'm very direct, and objective.'

Some of the women identified that they exhibited firm leadership, but this was always qualified by an element of empowering others or collaborating. 'Power with' rather than 'power over' is seen as typical of the way that women leaders in education might operate (Brunner, 2002; Blackmore 1999) and this attitude was fairly typical of the women interviewed. One woman in higher education indicated how she led from the front but was seeking to take people with her and pushing for values that she believed in:

> I've got vision, I am a strategic thinker. I can inspire, rally people round a cause. I've built up a groundswell of opinion about diversity where I am now. I try and empower other people and power then comes from those around you.

Another in broadcasting stated:

> I have a strong urge to make things better always. I have a natural instinct of seeing the bigger picture, the problems and blockages. My strong points – I am a really good shaper and a good leader. I get people engaged and don't dictate but collaborate.

The attitude of 'power with' rather than 'power over' tends to be underpinned by a consciously held set of values.

Values

In Chapter 2 there was some discussion of perceived differences between men and women in relation to values at work. Women in all types of work referred to the values that underpinned their leadership. In one case a woman in higher education felt that her career had been formed by a resistance to largely male values:

> At every stage in my career I had no intention to go higher, no plan, but a job would come up and I knew the men who might get it and I knew that I did not want to work with them. It seemed reasonable to apply. It was about values, I'm a values driven person. I did not like what I saw and so I just thought I would have a go and then I got the job. I have had little support, little peer support and no mentoring...If I felt that things could be done differently then I knew that I should have a go.

Also in education, a woman head teacher referred to her 'deep personal resources...resilience, determination, the belief that what I am doing is right' as helping her to cope with the accountability and high visibility that go with her job which she felt were experienced more strongly by women, who are arguably more 'visible' than their male colleagues:

> Very often the demands of the job are incredible. One thing the head teacher does not get is positive feedback. If everything goes wrong it is your fault. When things go well there is no feedback. Women find this more difficult than men, as men create their own little world of self-esteem and are more impervious to what is going on outside their little bubble.

A study of high-achieving women (Ruderman and Ohlott, 2002, reported in Burke, 2005, p. 19) identified five 'themes' from their stories, including:

authority: the need to have a fit between inner values and beliefs and outer behaviours;
connection: the need to be close and intimate with others;
controlling your destiny: being active (agentic) in achieving one's life and career goals;
wholeness: uniting and integrating one's varied life roles and having time to pursue them; and

self-clarity: reflecting an understanding of one's self (motives, values, behaviors, experiences).

The identification of the women with their own networks and families indicated 'connection' and the other 'themes' are well represented through the statements of the women about the ways in which they led and managed others.

Maintaining their individual integrity ('wholeness') was seen as important. A woman head teacher stated:

> Without wanting to sound arrogant, I have refused to not be myself. I have got a sense of humour and a sense of fun. I can't do the job unless I have a laugh on a daily basis.

Others referred to their 'authenticity' ('authority' and 'wholeness'). A woman in the media talked about how she had learned that:

> Women have to be more strategic in order to influence. It is like a game of chess. It is no good as a woman to be banging fists on the table or swearing. That does not work. Slowly, slowly and being thorough in thinking things through with a game plan and how to manage situations. For this you need authenticity and knowledge of who you are. In my early 30s, like many people I experienced a phase of asking who am I? Am I doing the right thing? What I have learnt is the more authentic you can be to who you actually are, the more successful you can be.

The theme of knowing oneself and of reflecting on your values and what you want ('self-clarity') came through strongly, as it does in the individual 'stories' of the women in Chapter 6. One woman who had qualified as a business coach commented that she did 'a lot of self-coaching, reflecting on what I am doing'. Another stated that:

> I have not managed my career by a route map, saying this is what I will do by the time I am 25, this by the time I am 30. It has been a combination of figuring out what I like and what I don't like, what I am good at and not so good at, bits of serendipity, bits of knowledge and experience that got you to the right place.

A small number of the women interviewed came from outside the UK and there was a sense among some of them that their different origins may have been advantageous, a view shared by Czarniawska and Guje (2008) regarding the relative success of foreign women professors. At a time when women were really outsiders in the boardroom, one woman commented on how not coming from the UK meant that there were no preconceptions about her, so that she was able to circumvent some of the challenges British women might have faced. In addition, experience of other markets was acknowledged as helpful in enabling women to 'stand out'.

In addition to their own determination and skills, the women inter-viewed were quick and generous in acknowledging the support of others, mainly in the form of informal mentoring and more formal coaching where that was available. Although personal agency featured most strongly in their assessment of success factors, mentoring and coaching and networking were almost equally important.

Support at work

In rare cases the women commented on the supportive culture at work as being helpful to their career. For example, one woman in higher edu-cation recalled a time when this had been the case:

> After this organisation got University status in 1992 we did have peo-ple at the top who were sympathetic to equality and diversity. I was chair of the Equal Opportunities Committee, and the only woman on the Academic Board at the time. But the senior management were prepared to listen and to help.

Another, in advertising, stated how she had not started out being par-ticularly ambitious, but:

> I set out to work hard and be good at my job. My career has unfolded in a very natural way, not because of an aggressive push from me. On the way, when I looked up I never thought I would get there. I had very good bosses. If you work for good people they recognise that you need to be both challenged and supported. A good job should provide a combination of support and development.

While a woman in the energy business stated:

> I was fortunate in the companies I worked in, that they are great com-panies. They have given me a lot of opportunities and development.

The thought never featured that, as a woman, you could not achieve your goals. It has been a two way street, I have been able to make a big contribution to those businesses with the teams that I have built.

The women were asked about professional development opportunities and many mentioned being able to attend training and management courses. However, formal structures for professional development apart from coaching were generally not highly rated. For example, when asked if annual appraisal worked well, one woman in broadcasting said: 'Not particularly, it's there. I think I have just been lucky and had good bosses who helped me with getting relevant training.'

In some cases the women at the top of their professions were maintaining a balance by ensuring that they also worked in a voluntary capacity, for example working for charities, acting as non-executive directors of other companies or taking secondments which might help them directly and indirectly in their career. One woman recalled:

I did some extra-curricular stuff and worked on a Government capability review. I spent 15 or 16 days over two months and then a follow up after six and 12 months. I have made quite a lot of contacts in the civil service as a result. They are quite an interesting network of people to have.

Taking on such additional roles enabled the development of further social and human capital.

Support through work structures was generally not rated highly, although once established in a senior role, many of the women spoke warmly about the usefulness of more formal, professional coaching. Initially, support had been more likely to be informal and offered by a more senior individual who typically had reached an agreement with the woman concerned to act as a mentor and champion.

Mentoring

Mentoring is usually defined as a senior, more experienced person giving developmental advice and support to a younger person who is new to the role (Carnell et al., 2006). It may be formally established as part of an induction process but this was rarely the case for the women interviewed. Understanding of the process, good matching of mentor and mentee and sufficient time for useful meetings to take place are all essential if mentoring is to be successful (Clutterbuck, 1992; Bush and Coleman, 1995).

Kram (1983) established that there are different stages in the mentoring process and that people have different needs whether they are in early, middle or late career stages. Most of the women who commented on mentoring had generally been picked out by someone senior who had seen their potential early in their career and then championed their protégée, for example:

> Everybody needs mentors and supporters. In newspapers I had two editors who helped me to write and improve my prose. Newspapers used to work like that. I was a newspaper journalist. In broadcasting I had supporters as well. They helped me move on – I was recommended.

The importance of mentors being active supporters has been emphasised by Ibarra et al. (2010) who make the point that in the USA study of 4,000 high potential women and men showed that more women than men were being mentored, but that more men were being promoted. The difference appeared to lie in the difference between giving advice (to women) and actively sponsoring (the men).

Some of the women interviewed were maintaining long-term relationships with mentors, and in these relationships the main purpose appeared to be obtaining honest advice from more senior individuals who are absolutely trusted, whereas earlier stages might have involved more general advice on career development. One woman in the media commented:

> I have over time found people that I trust implicitly. There is a professional coach who I trust and there are two or three people externally who I would trust. One is my ex-chairman. I can ask advice and he will give me a completely honest opinion. You need people who are older and wiser, who have been there and done it. I am not 'needy' but on something big I always take advice from someone who doesn't feel they have to agree!

In another case two mentors complemented each other. A senior woman in advertising said that:

> Mentoring has been important in the last ten years. I have two mentors I see regularly and discuss professional issues with. It is confidence building. One is an old boss and a luminary. We discuss all aspects of agency

work every six weeks over lunch. It is informal training and incredibly important to me. They are incredibly different. One is hard core commercial – 'how are you making money?' He is entrepreneurial and the other is much more on the human development and cultural development side but immensely successful and revered in the industry.

Older women were less likely to have been mentored. One who was now retired commented: 'one thing I did not have was a mentor; in my life in corporations I never had a mentor. It was not the done thing then.' More recently, formal mentoring schemes have been set up, for example the FTSE 100 Cross-Company Mentoring Programme established to encourage women who are in the 'marzipan' layer (Thomson and Graham, 2005) to make it through to the 'icing' of the boards of the FTSE 100 companies. At least one of the women interviewed for this book had benefited from this programme. Other formal programmes were mentioned, but usually in relation to the women acting as mentors to others rather than being mentored themselves. In the case of the Cross-Company Mentoring Programme the mentors are chairmen or chief executives of FTSE 100 companies and are therefore nearly all men. When the women interviewed had mentors, it was common for them to be men, although there were some exceptions. As one interviewee pointed out, senior women mentors are in demand and: 'it is difficult to find a peer who is female and who has time [for mentoring]. Most women I know who are professional are not peers so you end up supporting them'. Many of the women interviewed were mentoring other women and this is discussed towards the end of the chapter.

Where formal schemes had been introduced they had not always worked well. One of the consultant surgeons commented that:

they tried to force mentoring on our senior registrars in our region. I paid to go on a mentoring course to this end. It was a good course, but many people do not know what a mentor is. I don't think you can force things on people ... I have a personal network which is work based across the county, it is more of a social group.

Germain and Scandura (2005) have speculated that the more informal types of mentoring work best, where both mentor and protégée have made a decision to commit to the relationship and the protégée in particular is exercising self-determination. This means that they have taken responsibility for the development and success of the relationship.

In this case, 'Rather than assuming that the protégé is a passive participant in the receipt of mentoring functions, protégés may be viewed as shaping their own career and identity development through exercising self-determination' (p. 113). The current proportion of women in senior roles means that it is inevitable that aspiring women will be mentored by senior men. There is then a potential concern about the power relationship in the pairing. It is therefore particularly important that the protégée exercises some choice and self-determination in the selection of a mentor. It is also important that the mentor and mentee establish common understanding about the nature of the relationship. For example, Clutterbuck and Ragins (2002) discuss gender and ethnicity in mentoring arrangements and recommend that the mentoring pair come to an agreement about exactly how to deal with such sensitive issues in the relationship.

There can be ambiguity about the purpose of mentoring, as exemplified in the case of an interviewed property developer who commented:

> We are not mentored although we are trained with presentation skills and things like that. We don't tend to do mentoring in my firm. The only time people are mentored is where there is something wrong with the way that they work.

Mentoring is not usually associated with a 'corrective' approach but it is open to interpretation and development. Informal mentoring might have taken place through 'boundary spanning' (Gratton et al., 2007), where women make contacts outside the narrower confines of a job. One of those interviewed mentioned that:

> I never had a formal female mentor, but have made friendships with women and this meant I got information I might not otherwise have got. When I came back to London, I had a lot of conversations with women about what pay I could ask for.

Mentoring is normally by a more senior figure with the mentee being junior, but there are innovative examples of co-mentoring and peer mentoring. A woman in higher education commented:

> There are two women who work together, who are daring each other to apply for things, aiming at a level above where they 'should' be, and it is paying off. Co-mentoring seems to work.

For many of the women, mentoring had not been in place, but the examples set by role models were extremely important. A woman in the media summed this up:

> I have really good role models, men and women, who inspired me and taught me. They have been both in the company and clients that we work for. They have had a big influence on my career.

In education, a current head teacher commented on the importance of an example in helping her achieve her current position:

> It was very much due to a good female role model; the head where I was a deputy. She was a very successful head of a very, very successful school in demanding circumstances. As her deputy, there was no room for not being ambitious. She was the single most important influence, in the sense that without her encouragement and experience it may have been different.

Mentoring, coaching and the existence of role models are vital tools for the support and development of women who are attempting to access senior positions.

Coaching

Mentoring and coaching are similar and may overlap as concepts; mentoring may include an element of coaching (Bush and Coleman, 1995). However, a clear distinction was drawn by one interviewee who is responsible for coaching in a large institution:

> If you mentor, you are free to give someone advice, you have been down the same track, you share experience, open doors and are in the same field but more experienced.
> As a coach it is definitely better not to be in the same field. You would not give advice or suggest what the client could do unless all other exploration had drawn a blank. You could use coaching skills in mentoring, but mentors wouldn't be driven by the coach's belief that the client is their own best expert and helped most by questions which unlock their own thinking.

Coaching was thought by the interviewed women to be particularly helpful where there was a specific problem or issue in their career that needed to be faced and resolved. For example, one woman's difficulty with a boss:

> there was one boss I did not get on with. We did not share core values. I could not stand him and found it really hard. I had coaching during that period. It definitely helped but there was not a solution in it. I suppose that was the function of the coaching in that it teaches you to accept there is not a solution.

In this case coaching enabled the woman to come to terms with a difficult situation through realizing that it was not in her power to change things.

Unlike mentoring, which tended to be a long-term relationship which had usually been informally established, coaching tended to be used to address a specific issue and was time-limited. A woman in the media recalled:

> I had a life coach for about six months and it was brilliant. It was a couple of years ago. I found it hard to adapt to working here, I come from a very different background and that is why we thought a life coach might help. I saw her once a month for six months. Each time it was for half a day, it was quite exhausting but useful. I found a clear direction from the coaching. I may be ready to have that again.

As well as focusing on a particular situation or challenge, coaching was used by some individuals to reflect on the wider picture, and to clarify thinking:

> I recently decided to invest in some coaching. It was really interesting, half psychotherapy and half about professional matters, it really dealt with the whole of your life. I am taking a break from coaching now and then will come back to it. I had six two hour sessions over a four week period.

Coaching was used in innovative and creative ways, for example where a coach was used with a board of directors to work through the issues raised by the chief executive taking maternity leave. Given that women are often thought to be less aware of micro-politics at work (Morley, 2000) a further example of a specific and creative use of coaching that might be particularly appropriate for women was the following:

> Recently I have worked with an external coach to focus on how to manage upwards and manage reputations. It has been very helpful. It's been about building relationships with significant people. I have had six months with the coach...and I will carry on for another six or nine months.

In addition to the support that they received from mentors, coaches and other forms of professional development, most of the women interviewed were themselves keen advocates of supporting and developing others, often recognizing that they also benefited professionally from this process.

Developing others

The majority of the women were enthusiastic about supporting more junior colleagues. Since many of them belonged to women-only networks, it is perhaps not surprising to find this. In the current research, the support offered was often informal, for example:

> I mentor people. If people call me I have lunch with them, coffee with them, I offer advice, I give free advice, I do it all the time. I met with a woman the other week in New York, she was a banker, friend of a friend, I gave her advice, told her how to re-write her CV. I have lots of dialogues like that, with men too not just women.

It was common for them to point out that they were happy mentoring men and/or women. For example, a senior woman in a university pointed out: 'When I have line-managed women I have directed them to opportunities, but we work in mixed teams and I don't want people to feel I only support women.'

There were examples of more formal attempts to mentor and support women in particular, for example:

> I've brought on quite a lot of women now, on the senior team there are several women and I have a female business manager. I never set out to discriminate in a positive manner it just happened that the best people who came forward were women.

Several of the women interviewed had taken responsibility in their firm or area of work to provide support for women. One had chaired the organization Opportunity Now:

> the role was unpaid and I did it for seven years, encouraging employers to make sure there really was a level playing field, developing action plans, sitting on panels.

Some of the head teachers had mentored quite formally within national education leadership programmes.

Establishing mentoring for women might be particularly important in the context of countering informal male mentoring, for example that which might still be found in surgery, where the senior people are almost always men. One of the women surgeons commented that there is:

> informal mentoring that boys get in the locker room. They chat about: 'are you going to such and such a course, have you heard about this'. I wasn't in that locker room.

A woman who worked in the energy industry, another potentially difficult area for women, had made real efforts to mentor and encourage younger women:

> I have set up mentoring circles, mentoring about ten women at a time. It is brilliant. Different topics are covered, how to get 'stretch' opportunities, how to increase your political savvy. I have a whole lot of women who I talk to about how to deal with challenges. A lot of it is informal. One thing, given the need to manage time, I do take a view on who can I best give time to. Mentoring is also valuable for mentors. I learn a lot as well. I encourage others to mentor because of the benefit it brings.

It was widely recognized that mentoring and coaching would bring benefits not only to the protégée but also to the mentor and that the process was enjoyable. One woman in broadcasting said: 'Developing other people is one of the best parts of my job and this is it with knobs on.' The women were also very much aware of the need for them to act as role models to younger women and to show them that it was possible for them to 'make it'. For example, a woman in the media spoke about the need to be a role model demonstrating work/life balance:

> I chaired Opportunity Now for four years. I went to the media, banks, insurance, retail and manufacturing sectors speaking at their women's networks. I have mentored women either as a non-executive director or in my industry. It is really important to me to do this. Wherever I have spoken, the question I always get from women is: 'how do you do it?' These are women in middle management who want to get into senior roles. They want to know how I manage with my job and with three children. They want to hear about it so that they can visualise how they could do it. They want to see a role model.

The vital issue of the difficulty of having children alongside a responsible and senior job is the main focus of Chapter 5.

The main issues

These successful women rated their own agency – their determination, hard work and enthusiasm – as most important in building human capital and their careers. Secondly they acknowledged the support of others, mainly through mentoring arrangements which had usually happened spontaneously and organically rather than formally. In addition many mentioned the use of coaching mainly to deal with a specific problem or to take stock and reflect on their overall career.

Although they did not recognize themselves as feminists, almost all of them actively supported younger women, giving career advice and mentoring sometimes informally and sometimes formally. They acknowledged the importance of role models in their own development and recognized that they were now role models for others.

Both the challenges and the support that emanate from family will be discussed in Chapter 5. A further important source of support, networking, will be the focus of the next chapter.

4
Meeting the Challenges through Networking

Professional groups provided good contacts. I'm a real networking queen. I've always had extremely extensive networks, people I could talk to and bounce ideas off. People I could talk to as sounding boards. I was never shy about asking.

My advice would be for women to be more aware of what is available and find a network that supports you at a particular point in your career and where you can give and receive support. It's tough when your time is not your own and is deal-driven etc. Knowing what I know now, I should have prioritized one good women's network. It would have helped. Sometimes you feel like you are the only one who feels like this and I remember the relief I felt talking to my peers.

(views of two interviewed women)

In the last chapter we considered the success factors that the women identified deriving from their own agency and the support of others in the form of mentoring and coaching. The women also valued the support of partners and family, but they rated membership of a variety of networks as very important in their career progress. My review of literature (Coleman, 2008a, see also Bibliography on p. 185) identified networking as the single most discussed factor relating to women's career success, and networking is the focus of this chapter.

The two quotations that open the chapter illustrate the importance of having a wide range of networks of all types, but also the particular support that many women gain from an all-women's network. The first part of this chapter concerns networks in general, and the second part focuses on the importance of all-women networks.

Types of networks

All networks offer a level of emotional or 'expressive' support involving the support associated with friendship and trust (Ibarra, 1993; Perriton, 2006), but networks are also potentially 'instrumental', that is useful in promoting business contacts that will benefit the working practices of members of the network and build up their social capital. Networks tend to offer different combinations of these two main functions across a spectrum, but within this range women commented on three different types: the first two experienced in a work setting and the third in a social setting.

1. Expressive networks in a work setting. These networks could also be instrumental, but their primary function was expressive. They had usually emerged naturally from working with like-minded people in their organization or business context.
2. Instrumental networks primarily to promote business contacts which might incidentally offer some expressive support. These networks are often associated with traditional male socializing.
3. Informal networks of friends offering mainly emotional support, situated in a social rather than a work context. As these tended to be women-only groups they will be discussed later in the chapter.

Expressive networks in a work setting

Some of the networks that were identified as most successful were those relatively informal networks that had been developed through working with the same group over a long period of time, sometimes on long-term projects. For example, a woman in property development commented that: 'In the sort of work I do, you work for a long time on a project, say four or five years and build up a strong relationship with people you work with, e.g. lawyers. There is a relatively close-knit group of people who I work with who are in relevant disciplines.' A woman academic referred to a group of ex-colleagues and to an interest group developed over a number of years:

> In terms of personal support, the people I worked with in my first institution are important. I went on working with the same people for 15 years. Also my research network, which happens to be fairly heavily female, is important. We support each other in a different sort of way, we co-edit and research together and can talk about

other stuff. They are important because they are not part of my day job. There is no hierarchy involved as there would be if we were in the same institution.

In this case the supportive nature of the network was linked to the membership coming from a range of institutions so that the rank or seniority of the individual was less important than it would be if they were coming from the same institution.

Supportive and useful networks may be developed at the highest levels. In this example the variety of experience of members was also important:

> A board I belong to is a very diverse group of people of different nationalities. They are all CEOs. We spend two days together, communicate work-wise and socially. It is one of the best boards I have been on. Peer relationships are very important and sustaining. We recognize that people will see things differently and we will listen to each other.

These networks are really about good relationships within the context of work which are valued and then may be taken forward and continued beyond the work relationship where they were initiated. Finding people of a like mind provides a bond across the borders of organizations and helps to build social capital. As discussed later in the chapter, women found that they could identify easily with other women, in networks that were exclusively female, but they also mentioned forming strong bonds with male colleagues:

> I think I have found support through a network of business relationships as well. Forming strong relationships with people you have worked with through the years you find the relationships move beyond business. They are not your best friends, but in a business context you have a sounding board, but they are not in your organization and it's not going to get back to it. I am talking about a strong partnership relationship with people you are comfortable with. You identify kindred spirits who have values that are the same as yours, and these are not just females. If you give a little you get a lot back.

In one case, such a network came about through a formal initiative introduced by the company's training and development officer who provided an opportunity to join a self-managed learning group, which then maintained its support and development role over a long period:

> I was asked to join a group of directors from different companies and we would meet once a month and share our work, career and personal life and help each other. For the first year we had a tutor/ facilitator. We continued meeting for about nine years. There were five of us and the others were all men. There was total confidentiality within the group. Strangely I think that the men bared their soul more than I did at times. I looked at them sometimes and wondered about life in their boardrooms. We gave each other a lot of support. I wondered how different they were. Egos weren't required when we met. It was very supportive and non-competitive. It only fizzled out two years ago and we first met eleven years ago. It was just time really that caused it to finish.

In this case not only were there strong bonds between the woman interviewed and her male colleagues in the learning group, but there was an example of the type of expressive support where 'men bared their soul', which mainly seemed to occur with women-only groups. However, in this mixed group a culture had emerged that allowed a high level of honesty.

In some cases the continuing support of such a network can outlive even international moves. McCarthy (2004, p. 37) identifies 'diaspora' networks of women who have worked together then moved on but wish to still keep in touch.

Instrumental networks

More formal networks, existing mainly for instrumental purposes, exist within and across professions and industries. Some of the women belonged to these high-powered networks that offered beneficial contacts and useful and stimulating new information. A woman in finance referred to one such organization, which has 'regular lunch and dinner meetings with interesting speakers. It is educational and also good for client referrals.' Such networks are not likely to provide much expressive support. One woman working in a technical field commented: 'I have networks but they don't support me. I belong to technology groups and they are about informational support, not emotional support.'

Networks put people together in ways that allow them to make links that will be helpful to them in performing well and in developing their career. The opportunities to do this include regular meetings, possibly with a speaker at social occasions including dinner, lunch and breakfast meetings. Lectures and seminars include opportunities for receiving and giving information of all kinds. Networks also provide the possibility of offering training in the form of formal courses for members or aspirant members. They are often reported as the arenas where both formal and informal mentoring and coaching takes place.

Although there are many mixed networks which can carry out all these functions, the challenges that are recognized by aspiring women (see Chapter 2) are linked to a perception of the continuing importance of the 'old boys' network' and the associated entrenchment of male privilege. There is also a perception that networks that have been established by men, and were originally exclusive to men, are not easy for women to join and may not be comfortable for them to inhabit as members. Despite this, a small number of the women had successfully joined some of the old established, previously male networks associated with the City of London. A woman lawyer interviewed had been a member of six or seven City organizations, including the Institute of Directors in the City and two Livery Companies becoming the second Lady President of one. She commented:

> One of my two Livery Companies is very traditional as it is nearly 800 years old. The other is only seven years old as a Livery Company and is a modern company. There are some Livery Companies where they still do not admit women. I lead on the Women in the Livery initiative at the City Livery Club. I am keen to get more women and more ethnic minorities involved in civic life in the City of London. There are opportunities to do so but as with everything that you do in the City you need to do it diplomatically.

Although there may be what one woman termed 'integration' into such old established organizations, the women interviewed do perceive differences in the ways that men and women operate together. One woman head teacher talked about her feeling of isolation in meetings of peers who are mainly men, something that I found quite widespread in earlier research with women head teachers (Coleman, 2002).

Working in a predominantly male world, one woman commented on the 'naturalness' of male networking, which is not deliberately exclusive but unconsciously so:

> Since I have moved into a technical world I find myself in meetings that are all men. When I mix with colleagues they are all men.

There is something about men together and how they do business. Networking is an incredibly important part of what you do. Getting to know people in an informal way is important. They say come and have a beer in the technology world. You are not excluded, but it is a male type thing to do.

A woman surgeon commented: 'I don't know that women are natural networkers. I would never dream of meeting someone for a drink after work, there are children, the meal to think of, but for men it is a natural thing to do.' Stereotypical male interests such as sport, particularly the discussion of football or cricket and playing golf form another barrier for women (see Chapter 2, pp. 23–24). Of course there are women who share an interest in sport (see Chapter 6) or other areas, like technology, which are stereotypically seen as male, just as there are men who have no interest in football or in visiting the pub. However, the majority of the women interviewed felt that there were particular benefits for them from belonging to female networks, whether formal or informal. As discussed below, many but not all of the women interviewed were members of networks that had been set up exclusively for women, and the particular benefits and issues around all-women networks are considered here.

Identifying organizations that support women

Potential difficulties, particularly in the past, of accessing male networks, and the perceived advantages that men are thought to derive from networking, form part of the background for the existence and development of all-women networks. With a focus on the support and development of women at work, I undertook an Internet search for organizations that support women using the search engines Yahoo, Google and Ask and combinations of the words *networks, groups, women, organizations, support, development, leadership, work* for organizations that support and develop women who aspire to senior roles or who are already in senior roles (see Coleman, 2008b).

By definition, organizations that support women have women members and are run by women. They may have developed either as 'emergent' or 'prescribed' organizations (McCarthy, 2004). Emergent women's networks are developed bottom-up, usually by individual women who identify a need for an organization to support women in their particular area of work. Prescribed women's networks are established top-down by organizations actively seeking to recruit and develop more women. There are also women's networks which are a mixture of emergent and prescribed, for example women's networks within individual organizations such as Shell (Mays et al., 2005), which might owe their development to individuals but would not have come into existence without the active or at least tacit support of the organization. However, support for an all-women network in an organization is not purely altruistic. Such groups were found by Singh et al. (2006) to provide benefits to the corporation that are not generally recognized. They were found to be driving change and promoting 'organizational citizenship'.

I found that most organizations were linked to a specific profession or area of work, such as Women in Journalism or Women in Property, or had a slightly wider brief, such as City Women's Network, covering a range of professions in the City of London. These networks tended to be 'emergent'. Other networks which offered support to a more general category of business or entrepreneurial women were mainly prescribed. Good examples of the latter type of network are Opportunity Now which grew out of Business in the Community, one of the Prince's Charities, and Prowess, which emerged from a joint initiative of the DTI and Women's Unit (now encompassed in the Government Equalities Office). Such organizations are not restricted to the UK; for example, in the USA Catalyst works as the equivalent to Opportunity Now as a prime organization set up to support women and raise their profile, for example encouraging their access to board membership.

The Internet search identified the work of the UK government in supporting women through the Government Equalities Office and the Women and Work Commission. Policies aimed at fairness for families and for gender equality in the workplace are endorsed in recent publications which also include a specific aim of working with business to address the under-representation of women on boards (Government Equalities Office, 2010).

There are also long-standing pressure groups such as the Fawcett Society which focus on women's rights more generally, speaking for women as a whole at a national and sometimes international level. In addition, there are a number of university centres specializing in women and work, for example the Centre for Developing Women Business Leaders at Cranfield University, and the Academy for Gender, Diversity and Leadership at Lancaster University Management School. They, and others, undertake research on women in leadership, which also raises the profile of women leaders, and in some cases they also offer courses designed specifically for senior women, as does Ashridge Business School.

No Internet search can ever claim to be fully comprehensive. Different search engines throw up different results and in the case of this particular search, groups are constantly emerging or disappearing. However, there appeared to be more women's networks in professions or work areas that have been, or are still, largely male-dominated, for example: construction and property; finance; media and communications; medicine; science, engineering and technology; law; police; fire service; and the church. Most but not all of these networks were emergent, that is they are 'bottom-up', set up by an individual or a group of individuals in response to a felt and continuing need.

The place of networks in the research

Since networks appear to be extremely important as a source of support for women at work, I aimed to interview women who belonged to different types of all-women networks operating in different work contexts. From a practical point of view, accessing the networks offered a relatively efficient way to reach a number of successful women rather than making many individual approaches. However, not all of the women interviewed belong to a women-only network; about one-third of the women interviewed were approached individually. Those who are not members of all-women groups often offered an alternative and more critical view of such networks. Individual women who were not in all-women networks worked in finance, property, consultancy and the media including broadcasting.

Most of the interviewees came from five different networks, including two in education: SWISS (Senior Women in Secondary Schools) and TTGC (Through the Glass Ceiling), which is a network of women in leadership in higher education. Education is normally seen as a female-dominated area, but in contrast, WinS (Women in Surgery) represents a profession where women are very much in a minority. Although women now account for 40 per cent of all doctors (Driscoll, 2010), surgery remains a male-dominated field where less than 7 per cent of consultant surgeons are women. The fourth network from which women were interviewed is Forum UK (an organization of 'outstanding' women in all fields of work) which is an arm of the International Women's Forum, established in the USA. Women interviewed from Forum UK were leaders in finance, retailing, power industries and consultancy. The fifth and final network is WACL (Women in Advertising and Communications in London) whose members are leaders in advertising, marketing and publishing.

As women-only networks are a key feature of support for senior women at work, the latter part of this chapter focuses on the perceptions of members of the five networks, looking at their similarities and differences and what they have offered and continue to offer to their members. In addition to their membership of these formal networks, most of the women interviewed also identified the importance of informal female groups having a special and supportive place in their lives and these networks will be considered at the end of the section.

Women-only networks

Women-only networks emerged to help remedy the scarcity of women in leadership roles in the workplace, to support women in their career progress, particularly in male-dominated work areas, and in response to the informal and formal male networks which have helped to keep men disproportionately in positions of power. Although some professional women's organizations were founded early in the twentieth century, most established women's networks that are still current today were set up from the 1970s onwards, with the majority emerging towards the end of the 1980s and beginning of the 1990s. Although current women's networks are rarely feminist in their stance, the timing of their development links them with a change in culture following the second wave of feminism.

The origins of the five networks

Of the five networks identified here, only WACL originates from the beginning of the twentieth century. It was founded in 1923 by two men on the occasion of a convention of the International Advertising Association when it was realized that there were no established organizations where women could host formal dinners, so a club where lady members could invite guests was started and this provided the foundation for the network (WACL, 2008).

The other four networks were all founded around 1990. Although education may be seen as the province of women, in fact its management and leadership are normally dominated by men. In secondary schools most head teachers are men, although there are geographical differences with approximately equal numbers of men and women secondary heads in London and Birmingham, but only about 25 per cent of women heads elsewhere (Fuller, 2009). The initial impetus for the formation of SWISS was the recognition of the small number of women secondary head teachers in an area of northern England. The head who first thought of the network stated: 'when I became a head I went to my first conference of heads and saw rows and rows of men in grey suits. I said, "Where are all the women?"' The numbers of women heads in the area has now risen but is still less than the national average of 38 per cent (DCSF, 2010).

The other network in education, TTGC, was also established about 1990. One of those interviewed stated that: 'It was founded (1) to support those of us who were on a leadership trajectory through the glass ceiling, (2) to support us in changing cultures on that journey and, when there, (3) raising awareness with other women.' (For further details of the two educational networks, see Coleman, 2010.)

Women in Surgery (WinS) is a national organization founded through the Department of Health and the Royal College of Surgeons of England in 1991 as Women in Surgical Training (WiST) and then re-launched and rebranded in November 2008 as Women in Surgery. The organization(s) was founded in the context of surgery being a male-dominated speciality of medicine. It is therefore an example of a pre-scribed rather than an emergent network, although individual women surgeons are and were conscious of a need for such a network. The mission statement of WinS is: 'to encourage, enable and inspire women to fulfil their surgical ambitions'.

The fifth network, Forum UK, was founded around 1990 as an off-shoot of parent organization International Women's Forum, which was established in the USA in 1982. Forum works to promote networking among women of achievement and to promote opportunities for women in leadership. Membership is limited and is by invitation.

The functions of the five networks

McCarthy (2004) identified evolutionary stages in the development of functions of all-women networks:

Survival: first offering a 'space to breathe easy', where 'the climate is particularly hostile to women'. (p. 92)

Support: moving on to develop strategies for change and development, building confidence.

Voice: considering what the network can do about wider issues. This may involve moving more towards being a pressure group with less emphasis on individual support.

Another stage of evolution was termed 'exit', meaning that the network may help a woman identify that it would be sensible to leave her profession. However, it could be that 'exit' in the sense of the network being dissolved might occur because there is a perception that it is no longer needed. The two networks in education appeared to be moving towards exit in this sense.

Data from the networks in the current study indicate that there are differences in the way that they operate, but the functions of all the networks include, or have included:

1. Offering emotional support which may include the 'survival' element indicated above;
2. Providing practical instrumental help in terms of business/work information and contacts;
3. Offering professional development;
4. Exercising influence on behalf of women: 'voice'.

1. Offering emotional support

Networks for women seem to play an important role in providing emotional support. This is a particular positive quality of the 'emergent' women-only networks where their expressive function appears to provide an opportunity for speaking honestly and openly in a way that a mixed forum does not allow. Women highly value these opportunities which would not be available elsewhere. One senior woman in a university commented on the organization to which she belonged: 'It is a supportive, comfortable network where members can unload and be themselves which is very unusual.' Another referred to joining it as being: 'like getting into a warm bath'.

It was clear from the interviews that the all-women networks were most important in offering a channel for women to obtain support from other women, and that this support was of a special nature. Typical comments from the four emergent networks were:

> We are able to talk freely and get support ... it is more difficult to open up when it is a mixed group. (TTGC)

> It offers support when you have had enough. To know that there are women there to talk to, to say things you would not want to say to a man. (SWISS)

> There are absolutely fantastic women in it who are wonderful. It is a unique organisation, you can just be yourself, you don't have to sell or explain yourself. It is tremendously supportive in a unique way. (Forum UK)

If I have ever felt isolated, it is a great network. You can ring someone up and talk freely. (WACL)

WinS, which is a prescribed network, did not have the same function of being a safe haven for talk, mainly because it supports women at all levels of surgery, not just those at the top:

Not sure how useful WinS is. it has a role in the College to support women and enable opportunities. It is a bit broad based, talking about opportunities to students, right through training and then consultants, and therefore does not address specifics along the way.

However, one of the women consultant surgeons belonged to a more informal emergent network which provided her with a useful level of professional support from practising women doctors:

I do belong to a female doctors group. I was talking to a colleague on the train to London and he said you ought to belong to my wife's group. It includes GPs, psychiatrists and others. We meet around every six weeks. I like being in that, it is something I would never have done by myself. It is a very good group with a diverse mix of people outside of the hospital.

The prescribed network of WinS is in contrast to networks that are focused on the needs of a specific group, in this case of senior women. A woman belonging to Forum UK commented that:

Networks must be focussed, women's networks if they are too big appeal to no one. There are several on the street that invite everyone from secretaries to MDs and you will never get MDs to go, it is not relevant to them. For personal needs I want people who are facing the same issues as me.

In the four emergent networks, the ability to talk freely in an all-women environment is seen in contrast to mixed networks where women might feel vulnerable and exposed to [male] criticism.

You find you can talk in ways that are different. There is a sort of camaraderie. One is not let down. There is something about it. No one believes it till it happens.

Women in senior positions are aware that they cannot afford to expose potential weakness to male colleagues except those who are very close and trusted. They also perceive that women's groups may be belittled by male colleagues, for example: 'WACL have broken through barriers. Blokes try and "lessen" it but it probably has as much status as the equivalent men's group.'

This study seems to support the findings of Ibarra (1992) which showed that while men formed strong ties across many networks, the pattern for women was different. They obtained social or expressive support from women and looked to the mixed, possibly male-dominated networks only for instrumental support. Nevertheless the women also rated the instrumental support that they obtained through their all-women networks.

2. Providing practical, instrumental help

Networks facilitate the exchange of information, for example finding out about an unadvertised vacant position or receiving informed advice from a senior person in the field. A member of TTGC commented on how:

> A new member of Glass Ceiling came to a first meeting and was inspired by the confidence giving message. She e-mailed later that she had seen a post advertised and gone for it and got it. She would never have applied for it if she had not attended the day. Just one example of the fruit of the network.

The difficulties faced by women surgeons which make them more likely to leave the profession (Halliday et al., 2005) were identified as:

Less sociable hours;
More on-call commitments;
Paucity of part-time opportunities;
Continuing perception that women were not up to the job;
The presence of discrimination.

As part of their function, WinS has ensured that women surgeons are aware of the work of a Flexible Training Adviser to help them combat some of these difficulties.

Networks have been theorized (Granovetter, 1973, Ibarra, 1993) according to the extent of diversity of the members and according to the strength of their ties. Weak ties (Granovetter, 1973) are considered important as channels through which socially distant ideas influence, or information reaches the individual. They may act as a 'bridge' to parts of the social system to which members are not otherwise connected. Weak ties enable women to build social capital, offering the opportunity of making links with clients as well as with individuals in their own profession or organization (Suseno et al., 2007). Strong ties bind people and it is likely that information passed through them may not be new but already known. However networks with strong ties are characterized by 'trust and predictability'. (Ibarra, 1993, p. 63).

The networks represented by the interviewed women generally have strong ties, i.e. they all come from the same type of work environment and members have a lot in common. This is particularly true of SWISS, whose members are working within a region and generally facing fairly similar circumstances and issues. An exception is Forum UK, a network that is made up of 'outstanding' women from all work sectors who therefore have relatively weak ties, but are then able to make bridges between different types of business that may be advantageous to them:

> Forum over the years has been useful. I have found some good friends there, women you respect. It is nice to work with people who are not in your industry. I have met people from technology, astronauts, senators. It is an unbelievably pre-eminent organisation.

As Forum is an international organization there is also the potential for making international links.

> Its great advantage, even at 200 members, is that it is basically a peer group of women from different occupations and professions. If we didn't have a judge or a musician, we went out and got one. It's as diverse as we can make it so in my experience. For example, if you have a legal problem in Paris you can ring someone and say 'how do I deal with this?'

The usefulness of a network that you can trust was echoed by another interviewee: 'You create a wide network internationally. If I need something I can just pick up the phone and ask.'

Some of these successful women belong to other women-only groups as well as to mixed networks. One who felt that she benefited from them all mentioned how a similar group to Forum UK has: 'a different feel to it. It is a different cross-section of people'.

The networks of senior women in business appear to operate very much like male-dominated networks, in allowing people to meet others at the same level who might share the same interests. Establishing these links within the context of trust engendered by the network provides a ready route to access useful expertise and advice. However, although progress is being made through all-women networks, 'there is no simple way of overcoming the gender advantage held by one sex by recreating the behaviour (and social mechanisms) that exist for the other and assuming it will result in a level leadership playing field' (Perriton, 2006. p. 112). Women are still all too aware of the barriers they face, although they may be very slowly diminishing.

Instrumental functions seem particularly important for women's networks in the private sector, but all of the networks have offered or currently offer support to their members, and to more junior women who might aspire to membership, through offering professional development thus building human as well as social capital.

3. Offering professional development

Offering professional development to members is part of the support function of these networks. Professional development is inherent in the networks, in that the members are meeting for professional purposes and gain from discussion and exchange of information at any event provided. The extent to which this was recognized varied between the networks. The network that operates in higher education, TTGC, provided professional development through conferences and through the dissemination of their own research:

> it is useful in disseminating information about research in gender issues. Where else would you get this information? It is incredible to have access to academic researchers in gender. That has been wonderful, people like xxx who are able to give knowledge.

They also found difficulty in finding appropriate leadership development as senior women except within the network. One commented:

> When I was head of department in 1980 I was sent on a course for university heads of department. It was a very masculine course and not good. I then went on one for women managers and it was equally poor. I felt frustration, but when I joined TTGC it offered

an appropriate balance of support and self-development, along with keeping up to date with HE issues.

Another that:

> I see its [TTGC] functions in terms of staff development that I am not getting elsewhere, e.g. discussions about 'Where is HE going?' They are a supportive group of academics and you can say anything and it will not get out. Also they are people outside your institution which is always useful.

The other education network that operates in secondary schools moved in evolutionary terms from survival to support not only for the members, but also to meet a growing need for professional development among aspiring women leaders in the area. The four heads who set up the group invited deputies who were asking for further training, and then other women teachers also came forward. SWISS then provided twilight sessions, Saturday morning courses, residential courses on women into management and sessions on interviewing, financial management and timetabling. One founder member commented about the early years of SWISS:

> We could share how to deal with problems. Getting that confidence was magic. However, it was damned hard work organizing SWISS while running a school. The need for support for women kept on going. The junior schools wanted to join in. It was very rewarding, we believed in what we did.

However, the growth of professional development for leaders in the school sector has effectively removed the need for SWISS to provide such courses and they have reverted to support for the core group as the main function of the network.

Women in Surgery (WinS) developed from a model that focused on networking and running a conference, putting women surgeons in touch with each other and promoting role models. In the late 1990s research showed that women were put off surgery before medical school, so the organization expanded to work with school-age pupils and to show them that surgery was an option. The organization now works at all levels with their main priorities being school students, medical students, foundation and core trainees, speciality trainees, speciality doctors and consultants. Although professional development may be implicit in the model, the focus of the organization is on 'voice'.

Members of both Forum UK and WACL look outside their networks for their own professional development, sometimes to their professional organizations. Another source of development was identified through taking on an additional external role, for example as a non-executive director. However, both of these networks contribute to professional development of younger women through leadership courses and conferences.

4. Exercising influence on behalf of women: 'voice'

All of the networks in different ways have tried to raise the image of women as leaders. In TTGC the founder members articulated the need for change: 'It was not just about having more women leaders, it was about bringing change in the culture and the organization worked to support this.' However, both of the networks in education now look set to 'exit' (see Chapter 7 on change). Members of SWISS recalled how they had researched to inform local policy:

> In the early days there were quite a lot of questionnaires and getting figures, presenting statistics. We did reports for County Hall and head teachers' meetings. Lobbying and raising awareness that this was an issue to be taken seriously. Some heads were sympathetic and some not. The lobbying went, I don't know why. They didn't get a lot of women into County Hall.

In contrast to the education networks, WinS exists to speak on behalf of all women in surgery, including women consultant surgeons. WinS tries to have a media profile and is moving towards more political and lobbying functions. The chair of WinS stated that: 'we need to change the surgical infrastructure'. She has been co-opted on a committee with the Chief Medical Officer looking at 'Opportunity Blocks' to work formally on ways in which the medical profession can reform and attract women to specialities where they are badly represented. They are also aware of the importance of changing the perceptions of girls still in school who might reject the possibility of becoming a surgeon.

Their aim is to make the organization redundant. One respondent hoped that surgery would become as open to women as the field of obstetrics and gynaecology, which had been dominated by men 'about 20 years ago and it is just not like that any more'. In the meantime they aim to do more to support more senior grades as well as encouraging young women and nourishing their media profile.

Members of Forum UK and WACL are aware of the need for change, although one member of Forum UK stated that: 'I joined Forum because of seeing this real barrier [to women becoming leaders] and Forum does try and find ways to get through it.' Forum has also been influential internationally.

> Forum is a very interesting and strong group. They have helped the women in the peace process in Northern Ireland and have done other international work very well. For a women's group in a society like this to reach out internationally and be seen and to stimulate discussion about what women can do gives hope. The spin-off is all types of things like charities, helping in the disadvantaged world. That is what I see of value for these organisations [women's networks].

WACL has worked through the Institute of Practitioners in Advertising to carry out studies on women in advertising (Klein, 2000) and maintains a high profile in the industry.

Despite the enthusiasm of the members, particularly their appreciation of the support function of the networks, there are women (and men) who are antipathetic to the concept of the all-women network.

Antipathy to all-women networks

The women who belonged to the all-women networks were enthusiastic about the support the networks offered and the benefits that they received, although some were late converts who had been dubious about such groups until they joined. Some existing members of all-women's networks held ambiguous attitudes about the need for them, enjoying them on the one hand and on the other still expressing some doubts, usually relating to affirmative action. There was some perception that women are probably doing well enough and should not be receiving any special treatment. For example, it was reported by one of the women surgeons interviewed that: 'some women surgeons don't like the whole gender thing'. Another woman surgeon member of WinS commented: 'I need to network with my colleagues whether they are male or female. The main concerns are training etc. I don't have "female" issues. I network all the time with my colleagues.'

Perceived or actual antipathy to all-women groups took several forms. There was a perceived 'male' view trivializing a network that was composed only of women as being a 'knitting group' or for gossiping. The chair of WinS stated that:

> I hope for it to be seen as a professional organisation, to be seen as formal. It has been criticised as being informal, for gossip and chit-chat. I want it to be seen as a professional organisation with teeth, acting as a beacon and source of information and encouragement. I would like all medical students and doctors to have heard of us.

There was also nervousness that an all-women group would be perceived as antipathetic to male colleagues and that this would then rebound on women in a negative way. A woman in broadcasting commented: 'I also felt that in a male organization they would have been seen as a threat.'

There were references to the possibility that younger women were definitely less aware of women's issues and did not see the need for a women's group. A woman in TTGC commented that:

> Occasionally, we have had someone who is a young academic come along who has said they don't like women's groups, whose attitude has been 'I've made it here by myself and don't need a group like this'.

Others optimistically believed that there are no longer issues for women, although all of them were able to identify some aspects of male advantage in the workplace. A woman in the media stated: 'Women's issues have moved on. Now a lot choose not to be full-time, so therefore it is not an issue.' (The particular issues that women face in relation to work and family life will be discussed in the next chapter.) A woman in broadcasting, commenting on a 'women in news' network for senior women, stated that after a few years the increased number of women in the news meant that:

> It was deemed unnecessary. Chaps said: 'why do you need this, you are all over the place.' It was becoming a bit of a vestigial organ, we did not need it. We now have a lot of senior good role models who we can turn to.

However, as noted in Chapter 2 there were perceptions of particular difficulties relating to age for women in the media.

There were a number of women who felt only negatively about an all-women network of any kind: 'I did not attend women's networks because they met in the evening and anyway I never believed they would work. I have never felt the need to be part of the sisterhood.'

Some women expressed a preference for mixed-sex groups although this was sometimes linked to a reluctance to join any sort of group:

> I have not been involved with women supporting women. I even found the toddlers' group difficult. I would rather be in a mixed group. I don't like the clubbable bit. I went to a regional 'Women in Business' day and little of it felt sharp and relevant to me. On any occasion it has not offered the things I need. I am a joiner but not of women's groups. I don't belong to professional bodies of any sort. I get my support elsewhere from friends and family.

There were strong and negative reactions to what might have been seen as a more militant type of women's group that emerged from second-wave feminism. A woman in property development referred to: 'an organization which was started up in the late 1980s and I went along to it. It was horrendous, going on about men, and not helpful at all. It put me off.' This attitude is allied to the antipathy and backlash to feminism identified by Gaskell and Taylor (2003), and discussed in Chapter 1. A woman lawyer stated:

> I am wary of organisations that wanted to get into a huddle to tub thump and who worked on the basis of 'we are entitled to ...' You are only entitled to that which you deserve. Professionally I could see that it was better to get in and work from within rather than rant from the outside. Some of that behaviour emphasised the differences rather than the similarities.

However, there was also antipathy to the perceived exclusivity of male as well as female networking:

> I don't like them [networks]. Men have dominated for so long, for example the livery companies, although I have integrated into those. My feeling is: don't let us go the wrong way round and sit in a room with all women. I am not comfortable with that.

Several of the women interviewed were from the USA or had experience of work in the USA and they commented on the differences between US and UK experiences. One who worked in finance stated:

> I have a passion to bring more women into business. In Europe, women's networks are much less developed than in the States. I tried to set one up in the organisation where I worked, but no one would

come. I met women in the corridors and they said they wanted to network but did not turn up. When I dug under the surface, I realised they would be viewed as being at some sort of knitting circle or something negative if they went to a women only group.

Cultural differences may make networking more difficult in the UK, where the individual is less encouraged to talk about themselves and there is some reluctance to talk openly. One of the women referred to herself as 'a private person' and went on to say:

In the States they are brilliant networkers. I'll sit there rapt while people tell me all about themselves and I just tell them my name and where I am from. I'm learning they need to know all about you to place you. That's the way they work. It does not come naturally to me.

Perhaps this reticence means that the more informal networks of friends and families have a particularly relevant role for these successful women. The place of family will be discussed further in the next chapter, but many of the women interviewed commented on the social and informal groups of women from whom they gained support.

Informal support networks

All those interviewed talked about friends and family in the context of support. For example:

My family are important, husband, children, sister and parents. My sister and I are incredibly close. If ever I am miserable I go and talk to her and we go and buy a pair of new shoes. She is an absolute rock.

But some mentioned other informal groups, who had kept together over the years through having common experiences, attitudes and interests. For example, a member of TTGC stated:

I belong to a book group and we all tend to be professional women. We talk about the book we have read for half an hour and then 'do' the rest – family, career, aging parents.

Another that: 'there are another couple of women VCs [Vice-Chancellors] I have lunch with every two months or so'.

Several women mentioned support through the church. For example, a woman in broadcasting said:

> I belong to the church locally. It is a fairly modern C of E and a lot of professionals and their families go there, what I call 'normal' people. I have made strong friendships and get support there.

Others had retained links from their student days:

> There is my old college, I go back there and have quite strong friendships from university days. We share ideas and understand each other as we are all working women in high powered jobs, not making jam, although that would be wonderful.

Some had links initially made through having children:

> I have a post-NCT group who are real friends now. We give each other a lot of support. We are all working mums and often talk about work and share ideas. Actually we rarely talk about the children any more.

For one woman, a chief executive officer who had a child relatively late, the informal group of local stay-at-home mothers had proved vital for support and mentoring:

> When I moved my neighbours came to see me and they told me afterwards that they expected me to be hard. They helped me raise my kid. As a parent you wrestle with guilt. I'll always be grateful for that friendship. I entertained a lot and did my best to do things for them. I had a kid at day school, and they rang to remind me I needed to send a dozen cookies to school tomorrow. They were housewives but they were real guides on the parenting side and school network. I am still in touch with that group today. People think what an unlikely group for me.

The conflict that working mothers experience, and the gap in experience between career women and women who have chosen to prioritize their role as mother, is apparent.

Working in media tends to involve women and men in socializing as part of the job. The women working in this area commented on the sociability of the industry and typically they would have good female friends but also belonged to mixed informal networks. A CEO explained:

> I have an informal network of about 30 women who meet four times a year and lots of female friends I can talk to. We have a girls' night out, they are senior women in TV who meet up and moan and put the world to rights. We take it in turns to organize a dinner and we could always ring each other up for help. I also have different informal networks that include both men and women. The people I am closest to in this industry are two men who I would talk to if I had a big business issue. I am proud of being a woman and like other women, but not to the exclusion of men.

However, women from different work backgrounds tended to appreciate the uncritical support they received from other women with similar experiences. One of the head teachers' comments sums this up:

> I get support from very good friends who are doing the same thing and they are empathetic. They give you a coffee and a glass of wine, while men will tell you how you should do things.

The main issues

Networks at work tend to be identified with male privilege and exclusivity. Changes in the workplace mean that the barriers for women at work are generally reducing, but not necessarily for the top echelons and not in certain 'hard' industries, for example, engineering or power. Nevertheless women are joining some of the more formal and formerly male-dominated networks, although more informal male networking through, for example, sport tends to remain more exclusive.

Networking is generally seen as a positive force for women's careers (see for example, Hackney and Runnestrand, 2003; Pini et al., 2004; Suseno et al., 2007). However, there is doubt that women benefit from networks in the same way as men (Fletcher et al., 2007; Perriton, 2006; Tonge, 2008). Despite this, women tend to grow in confidence and benefit from belonging to an all-women network (McCarthy, 2004). Women's networks will not by themselves change the culture or structures that restrict the access of women to positions of power. Women-only groups are not perceived as being as powerful as their male counterparts because of entrenched male advantage in the workplace. The situation is summarized by Pini et al. (2004, p. 286) as follows:

> [that] networking is integral to career success ... [that] the networks to which males belong tend to be more powerful and [that] women typically have difficulty in accessing these male-dominated networks. (Pini et al., p. 286)

Most of the interviewed women belong to all-women's networks, and find that they offer a very special type of support that is very much valued. The emergent networks in particular offer a great deal of expressive support but also provide instrumental help, putting women together in ways that allow them to make links that will be helpful to their careers, building social and human capital. Networks provide opportunities for women to compare experiences, gain support and grow in self-confidence:

> Anything and everything could happen to a woman who connects with another woman in this space. She might get a new job, a business tip-off or the promise of an introduction to a useful contact; or she might hear an inspiring story of female success, or access advice on how to negotiate reduced hours; maybe she'll come away with the name of a reliable babysitter or a good plumber. And, more likely than not, she'll have shared her own experiences, strategies and knowledge with other women too. (McCarthy, 2004, p. 90)

Although some women remain doubtful about, or even antipathetic to, women-only networks, they provide a special type of support that may be hard to reproduce through any other channel.

5
Women and Choices

Not being married meant that I put 100 per cent of my life into my job. I have no regrets. The way it's been is the way it's happened.

I think you have to be driven to succeed. Some people want to achieve and some don't. I don't know what makes that difference. When I had children, I loved being a mother, but it never occurred to me not to go back to work. I thought if I am happy, my kids will be happy.

(views of two interviewed women)

Women and men both make choices about the sort of work they do and the type of career that they want, and their choices are influenced by such factors as location, parental example and their own specific talents, qualifications and interests. In addition, choices tend to be influenced by expectations of what is an appropriate job for a man or for a woman. For both women and men there are also choices to be made about work/family balance which are usually based on assumptions about male and female roles.

Gendered career choices

Although driven by many of the same motives in making choices about work and family, women and men make career decisions that are contextualized by gendered expectations. Adopting gender roles, gendered behaviour and gender discourse is part of identity formation throughout childhood and adolescence (Davison and Frank, 2006; Eagly, 1987). Specifically, choices about specialization at school to some extent determine career choice, and subject choices still tend to be gendered (Myers and Taylor, 2007). For example, more boys specialize in science, technical subjects and ICT while more girls specialize in English, modern languages and the humanities.

One of the women interviewed was a rarity in that she had worked in engineering. She was the exception as she recalled how she had escaped being pigeonholed by her school through a combination of 'the accidental and my obstinacy'.

> I went to a traditional girls' grammar school where they only let you do the normal subjects if you were good at everything. I was only good at Maths and I was made to do subjects like domestic science. I had no career advice and no science qualifications so I looked at what I could do. I got into computing and electronics at university. The school system moved me into it by accident and then I got on when I got there. I went to university to do something applied, and found out I was incredibly interested in it.

This woman was unusual in her career choice. Women and men tend to gravitate to particular areas of work, as we noted in Chapter 1. Men predominate in industry and in careers associated with science, technology and engineering, while women predominate in the three 'C's of caring, clerical and catering, offering support where appropriate in male-dominated areas and to male roles at work. Where vertical differentiation is breached so that women are working in a 'male' industry, the tendency will be for them to specialize in a 'feminine' area like human resource management rather than in the core business. A woman in a power industry felt that:

> The barriers have been around the fact that I was neither an engineer nor an accountant. That might have got me to the main board. They tend to be chosen to run businesses rather than lawyers or human resources professionals.

Another woman commented on the importance of breaking down the stereotypes that associate men with the 'hard' and women with the 'soft' jobs. She said that success at work came from measurable results and went on to say:

> I do scold women and girls and ask: why are you not taking on line positions in charge of revenue and results? If you take soft jobs, results are not measurable. It is important that women take on technical positions. Women so often go into HR. It's not surprising, they

are good at it. But if you can grow a business and show results that is how you get on.

In these two cases the women were aware of the impact of gendered career choices and to some extent 'blamed' other women for taking jobs in the 'soft' feminine areas and were also accepting the value judgement that the feminine 'soft' areas are less worthy. However jobs are valued, it is difficult to transgress gender barriers and break through layers of social expectations.

In addition to vertical differentiation linking gender to type of industry, there is horizontal differentiation, so that men tend to occupy the senior roles even in areas dominated by females. For example, although men account for only 13 per cent of primary school teachers, they make-up 30 per cent of primary head teachers (DCSF, 2010). The image of the manager and leader remains male (Schein, 2007; Karau and Eagly, 1999).

It is clear that there is male domination of leadership roles (see Chapter 1) and from the social justice viewpoint this seems inequitable. There is also a business case for ensuring that more women are involved in decision-making at the highest level (Gratton et al., 2007; Kramer et al., 2006). In contrast, the impact of gender is seen by Hakim (2004) as being to the benefit of women. She takes the view that women can choose whether they want to be home-centred or work-centred, whereas men generally do not have that choice. Her preference theory is based on the assumption that only about 20 per cent of women are truly employment-oriented, with the rest content to put family first, and that when they choose to work it is likely to be primarily for some additional income for the family rather than to build their own career. Hakim dismisses patriarchy as a reason for women's poor representation in senior positions at work, and considers that women have a free choice in whether they choose to be work- or home-centred. It is notable that the women interviewed for this book, who could be deemed to be work-centred, were all aware of male privilege and the structural and cultural barriers to women's career progress (see Chapter 2) and the resulting difficult choices that women make between family and career and the problems in trying to combine family and career.

Work/family career choices

A changing culture

The choices about career and family made by the interviewed women depended to some extent on their age group. The women interviewed ranged from late 30s to early 70s, with the majority being in their 50s. When the older women started their careers there was no gender equality legislation and attitudes to women at work were much more along traditional gendered lines. When I surveyed women head teachers of secondary schools in England and Wales in the mid-1990s I extracted a typology of the discrimination that they reported when they were then looking back over their careers. These included:

Overt discrimination, e.g. 'the headmaster wouldn't even consider appointing a woman to this post'.
Direct discrimination, e.g. 'I was told I would have to be better than the male applicants.'
Sexual harassment, e.g. 'comments on my long legs and pretty face'.
Indirect discrimination, e.g. 'the sportsmen have the real advantage'.
Prevailing social values, e.g. 'I am still receiving post addressed 'headmaster'.

(Coleman, 2002, p. 47)

The appointment boards for these head teachers were very conscious that there would be clashes between the demands of the job and the needs of the women's families. At an interview one governor asked a woman candidate: 'What does your husband think about this headship lark?' (Coleman, 2002, p. 44). Only about half the women in this national survey had a child or children, although by 2004 when the survey was repeated (Coleman, 2005) the proportion had risen to around 60 per cent, perhaps reflecting a change in culture over the years, at least in the field of education. Some of the more practical aspects of this change in culture were mentioned by one of the older women interviewed for the current research. She did not have children herself, but commented:

There is now an infrastructure, like child minders and it is acceptable that people take that route. I know loads of women in their thirties and forties who very successfully have a family and a career, where it was impossible in the 1970s. I suppose it may still be perceived as a barrier if you want to run the traditional sort of family, but if you want to use the support structures that are there you can and you couldn't before.

The introduction of maternity leave following the equal opportunities legislation of the 1970s paved the way for the acceptance of women returning to work after the birth of a child. This had not been available for all the older interviewees whose choices were therefore more limited. Even for women now in their 50s, there were difficulties. One woman commented: 'Unfortunately in the 1980s when I was a director for the first time it really helped me that I didn't have children. That would not be the case today. People would not ask about children now and would not discriminate.'

Approximately half of those interviewed who were mainly in their 50s did not have a child or children, compared with ten per cent of the general population of women born in 1945 and 19 per cent of women born in 1960 (Portanti and Whitworth, 2009). The fact that almost half had children masks a more complex picture. The number of interviewees is insufficient for statistical analysis, but within the sample interviewed the women employed in education, medicine and parts of the media were more likely to have had children than the women in finance, retail or energy. It is possible to hypothesize that the work culture of sectors differs, particularly with regard to flexibility over maternity leave and work hours.

Domestic responsibility including childcare

In the current work culture, having a child means taking many decisions. The initial decision of who will be the main carer is usually decided in favour of the woman, although a small proportion of fathers take that responsibility. There is then the question of whether both parents continue in full-time work, or whether one or other or both reduce their time commitment to work. It also means taking decisions about the extent to which parents prioritize work or family life to obtain the elusive work/family balance that they seek. One way of prioritizing family life might be for one or both parents to seek flexible working hours. In the UK, a statutory 'Right to Request, and Duty to Consider, Flexible Working' was introduced in 2003 for parents of young children or individuals who have caring responsibilities for dependent adults. In 2009 the right was extended to parents of children under 16. A comparative review of flexible working practices (Hegewisch, 2009) found that the take-up of flexible working is predominantly in the public sector and where the workforce is mainly female. In all countries where flexible working is possible the option is generally taken up by women. Purcell (2000) identified the importance of 'control factors' for women who are working. These refer to the extent to which women can control the hours they work without endangering their career. For example GPs are usually able to control their own hours without endangering their career progress and thus have high control factors, with the result that many women doctors have chosen the GP route (Driscoll, 2010). Women experiencing low control factors, such as those who have high-powered jobs in finance, are likely to damage their career prospects if they take maternity leave and are less likely to be able to arrange flexible working hours.

Career decisions taken by women and men in partnership are generally influenced by expectations that women will take prime responsibility for the home and the raising of children while men prioritize work. For example in a national survey of men and women secondary head teachers 94 per cent of the men were married with 72 per cent stating that their wives/partners took major responsibilities for the home and children and only 4 per cent saying they took major responsibility. Of the women head teachers, only 78 per cent were married or partnered but one-third of these took major responsibility for the home (Coleman, 2005). Most of the wives/partners of the male head teachers had put their careers on hold and opted for part-time work while children were young while the husbands/partners of the women head teachers usually had a full-time professional job, except for those who had retired. A large-scale Canadian study (Duxbury and Higgins, 2005) showed that, for professionals, motherhood remains more stressful than fatherhood with mothers in professions feeling both more stressed and depressed than their male equivalents.

For women who have a child or children but decide to stay in full-time employment in a demanding job there are tensions which may be increased by the fact that women at work are often identified with their domestic role and as a result overlooked for promotion or excluded from positions of responsibility or seniority. Gatrell (2006, p. 90), having reviewed the literature and research on the impact of maternity, concludes that it brings about discrimination, with employers making 'a negative link between a woman's reproductive status and her employment orientation'. An interviewed woman working in media commented on how perceptions of others were affected by the change in status to motherhood. For example:

People make assumptions, S won't be able to do that. The decision is taken without me being involved. Initially I took umbrage; now I am more flexible and sanguine. You do fall into the position of not being considered. Assumptions are made about women who have children of a certain age.

Another woman recalled similar experiences:

> It is hard to continue to rise at work whilst having a family. Taking the decision to be a parent is difficult. In our work you have to drop everything to put clients first and this is a real barrier to combining work and parenthood. It causes the men around you to take a sceptical view when you have to take the needs of children into account.

There is no doubt that the complications of combining family life with a demanding job are seen by the interviewees as the single biggest potential obstacle to the career success of females. One of the interviewed women commented that much depends on the employer, but: 'You do hear some horror stories and most of them revolve around having children and coming back to work.'

The relatively small proportion of women who are in senior roles in work, including those interviewed for this book, have overcome successive potential barriers including gendered choices in their education, gender stereotypes about women at work and gendered expectations of employers, particularly for those who are in childbearing years. At some stage they have to make choices about family life. For those who decide to have children there are decisions about when they would like to have a child and then whether they can manage the demands of a second or more children, how long to take for maternity leave, the type of childcare they prefer and can afford, and whether to modify their working arrangements.

Some of the women interviewed have either chosen not to have children or knew that they could not have children and so have concentrated their efforts on their work. However, those without children were still very much aware of the difficulties of managing a career and a family. For example, one woman who was childfree stated:

> I don't know how people do it. It is not a problem to me as I did not want to have children. They [women who have children] are better at juggling, more efficient, but it is really evident that they are more stressed.

Some of the women commented on the learning experience of managing a home and children on top of work. Although rarely recognized, such experience can hone skills that are then useful in the workplace. One woman commented:

> I am very wary of stereotypes, but I do think that there is an element contributing to success of the immense amount of juggling it takes

to manage a job and a family. There is the prioritising and making choices, making judgment calls on what is the most important thing. From that there is learnt a strong ability to look at things and say 'what are we going to focus on?'

Although it may now be acceptable, even expected, for a woman with young children to work, women who aspire to senior roles, particularly in the private sector, are often operating within a 'male' career model that makes no concessions for families and childcare.

The challenge of the male career model

The 'male' model of work has no toleration for part-time work or flexible hours. It archetypically includes working long hours, well beyond the statutory maximum, and may involve travelling that is disruptive for family life. In some service industries it may also include an expectation that clients will be entertained, so that work commitments extend to evenings and weekends. For women who aspire to having both a senior work role and a family, the male career model is problematic.

Decisions about children and taking maternity leave

From a biological point of view women are best advised to have children in their 20s and early 30s with fertility waning and potential problems arising once past the mid-30s. From a career point of view the late 20s and early 30s are likely to be the time that career breakthroughs occur when individuals have built up meaningful experiences that enable them to move on and up the career ladder. The conflict between career needs and the desire to have children is therefore strongest at this time. Taking a career break is likely to lead to a reduction in status that may never be fully repaired.

White (2000) has developed an age-linked stage model of career development of successful women. Once their career was well established, in their early 30s, was when the women took decisions about having a child. They generally took minimum maternity leave. In their late 30s these women then began to feel the strain of managing both a career and family. At this stage some opted out to become self-employed, and others felt that they met the glass ceiling.

There is not quite such a clear pattern among the 60 women whose views are represented in this book. In some cases they had prioritized their careers either because they chose to be childfree or could not have children. Approximately half have a child or children and the difficulties of taking maternity leave in their late 20s or early 30s are well recognized, as this is a time when a woman can fall behind even by taking a minimum maternity break. Those who had children had used various approaches to planning family around their career. All of the women interviewed were in, or had retired from, senior roles, and only two had taken the option of becoming self-employed. Although the majority had their children in their 30s, more had children early and late than in the study by White (2000). There were three separate approaches apparent among the interviewed women who were mothers.

- Having their children before they started building a career. They then had time to carve out their career afterwards.
- Waiting until their career was well established. One of the benefits of having children at this stage is that financial security means that the relatively expensive but flexible mother substitute of a nanny is affordable. Having children relatively late means that the women have enough credibility and seniority to combine work and maternity relatively smoothly.
- Taking minimum maternity leave and carrying on working with support (see later section in the chapter).

For one head teacher, having children early had been advantageous:

> I married when still an undergraduate and had my first daughter not long after graduating and my second daughter before I really started professionally. I went into teaching when the children went to school and went up quite fast. I think for people who had a career break it was more difficult. Once in the profession, I was a deputy head and head quite quickly. I did not meet the barriers.

One of the senior women in higher education had a similar experience:

> I had my children young and then went to university in my early thirties. I might have found it harder if they had been younger, with all the out-of-hours demands [once she was working in HE]. It would have been harder to go to international conferences etc. if my children had been younger.

One of the women surgeons had a child both early and late:

> I had the first before I started training and one when a consultant. Anything in between would have been a serious problem. The general opinion of women with children is that they can be a bit dodgy.

Changes in the structuring of training for surgery means that now the ideal time to have children was once in post as a consultant, as one of those interviewed confirmed: 'As a consultant it is easier to organize your own time than when you are a trainee. People now wait till they are 30 and have a baby.'

In the cases where the women were very much established before they had a child, combining motherhood and work was much smoother:

> It was lucky for me that I had children when I did although it is tiring having them when you are older. I was already Managing Director of xxx when I had my first child. I think it is easier when you are more senior, respected and already promoted. You are in a position where you are calling a lot of the shots. You can say: 'this is how I am going to do it'.

Whether children arrive early or relatively late in a career, one of the choices for the mother (or father) is to move to part-time work.

Part-time versus full-time work

Part-time work while children are very young would seem to be an ideal solution for women who want both work and family and many women who have young children opt to work part-time for a while. However, the part-time option is anathema for those who are ambitious, since inevitably the male model of uninterrupted career progress with a main focus on work is regarded as the norm. A woman working in the retail industry who had been appointed an executive just before having her first child commented on how 'everything I had achieved making the transition would be lost if I had gone part-time'. A woman in the media stated:

> I had a great nervousness about coming back part-time or having a career break. I came back full-time and felt I would not be able to do the job properly if I went part-time. When I got into full-time I could not see a way of being part-time.

The view is often taken that part-time work means a lack of serious-
ness about the job. A woman in property development commented:
'part-time working is seen as a barrier to commitment and to doing
your job properly'. She stated that after maternity leave:

> I felt that I had to come back full-time. I had three months maternity
> leave with the first child and four months with the second. I knew
> that if I didn't go back full-time I would not have been accepted. I
> had a full-time nanny. It was horrible for the first year, but I could
> not have done it any other way.

There are particular difficulties involved in going part-time when the
culture of the business involves longer than normal hours. For example.
in publishing, one of the interviewed women employed three editors
with children who were each trying to work a four-day week. What she
and they found was: 'scope creep', a failure to limit the scope of their
work to fit the shorter week, so that:

> they always end up working on their days off and in the evenings.
> It is really hard to get out of the five day week mentality. We still
> expect them to do the job full-time. We need to say, here is the scope
> of a five day week, what are we going to take away to make it a four
> day week?

There are also management issues relating to colleagues who may
have to support the work of a woman trying to keep family-friendly
hours:

> They see her go at 5 pm and then her peers might pick up her work
> till 6.30 pm. She is not working the extra hour and so there is an
> increase in work load for them. We need to think what is each per-
> son's scope of work? If we take it away who do we give it to? How do
> we pay them?

A woman who had taken the unusual route of working in production
in industry felt that she had to change her career route after she had a
child: 'I was offered shorter hours, but felt I could not stroll in at 10 and
leave at 3 in a factory where people were working hard. I opted not to
go back after maternity leave and used the opportunity of having tiny
ones; I had three under 5 at one time.'

Becoming a freelance consultant might be a way of working flexibly, but there may be particular issues when it is necessary to keep up to date with technical matters including new legislation. For example, in the property development area:

> We have taken on some women in the past as consultants on one-off projects, but it is hard for them to keep up to date. After a while they lose touch. Then it is quite hard to dip in and out of work unless they retrain. Some go off and do different things altogether.

Such practical difficulties could be remedied through professional development, but the commitment to a lifestyle that prioritizes work over every other aspect of life causes almost insurmountable difficulties for women with children.

24/7: Full-time work plus

The commitment to a life based primarily around work is most obvious in areas where client demands are strongest, particularly where business is global, so that work hours transcend time differences. However, Ogden et al. (2006) found that in the financial services sector the long-hours culture permeated through from areas where client relationships were important to areas where they were less so. A woman interviewed, whose career spanned law and business, looked back on her experience to comment:

> I think there are professions where women have to assimilate. If you take the top law firms and accounting firms, the pressures of hours and time are just too much. Some do succeed but they have to work ridiculous hours. The answer [to life/work balance questions] is if the basis of your business is to run for 24 hours there really aren't any answers. I don't see what they can do.

Although not necessarily as dramatic as this example, women in all areas of work are confronted by the tensions between working late or during the evening when the demands of home and family are strongest. Even in schools which might be seen as relatively family-friendly, one woman head teacher recalled: 'In the [school] the barrier was that I had a life at home. If they had a meeting that went on into the evening they sent out for pizza. I was seen to be the person who was the odd one out because I did not want evening meetings.' A woman surgeon commented on the traditional culture of doctors of 'the old school', who 'do not see the need for different hours', whereas younger women and men want to spend more time with their families.

The clash between the demands of motherhood and the need to work longer than statutory hours in many jobs is a difficult one. A CEO gives an example here of the problems and issues for both the young mother and her employer where the normal eight-hour day is seen as being 'flexible hours':

> I love these women and they go off and have wonderful babies, but I've still got to run the business. I have one young woman who is brilliant and who got pregnant and wanted to come back on a three or four day week. The job would just not allow that. I felt so mean, I felt like the wicked witch of the west. In the end I had to put my business head-on first. She came back on a five day week. Now she is back we are trying to work out some flexible hours for her, 9.30–5.30. They all work a good hour on top of that, often at each end. A lot don't get in until 9.30 but will not leave till 6.30 or later.

Where full-time work demands that clients are entertained, some sort of compromise has to be reached. For example one woman in property development commented: 'When I came back to work after having children I said I would only do one night of entertaining clients each week. You do have to do entertaining, but you can be disciplined about it.'

Travel and changing location

One other aspect of how high-powered life can be in conflict with family life, and lead to a choice of prioritizing one over another, is that of travel, both where international travel is part of the job and where it becomes necessary to change the location of the family because of a career move. A woman CEO in the media who was relatively optimistic about changes benefiting women at work still felt that:

> the only other barriers that are increasingly significant ones are international barriers. Whatever sector you are in being able to travel is important and that does not sit brilliantly with kids. Often these are the routes through to top jobs.

Several of the women who had children commented on their inability to move geographically because of uprooting children, or their choice to move despite having children. For example, one head teacher stated that: 'I haven't been someone who said we have to stay in one location.

I have been a bit ruthless. My marriage broke up so I have been able to move round the country. I have been a free agent to go.' In other cases the career demands of a partner plus the needs of children were instrumental in reducing career options:

> One thing inhibited my career development. I was not prepared to make the sacrifice of moving to other institutions. It was a choice I made. I had three children and a partner also working in the University sector and it was difficult to find an opportunity to move together.

For others, the attraction of international travel as part of work contributed to a decision not to have children:

> I just could not have done it, the juggling of career and children. When I was in Asia I travelled two thirds of the time. The others in the team were all men and one was a new Dad, he found it horrendous. There were no women with kids in those jobs. They just could not do it.

However, there were examples of women who had undertaken international travel for their work, but only when backed up by family who stepped in to cover:

> My first job back was making a film in Africa. I quickly saw that I would have to go there. My bosses were surprised that I was prepared to travel, but what needs doing I will do. I always have a set up at home for the children. My Mum helped a lot after they were born and we have always had live-in or live-out professional nannies and au pairs, people who have come and lived with us. My husband is a cameraman so he is never sure of when he will be working and he is at home sometimes. I have made sure that there are always two people at home to look after the children.

Guillaume and Pochic (2009, p. 33), who conducted research in a major French utility company, regard ability to undertake international travel as a 'key factor for promotion'.

Women combat the difficulties of combining family and work through their fierce determination and drive, but experience negative emotions including guilt and awareness of what they may have sacrificed in having to work within a male model of career.

Dealing with the male career model

As with the reasons that they perceive for their success that were exam-ined in Chapter 3, the women interviewed see their ability to rise above the difficulties of managing career and family as due to their own deter-mination and drive. One of the head teachers commented: 'I've been ambitious all the way through; that has been a driving force. I am not someone who is happy staying at home.' The determination to maintain career has led in some cases to fairly brief breaks for maternity leave. A woman in broadcasting commented: 'I have been extremely dogged in pursuing a higher grade from about ten years ago. I took the minimum of six weeks maternity leave with both children.' This stereotypical male model of career involves putting work first at all times, even when babies are very young. Smithson and Stockoe (2005, p. 160) talk about 'doing macho maternity': in extreme cases where women take less than two weeks for maternity leave. The example they give is of women bank man-agers, but women head teachers in earlier surveys (Coleman, 2002, 2005) made similar points about timing their children to arrive in the summer holidays, and taking the absolute minimum of maternity leave.

Trying to prioritize both work and children brings inevitable ten-sions and there were women who referred to potential sacrifices and compromises that they had to make. In some cases this inevitably led to feelings of guilt. One woman head teacher commented: 'I have sacrificed things at home with my own children. I might have liked to have three children but did not dare take another maternity leave.' She went on to say: 'my kids say now, "you missed out on that per-formance of mine at school". That was a price to pay'. Similarly a woman in finance recounted how her sons 'tell me about things they resented when they were young. I made some mistakes, but it is dif-ficult not to.'

Another woman who did not have children recounted how she had:

> a friend with a one-year-old. She works three days in the office and two days at home. She said to me that when she gets home he comes running to me, but five minutes later he wants his nanny. I think I would find that very hard. It is tough doing both, work and family.

A study of women who were both head teachers and mothers (Bradbury and Gunter, 2006) showed that they felt guilt and role strain at times but they found ways of reconciling their conflicts without constantly prioritizing one of their identities over the other so that their identities were:

> Not combined or integrated but coexist[ing] in a flexible state, with one sometimes growing and encroaching on the territory of the other, at other times vice versa, and at yet other times overlapping, underpinning or supporting each other. (p. 501)

The women interviewed who had children seemed able to operate in this way, combining their roles as senior women at work and as mothers, sometimes feeling that one role informed the other. For example, a senior woman in publishing who had her children fairly late felt:

> I'm far more balanced about other people and what to expect since I had the children. I found I was much more empathetic with women with children and with people with other interests. I saw that they had a good balance. For me having children gave me more balance in my life. When I was younger I really enjoyed working the sort of 23 hour day. I will still do that if I have to but not for 'fun' as I did before.

In some cases women were breaking fresh ground in trying to combine motherhood with their career, for example a consultant surgeon wanting to know in advance when she might be free to pick up a child meant that for the first time a rota had to be devised that allowed the woman to have the same night on call each week (see Chapter 6). The world of surgery is still male-dominated but establishing such new precedents and making working life possible for women who have children is helping to change the culture.

The need for support and organization

Managing both a career and a family is recognized as difficult and therefore a potential barrier to women's progress (for example, Gatrell, 2006). Merely having caring responsibilities, including for older dependants, may act as a disadvantage and be seen to be a woman's 'problem' (Grummell et al., 2009).

Support from family, or others who are trusted, is vital for many of the women, particularly when it comes to the inevitable crises that arise with children. One woman who did not have children said that the final straw in making the decision not to have children was seeing:

> a colleague with two small children whose husband was a session musician. She needed an extra day filming out of London and her husband could not be there and the normal child minder was not available and she used one she did not know to leave the children over night. She was so stressed.

Many of the women with children talked about how vital the support of partner and family was to them if they were going to be able to carry out their dual roles as mother and career woman. An alternative for some was a strong relationship with grandparents. In the case of a senior woman in broadcasting: 'My children have never spent a night away from me, my husband or my parents. The bond with the grandparents is very strong. It is hard when both partners are in high-flying roles.'

With or without close family support, being organized was seen as essential. As one very senior woman put it: 'If you are in the top 50 in an organization you have to have it buttoned down so that you are not worrying about what is going on outside of work all the time.' Where there is no partner or grandparent readily available, the need for well-organized support is paramount. A senior woman in the property world recalled:

> I remember once I was rung by my daughter's school, saying: she has nits, you have to come and take her home at once. I was about to go into a huge meeting and of course I could not just come at once. I had to find someone to pick her up. We had no help available from grandparents, so I had to be sure I had people in reserve.

Even when children are older such crises can occur. One senior woman in advertising gave an example:

> I have had a happy, healthy set of children, but there are flashpoints sometimes when the kids are ill. When they are seriously ill you have to drop things suddenly. It is not any easier now they are teenagers. I had a call today to say that my daughter is fluey. It happens that we have a bit of a crisis and I have to work this weekend. These are the sorts of occasions I could count on one hand. Kids have to be happy and healthy.

No matter how good the support structures, such rare conflicts are difficult to manage. In many instances a supportive husband/partner was mentioned as enabling the woman to have a career and in some cases there has been an element of role reversal with the woman's partner taking on a major role in childcare. In the case of one of the women surgeons, her husband was a nurse, 'so he can drop hours and that helps'. In another case a senior woman commented that: 'I've got three women in my team who are the main breadwinners in their family; their partners are either less well paid or are part-time "stay at home".' A woman in broadcasting explained that:

> I want to protect my family from work, although my husband does take all the guilt away. I met a senior woman in marketing who was fighting the same battles as me. Her husband also stays at home and looks after the kids. It may be a bit more common than I appreciated.

In a practical example another woman explained how she and her husband worked arrangements out between them:

> I do think that men are starting to play more of a part [in childcare]. The only reason that I could do it was that my husband was prepared to share on coming home on time. We used to split the week between us, he would do Tuesday, Wednesday and Friday and I would do Monday and Thursday and then we would swap. We had a system. It was important that we did this and it guaranteed that we both saw and spent time with the children.

Support might then come from a husband/partner, grandparents, or nanny or some other form of paid help. However, one senior woman in the media gave an example of how difficult life could be:

> I have a fantastic nanny who is a grandmother figure who really loves my children. The toll on me over the last five years is really difficult. I was very ill and had to have six weeks off. I have tried hard to be a good mother and to run a company. I would be distressed if my kids went through the same thing. Working mothers finish a day at work and then come in and move straight into mother mode. It's hard. However, I would not want it any other way. I love my kids.

Knowledge of just how difficult it is to manage parenthood and a demanding career has given the women interviewed a special insight into the management of their own staff in relation to childcare, maternity leave and other work/family balance issues.

Managing work/family balance for others

The women were each enthusiastic about their careers and several of them made the point that 'work' could not be separated from 'life' as in the term 'work/life balance', but that there was a tension to be managed in finding the balance between work and family. One woman CEO stated: 'The term "work/life balance" is one of my pet hates. After all, work is part of life. Work/family balance is important.'

Although work/family balance most often refers to families who have children where the mother is working, several of the interviewees pointed out that it is not just children but also parents who may require care, and that there was a need for balancing work and other aspects of life for those approaching retirement.

In different ways the interviewed women had found their own balance between the demands of work and family. All of them, whether mothers or not, recognized that compromises and choices had to be made. They were also aware of how best to help the women and men working for them to achieve a good balance in their own lives. They recognized that a good work/family balance was something that both men and women aspire to and, although in the end women are likely to carry the final responsibility for children, modern men also want to prioritize family. One woman who was in consultancy went so far as to say:

> The work/life balance issue is in some ways more serious for men than for women. Society has a problem; it is a disaster. It is more extreme if you look cross-culturally. There is an extreme work orientation in London compared with Germany. We cannot assume it has no effect on the family, personal well-being and society. A lot of our problems are due to that.

There was also awareness that women in general do not necessarily benefit if it is assumed that they are the main carers for children. One respondent commented: 'If you want to help women you have to help men to be better dads. It ends up working against women if too much is given to them [in terms of flexibility to cope with children].' This observation is in line with the criticism of current UK maternity leave which gives women the right to take up to one year off after the birth of a child but caps paternity leave at two weeks thus, further reinforcing the idea that childcare is the mother's responsibility.

There were two main aspects to the ways in which the women helped others to achieve a work/family balance. One was by being as flexible as possible over maternity leave and while children were young. The other was through the women themselves offering a positive role model to their employees.

Flexibility

As noted in Chapter 2, some of the women referred to breaking the mould of stereotypical masculine leadership and ensuring that they were leading and managing in a collaborative and caring way. This was apparent in some of the examples they gave about how they handle work/family tensions of employees. Head teachers gave examples of how they ensured that their teachers got away to see their own children in nativity plays. For example, one head stated:

> I never say 'no'. Staff who have little ones ask if they can go and see them in a nativity play. We get the ones with children to cover for each other. It's about being woman-friendly and understanding. Job shares, part-time work. We also do the same for fathers.

Life/family balance is not just about young children and one of the head teachers in an all-girls' school with predominantly female staff had an innovative attitude to ageing and retirement of her staff:

> I provide support for all of the staff and the most important thing is to support women who are menopausal – just managing their well being and the stresses of the job. Also coping with early retirement is important, allowing people to graduate down, rather than going from all to nothing. I have done quite a lot of that because I want to keep them. They are superb teachers and I don't want to lose their expertise. Also I am getting them to mentor and bring younger teachers on.

Although the demands of a business culture may mean that less attention is given to this type of human resource issue, the culture in some work sectors like media and advertising has become more family-friendly. One CEO stated:

> This is a family friendly organisation. Lots of people have children. There is flexibility for women on maternity leave; they come back

full-time or part-time if we can accommodate that. We understand the needs of mums and dads. For example, I can nip out to a carol service; this is not just a function of my seniority. Lots of people here have kids and we understand. There are pressure points sometimes when it all rains down on you.

Working in broadcasting, one woman recounted: 'I knew I was pregnant within about three days of getting the job at xxx. I told my boss who was a woman and she said it was fine and I was never made to feel bad about that. For me gender has never made a difference.'

Despite good intentions with regard to supporting young families it was impossible to ignore the difficulties that could arise from women taking maternity leave and wanting flexibility. One CEO stated how important it was for a woman taking maternity leave also to be flexible and cooperative with her employer, commenting:

it is a pain for small companies and difficult to manage well. The way that women behave when they are away and when they come back from maternity leave is very important. If they would not take a call when on maternity leave or come back for one month and then resign, it affects the way you view women.

This same CEO expressed with great feeling the sort of compromise that women with young children might have to make: 'Until you have felt that physical visceral ache of "Why can't I be home at 4 pm?" it is hard to fully understand, but it does pass. I came back after 11 weeks [of maternity leave] and I would never ask anyone to do that.'

Although from a work/family balance point of view it would be ideal to allow women and men all sorts of flexibility over hours, in practice it is difficult when a work culture demands long hours at a time in life when motherhood and work both need to be prioritized. One woman stated that it is impossible to take time out and progress at the same time:

If they are off for a year and then for another year try and give them flexibility then they will be back properly. However, if you make concessions it is unrealistic for them to think they can be promoted at the same rate. They should not have to go backwards, but it is unrealistic to go forward if they are unable to give more to the job.

Providing a role model

Women in surgery are consciously trying to provide positive role models to girls and young women in an attempt to alter the popular perception of the maleness of surgery both through their own lives and through the activities of WinS. Women working in both secondary and tertiary education are also very aware of providing examples and role models to younger women and men. One academic stated: 'as a feminist I think women should get up there and show we can do it, be role models to younger women'. Others in academic life were keen to model good family-friendly behaviour in practical ways. A senior administrator commented: 'I never convene meetings early in the morning. I leave the university at 5.15 pm. OK, I do work at home, but I want people to see I have a life, or you are no use to anyone. This applies to men and women.' Similarly, a vice-chancellor stated: 'Work/life balance is a challenge. It is important for me and the people who work for me to set an example that there's life as well as work. I try not to reply to emails at 11 o'clock at night even if it would suit me to do so. I don't want people thinking that's what is expected.'

Being a good role model was less discussed by those in the private sector, although a senior woman in newspaper publishing who became pregnant took the advice of one of her staff, who said:

> I hope you don't mind me saying this, but it is incredibly important that you take three months off and that you don't come in and that you don't set an example for other women of coming back to work too quickly.

With a few exceptions, examples of flexibility, family-friendly policies and acting as a positive role model to other women in relation to work/family balance were generally found much more in the public sector, particularly education where control factors (Purcell, 2000) may be stronger, rather than in the private sector where they tend to be weaker.

The main issues

To an extent, gendered expectations contextualize women's career choices with the result that women and men often occupy different industries (vertical segregation) and different levels (horizontal segregation). The women interviewed for this book are generally found in 'female' occupations, although not in all cases, and they have overcome horizontal segregation to hold senior posts.

Those interviewed are keenly aware of the difficulties associated with having children at the same time as attempting to maintain their status or climb the career ladder. Some were not able to have children or made a decision to remain childfree but about half of them made the choice to have children and were then faced with a range of choices about how to manage their care. Since the optimum time for having children is also the optimum time for career progress, options included having children early and establishing the career later, or having children later once they were in a secure senior position. Otherwise they had taken maternity leave and relied on family, including grandparents and in some cases their husband/partner, to take major responsibility. The alternative was to engage a nanny, which can be an expensive choice, made easier when mothers are very well paid. For all of them, the combination of stressful work and motherhood required intense organization and considerable support.

The women were generally operating within a male model of career where working part-time was not an option and where in the most extreme cases they had to be available virtually round the clock. Being able and willing to travel was also an issue, with most of the interviewees considering that international travel and having young children were incompatible. The inability to combine the two was seen as a major career obstacle for women in some cases.

Although most of the issues around work/family balance concerned children and mothers, the traditional paternal role was seen to be changing, with men wanting to play a bigger part in parenting. Also finding a work/family balance might include caring for older people and preparing for retirement.

The women interviewed were all in positions of power and influence and were aware of work/family balance for their employees. In some cases they took care to model what they thought of as good practice, ensuring, for example, that they kept reasonable hours of work. Some also indicated the tensions that arose when younger women took time out to have babies, describing the conflict between their wish to ensure that work is sufficiently flexible for young mothers and the 'male' norms of long hours and total commitment to work. Despite this continuing conflict, society has changed considerably and continues to change in its attitudes to women, particularly young mothers working, and Chapter 7 focuses on the changes observed by the women and their expectations of the future for women in leadership at work.

6
Individual Voices on Challenges, Choices and Change

This chapter takes some of the individual 'stories' of six named successful women from different work areas to provide rich illustration of many of the issues discussed in the book. The text has been drawn directly from their interviews. The sub-title of the book: 'challenges, choices and change' provides the main structure for each of their 'stories'.

These individual women exemplify attitudes and views from different perspectives of age, family circumstance and profession but all have career success in common. The age range of the women is from early 40s to late 60s. The older women have worked through a time during which attitudes to women at work have undergone many changes. Four of them are married, one is partnered and one single, so they bring different experiences to questions of work/family balance. Two of them are mothers. Their breadth of experience in work includes both public and private sector, specifically education, medicine, broadcasting, publishing, advertising, finance and energy. Although all have worked and currently live in the UK, two of them originate from other Anglophone countries.

They are Helen Boaden, currently Head of News at the BBC, Stevie Spring, CEO of Future Publishing, Marisa Drew, a Managing Director in the Investment Banking Division of Credit Suisse, Helen Fernandez, consultant surgeon at Addenbrookes Hospital, Carol Peace, now retired but formerly a secondary school head teacher and Judith Hanratty who trained as a lawyer and has worked in finance and in energy.

Helen Boaden

Helen Boaden took up her role as Director at BBC News in September 2004, having previously been Controller of Radio 4. She was the first woman to be head of Current Affairs at the BBC. She worked as a reporter and then editor of BBC Radio 4's weekly current affairs programme, *File on 4*, regularly presented *Woman's Hour* from Manchester and produced and presented a range of features and documentaries for Radio 4.

Her distinguished BBC career has been recognized with some of the top industry awards. Helen has been awarded honorary doctorates by the University of East Anglia (Suffolk College), the University of Sussex and the University of York. She is a Fellow of the Radio Academy.

Challenges

Asked about the challenges she had faced as a woman in broadcasting, Helen identified that they had been more obvious outside the BBC: 'In the "external" world I've encountered environments as a reporter where I am interviewing someone who only looks at the male producer, and people can look through you until they realize what your job is.'

But she was still aware of subtle challenges within the BBC due to preconceptions and stereotypes about women:

> In the 'internal' world of the BBC there can be a sort of nervousness about women who are passionate and articulate. They are sometimes written off as over-emotional.
>
> Occasionally you encounter a more defensive attitude from the men you work with. Of course it is easy to kid yourself that every man you work with treats you as an equal. I regard myself as very lucky with male bosses and men I have worked with – in the News there are a lot of men – but every so often you come across someone who regards you in clichéd female terms – too outspoken, too indiscreet, too emotional. The trick is to work out where it is a justified criticism and where it is an unconscious reaction to being a female.

Helen was also aware of the barriers that may arise from women's socialization, such as a lack of confidence:

> The barriers can be internal as well as external though. There are some clichés about women which are clichés because they are true. I know from my own experience. Women fall into holes of 'unconfidence'. That may be true of men as well but I see it in younger women who work for me. Also women still tend to undersell themselves. I nearly did not go for the job of Controller of Radio 4 – the job I most wanted in the world – because I was almost fearful of wanting it too much. My husband shrewdly asked: 'And what will you do about

your ambition? How will you feel when someone else gets it and you haven't even tried?' Of course he was right. I had kind of discounted myself before I even thought of it.

She particularly identified the challenge women face as they get older:

Of course as you move into middle age, outside the authority of the role the more you disappear, both in and out of the work situation. Doris Lessing wrote brilliantly about this in *The Summer before the Dark* and it remains true and a shock to all of us. Within the organization, the power of the role and the way you use the power means you are not remotely invisible. There is a contrast between the institution and the outside world.

I'm sure every generation of women thinks it won't happen to them, but so far it does not seem to have shifted significantly. You could argue that one sign of feminism having any impact at all is if women were no longer to 'disappear' in their 50s.

Responding to the challenges

What did Helen regard as the reasons for her success as a woman? A feeling of what was 'right' for her was important, as was flexibility and drive:

I don't start from the point of 'as a woman' as being most important, although gender is incredibly important to an individual's identity. I suppose I start from my strengths, weaknesses, fears and desires. I am tenacious and fairly driven. I always knew what I did not want to do – even if I did not know what I wanted to do – and have turned down opportunities, even when they have seemed really attractive, if I felt that they were not right for me.

For example, I was working on *File on 4* as a reporter which was a flagship Radio 4 programme and was asked to become a reporter on the *Today* programme which I declined. I did not think it would be right for me, but it was regarded by many as an eccentric move. I turned down the opportunity to be a reporter on *Panorama* because I liked radio, which was also regarded by some as a baffling move. And I went back to radio from TV because I liked the intellectual stretch of radio current affairs. I made these decisions trusting my instincts, even though they seemed irrational to many and certainly not the way to build a career.

I have always tried to be flexible because it matters in this profession. I came off staff to be free lance, which was not good for my pension but right for me at the time. You must trust your instinct about yourself. I've never had a game plan. I think having a game plan implies astonishing levels of self confidence.

I always had a deep fear of failure. I am not sure where it comes from and I don't think it is gender specific. I was very driven in my 20s and 30s – I am driven now but not to quite the same extent – although my husband would probably dispute that!

She was also aware of the good fortune that she might have been in the right place at the right time:

I have hugely benefited from being at the BBC at a time when there was an awareness that there was a need for more senior women. I have always found the BBC a fantastic place to work, with lots of opportunities.

There are elements of luck and timing that you have to exploit. It is hard now for young people in the media to be working at a time of contraction. In every job there is the importance of you as an individual but you can't ignore the external context – whether it is benign or hostile.

Helen felt that she benefited from the right mixture of a work culture and her individual qualities:

It's helpful if you find a culture which works for you and has values with which you identify. I love being part of a team, for example, and I like leading teams. Some people are lone cats, but I love being part of a big organization. I build teams and try to give space to people to let them get on with the work.

I enjoy connecting up and networking. People think networking is about networking upwards, but I don't think that is as useful as networking across and downwards. That is the way I get my understanding of how the organisation works.

Family background, upbringing and early experiences were also important:

Someone once told me that I didn't come with a deference gene. I can be blunt to a fault and that isn't always a good thing. You can miss the subtleties or hurt someone without meaning to. I had a tough, difficult Yorkshireman for a father who probably raised me as he might have done a boy. It was a very fresh air and no whining Fifties childhood, very rigorous with few comforts or compliments in case they made you self regarding or big headed. It was testing at the time but I am curiously grateful for it now. Getting through it probably made me more resilient and self reliant. It certainly means that I am not overly impressed by men who assume the right to rule.

Choices

Helen does not have children, but like all the women interviewed recognized that there are tensions for a woman with children who is ambitious at work:

> The age old feminist dilemmas still exist. The family life/work balance is a big dilemma for women. It has not been as issue in my life because we couldn't have children, so effectively I lead a very atypical life. I can pretty much suit myself. The men I work with care passionately about their children but most rely on a wife who takes on the majority of the family responsibility. But it's not just that. I think that a lot of young women colleagues under-estimate how much they will fall in love with their babies. They say funny things to me when they go on maternity leave like that they intend to write a book in their free time. I just nod thinking 'But you won't have any free time!' What's more they will *want* to spend time with their child. People underestimate the world of emotions.

She drew attention to the crucial time when women are likely to have babies, but when work is at its most demanding:

> Some young women don't even think of applying for senior editorships because of that juggling. They are making complex decisions about their work/life balance. Often the editor jobs come up when you are in your 30s, which is very tough in relation to kids. Many make a choice not to pull themselves in too many directions. I don't know what I would have decided had I been in that position.

However, she paid tribute to women who have combined an important role at work with motherhood:

> Senior women colleagues have done amazing things while raising small children. Jenny Abramsky ran the *Today* programme with small children; she was the first and, so far, only female Editor of *Today*.

Jay Hunt, the Controller of BBC One has a young family and Anne Sloman, who also broke through the glass ceiling, worked when her boys were young. She once told me that the only way to do it was to accept that you would miss out on some of the important things – the first step, the first smile. I have huge admiration for them, but it's not easy. Lots of women balance it, but it is not easily resolved.

Change

When asked: 'Do you think things are changing for women?' Helen answered first in relation to earnings and the pay gap:

> I don't know. Economically women are still behind. There are more women in more senior roles, but women do the least well paid jobs in society. The rise of some women can give a misleading impression of what is going on in the broader economy. The dilemma the women have to deal with between work and home has not been remotely resolved. It is not about victimhood, but the broad economy of the world we live in.

Helen was relatively unusual among the women interviewed in describing herself as a feminist, but one who is aware of improving circumstances for women:

> I would count myself a feminist, though I dislike labels and worry that there can be too much self-proclaimed victim hood involved. There are real victims, but to say that as a gender we are all equally victimised doesn't stand much scrutiny. Mind you, intelligent feminists have never argued that.

She pointed out that positive changes for women are not equally distributed across all jobs and sectors:

> My life isn't always a bowl of cherries, but compared to many, I have a lot to be grateful for. I sense that very little has changed in the City, for example, and I am not sure that much has changed for women doing the worst paid jobs in society.

She sees things generally improving for young women, but is worried about the current concern with body image:

> I do see some of the young women having greater confidence in being themselves, but it is hard to generalise. There are still some who are

very unconfident. How do young women internalise the pressures that are on them? You read about their obsession with self image and their eating disorders and the peer pressure and you think, whatever happened to 'Fat is a Feminist Issue'? I am not an optimist or a pessimist, but a realist.

Key points

Helen identifies two main challenges: stereotypical assumptions that might be made about women, and women's lack of confidence that then impedes their progress at work. Working in broadcasting she is particularly aware of the additional challenge faced by women as they age. She has been sensitive to what she feels is right for her in building her career and feels that she has benefited from being in the right place at the right time. Her own determination and upbringing have played a part in her success.

She recognizes the difficulties of combining motherhood and a career, and is generally positive that things are changing for the better for women, although she sees that the pace of change is not even across industries.

Stevie Spring

Stevie is Chief Executive of Future PLC and since 2008 has also been Chair of BBC Children in Need. She was previously Chief Executive of Clear Channel, UK and has been part of the management team at advertising agencies Young and Rubican and Gold, Greenlees Trott. Prior to that she was at Grey Advertising and TV am. Stevie studied Law at the University of Kent. She is a Fellow of both the Institute of Practitioners in Advertising and the Marketing Society.

Challenges

When Stevie started work in advertising, barriers for women were more overt. She gave an example that included sexual harassment:

Without a doubt I met career barriers as a woman, particularly early on in my career. When I was an account director at an advertising agency, I was working late and the client offered me a lift home. When we got there he said: 'Shall we have a night cap?' I said 'no'. He leapt on me. I went to see the chairman of the agency to complain, I had been really upset, and the response was: 'When will you understand that you are not here to collect boyfriends, but to work?' I took it up with his boss who was more understanding, but the solution was to take me off the business, not to disrupt the client relationship.

Such male behaviour would be unlikely to be condoned today. The culture has moved on. However, Stevie pointed out that there are still important gender issues, for example the pay gap between men and women, although she feels that this is partly the fault of the women:

> I earn more money than I ever dreamed I would, but there is a very real pay gap between men and women. I probably earn less as a woman than a man in this job. You can get an excellent woman for the price of a mediocre bloke. There is a definite inequality of pay still. That is our fault as women. We are not sufficiently assertive. We fight for people who work with us and for us, but are less good at it for ourselves.

She speaks as one of the limited number of women who are in the predominantly masculine world of a FTSE-listed company:

> I go to dinner after dinner, meeting after meeting where you can count the women on one finger. It is interesting how supportive and collaborative these women [on the boards of the FTSE companies] are to each other, contrary to what you might expect. When our financial results are out, I can guarantee that by 7.30 am Sly Bailey (Trinity Mirror CEO) will be one of the first to send a congratulatory email. There is a camaraderie about it all. However, inevitably if we are talking together we get the comments: 'What's the witches' coven talking about?' You have to be pretty thick skinned.

She is in a position where as an 'outsider' in a leadership position she is judged differently from male colleagues by other women as well as men:

> When I went to Clear Channel, I inherited a PA. When I met her, she had a face like thunder. She said: 'You need to know that I worked for a woman before and I didn't like it.' I asked her if she had ever worked for a man who she did not like and she said: 'yes, lots'. There is a burden of having to represent women when you are in these situations.

Stevie is also aware that women will tend to lead differently from men and may therefore be disadvantaged, even if their ways of working are good ones:

> I think that women have a natural bent to a collaborative style. However, in a situation of changes and a fast pace, we have to take a decision and then either pick up the pieces or get people on board afterwards. Women are not naturally good at this sort of decision making. You have to teach yourself to be able to do it.
>
> This is a gross generalisation, but I think that women's strengths tend to be in multi-tasking, collaboration, communication, diplomacy rather than 'I say so' and nurturing people to give the best of themselves. I can see that these traditional female values should be more prevalent in the work place. There are lots of men who share these skills.

Responding to the challenges

Why did Stevie think that she had been successful in meeting challenges? She credited a combination of personal qualities, opportunities and mentoring:

> I refuse to say luck, which is what all women say, but I genuinely believe that if luck is opportunity meeting preparation, the individual is half of that equation. That means being ready to take the opportunity when it presents itself.
>
> I think that I am infinitely curious, I have an amazingly good memory, I am not scared to take decisions and I have had enormously supportive mentors. My mentors have supported me, but they have thrown me in at the deep end to sink or swim and I have swum.

She gave particular importance to having the confidence to be honest:

> Deep in my soul I do believe that just because you haven't done something before does not mean you can't do something. Not many women think like this. I never have a problem in saying I don't know, I don't understand. It makes it easier to do something for the first time.

Stevie sees the benefit of standing out as a woman in a 'man's world'.

> In my current job it is a distinct advantage being a woman. It is a male targeted company and having a woman in charge has the creative dissonance of that. I am not the target market for any of the

products and I see that as an advantage. I can be dispassionate from a management perspective. It would be difficult to run Vogue (laughs). An advantage being a woman gives you, is that you have 'stand out' and rarity value. It can be good and bad of course. There is quite a lot of 'silly old tart, menopausal cow'. But we (the company) do punch above our weight comparatively.

Stevie reflected on advice she might give to younger people:

I have been incredibly fortunate in having a diverse set of experiences. My key advice when I talk to younger women or men is to explain the difference between five years' experience and one year of experience repeated five times. It is about recognizing that if you have favours in the favour bank where you work you will be given more opportunities than you would be if you were starting somewhere else. Head hunters are conservative about this. They want someone who has done the job before. For most jobs, core skills are infinitely transferable, managing a team, being literate, being numerate and being brave. Brave is important.

Choices

Stevie pointed out that people at the top of their professions do not necessarily make a separation between 'life' and work and that balance in life could vary accordingly:

I have had an eclectic and interesting life. I was going to say an eclectic and interesting work life, but I mean life. I don't believe in work/life balance. People in our positions don't have a work/life separation. If you work in a factory the separation between work and the rest of your life may be true. We can time shift, and work flexibly. I prefer to talk about life balance.

However, she was very much aware of the tensions that arise between a woman's career progress and her wish to have children:

You can't ignore the hippopotamus in the corner of child bearing and child-care. Just at the point when the hierarchy of management is coming to its zenith, is when women have to absent themselves from the work place.

Also, certain jobs make having responsibility for children extremely difficult:

> When you look at the City jobs, they do expect their people to work through the night to sort out a problem when things are time sensitive.

Stevie thought that the different ways in which women might combine work success and having children were: having a supportive partner who might take major responsibility for childcare; being able to pay for the best childcare once successfully at a senior level (risking being too old to have a child); or having children very young and building your career afterwards:

> In the early years it is women in particular who tend to be the primary carers. Successful women often have husbands who are the primary carer [thinking of the successful women she knows] one has to be cognisant of the role of partners in the households of successful women where children are involved. The role of the spouse and the structures that are in place to support the household are often unspoken. When you have children and you are in a senior role you can afford support. The difficulty is that you might leave it too late. It is tricky for women. It is a massive life risk that women have to take, leaving having children too late.
>
> The alternative is to have them young. Denise Kingsmill had her children young and studied law while at home. She ended up as deputy head of the Competition Commission and is now Baroness Kingsmill.
>
> It is the bit between middle management and being absolute boss that is so difficult. At the very top you have much more flexibility and choice. But then you tend to be old!

Stevie was also aware as an employer of the tensions and difficulties associated with senior women taking maternity leave:

> If you have built up credibility and a reputation it is easier to have children. There are very few senior women here, but one of our senior publishers has had two lots of maternity leave in the three and a half years that I have been here. I was thrilled for her personally and thrilled when she came back, but less thrilled as an employer

when three months after she came back she announced that she was pregnant.

A while ago I promoted a woman to a senior post of client services director and regarded her as a case study of how to manage things through a pregnancy. We did everything right. We kept in touch throughout and sent her a weekly report and it worked well, although I was there at one in the morning covering her work sometimes. When she came back she did not say thank you. In a service industry you have to do stuff after 6 p.m. so when she left at 6 p.m. for childcare reasons, others had to pick up the slack. After six months she resigned and took a job nearer home. I could not have done any more to build a job round her. It was worth doing; she was massively talented. I was thrilled for her at an individual level, but my heart said different as an employer.

Indeed there are difficulties around any women taking maternity leave:

We have 1,000 employees in the UK and the majority are male, but still at the present time, 90 of our employees are pregnant or on maternity leave. Managing that is not funny. In a small business God knows how you do it.

Change

When asked: 'Do you think things will change for women?' Stevie stressed the importance of having a critical mass of women in management and having a range of successful role models:

Yes, as a consequence of scale. The more young women are able to see a range of role models, with as many differences among women as there are between men and women the better. When they can see: there's one with children; there's one without; there's a triathlete; there is one who is gay. They need to see that not all women who get to the top are one particular way. Seeing more women helps other women. There are so many good women now in middle management, inevitably more will get to the top. Numbers will make the big difference.

But she remained aware of the continuing barriers, particularly in relation to the major choices that women make about children, childcare and their own balance:

The barrier is where the job makes it impossible to do young childcare. There are women who will not want to give that up and I respect that. Women make fantastic entrepreneurs partly because they are in control of their own destiny.

Recognizing the dominant 'male' model of career, Stevie commented:

> Women choose not to play the game in the way it needs to be played. I would never criticise anyone's choice to take a lesser middle management role.

Key points

Stevie identified a range of challenges for women at work, from sexual harassment to the pay gap. She saw her success as being due to a combination of her personal qualities and her ability to recognize and take opportunities, including those offered through mentoring. She obviously loves her work. She recognizes the tensions and difficulties for women who have or wish to have children and a career. She believes that change for women will occur when they reach a critical mass and through there being many and varied women role models in senior positions.

Marisa Drew

Marisa Drew is a Managing Director in the Investment Banking Division of Credit Suisse, which she joined in 2003. In June 2008, Marisa was the recipient of the Women in Banking and Finance (WIBF) annual award for achievement. She has also been recognized by Financial News in its annual 'FN 100 Women in Finance' publication as one of the most influential women in European Finance each year since 2007. Marisa is American and has been in the UK since 1999.

Challenges

Working in the masculine world of finance for over 25 years, Marisa has met prejudice against women, but also believes that she has benefited from being a woman:

> I believe that the position of women in finance has significantly improved since I started. However, there most certainly have been situations over time where clients or even colleagues appeared to have a negative bias about women. I could have seen them as barriers, or figure out a creative way to get around them. I found that you can establish a relationship with someone not positively inclined to work with a woman, you can find another angle with a man who

first tries to identify you as a wife, daughter or mother. Being female has benefitted me. Some clients are actually more comfortable with a female advisor. They trust me more. They believe I 'own' success or failure in a way that a man might not. Some male bankers are more laissez-faire or come across as more mercenary as if 'it's just another deal for me'. If I can't deliver on a price for extraneous reasons, I feel it. It keeps me awake at night. There may be something a little different: it could be empathy; it could be a matter of emotional intelligence that impacts how women interact with clients.

One of her biggest challenges involved a feeling of isolation relieved by the advice of a mentor:

It was most acute when I almost left the business. I was a junior associate working on a transaction, working round the clock. Another employee above me was made redundant and I was left in charge on a very high-profile, complex and risky deal. I had no sleep, I felt exposed, and lost perspective, most likely through exhaustion. There was no one I felt I could talk to. I did not want to show weakness to my peers. I guess I give credit to a person who became my mentor, a man who must have sensed my vulnerability and reassured me to hang in there. He told me that they had confidence in me, which was why they were able to let the under-performing employee go. He told me to go and get some sleep and I slept for most of 48 hours. I realised I liked the work and could do it. Before he spoke to me I had no one I was close enough to who I could vent with. That one man reaching out made all the difference to me. He became a mentor, a champion and a friend now.

She commented on how the same women's and men's attributes can be characterized differently.

I have sat in meetings and if the room is dominated by males a woman's characteristics are often debated. If she is aggressive, she is often characterised as sharp-elbowed, whereas a man would be thought of as assertive. If not, she is considered too 'meek', whereas men sometimes get the benefit of being considered 'collaborative'. Champions for women have to take the responsibility to shine the light on these biases and make people aware of the double standard when they see this go on. Often raising the issue in a public forum is enough to get smart people to re-examine their ingrained thought patterns.

Responding to the challenges

Marisa was very aware of the importance of mentors in career progress, in addition to the mentor mentioned above:

Also one of the people I worked with early in my career was a woman with a difficult personality. She was acting like a male – big shoulder pads, chain-smoking and very forceful. She was one of the first few senior women on Wall Street. People said you don't want to work with her, but I did. She and I became friendly. I worked my tail off to prove my worth to her and she became a supporter. People thought, 'She's tough, if she says you are OK you must be good.' That was helpful. I admired her, but her personal style was not something I wanted to emulate. I wanted to be my own person. I felt that if that was what you had to be to be successful, I don't want this. I asked myself 'Is that required? Do you have to sublimate your personality in order to be more like a man?' I decided to give it a try to be a different kind of operator.

With the second mentor, I felt I had to earn his respect day to day, but once I had, he was a great supporter. I had to earn that, but it is important to have someone above you who will be your champion. It is almost more important for women than men because women have fewer natural opportunities to bond with senior people of their gender, given their lower numbers in the business.

In addition to mentors, Marisa rated her excellent qualifications, range of experience and thoughtfulness about what she wanted in life:

I did a number of things before coming back into investment banking. When I started out I 'fell' into investment banking. I did things out of order: I did the analyst programme in New York, where I trained for two years and it was assumed that I would go on then and get an MBA, which was what analysts were expected to do. Instead after two years I was intrigued by the buy side and went into private equity for two years. Following this experience, one of my former colleagues in the investment bank called me to say that they would put capital behind a business if I ran it. I ran a business for two years and learned a lot about myself, including the fact that I did not want to be an entrepreneur. I sold the business and went to Business School at Wharton, where I did a lot of soul searching during the two-year programme. I asked myself, 'What did I really like and dislike about the various work experiences I've had? What am I suited to?' One of the reasons I believe I have been successful is because I was very methodical about choosing my next job. I returned to investment banking in a careful way. I wanted a high velocity of transactions and I wanted to work with clients, particularly young dynamic companies who satisfied my entrepreneurial bent. I did not want to be doing large company corporate coverage. All these prior experiences taught me what was most aligned to my personality. I was focused in my search to find a home best suited to who I am and where my passions lie.

As with some of the other women, Marisa has been guided by her intuition in deciding what was right for her career:

Am I lucky? Is it the company? Am I at the right place at the right time? I looked seriously at two firms before coming to this one and I first accepted the offer of the other firm but I had a gut feeling that it was wrong. They were similar organizations, but something was niggling at me. Sometimes you have to trust that little voice. I then changed my mind and decided to come here. Looking back I don't think I would have had the opportunities I have had here at the other firm.

She has been equally thoughtful about how to maintain success as a woman:

The criteria for success have changed over time. Initially I recognised that my role was product-specific and I brought mostly technical expertise to the table. I focussed on knowing my stuff and being an expert in my field. I made sure I was top of my game – 'she's the one who can always answer the question'. I made sure I was over the top in being informed.

I also tried to create a presence for myself. In the start I was in a pool of junior bankers and individuals were picked out for a given assignment. It is easy to become faceless in that environment. I tried to create a way to be more visible. Of course as a woman I stood out anyway, but I felt I needed to take the extra effort to ensure I was noticed for the right things. I tried to participate in conference calls and meetings and volunteered for things that were non-revenue making, e.g. recruitment, philanthropy, culture building activities over and above my defined 'job' that allowed me to build networks and interact with people outside of my sphere. Then as people rose in the hierarchy there were people throughout the firm who knew me. It was helpful for my career.

Choices

Marisa feels that she has a balance between the work that she loves and her life with her husband:

> I love what I do, absolutely love it. I have been given other offers and turned them down on numerous occasions. I get a huge amount of satisfaction from what I do. I am totally committed and this drives my success. People feel it, and see you are committed and this is important for those you lead.
>
> From the family structure standpoint, I give credit to my husband. He knew I was a passionate career person and that I knew I needed to be in an all encompassing career. He supports me in all that I do, for example never complaining about my work or if I do something like book a conference call at the weekend. I never feel guilty about work, he's always behind me. If I look at female friends, almost all of them have a supportive partner. It is a big piece of a successful career.

She feels that although women have to make trade-offs between work and family a more important factor in the development of a woman's career might be seeing women in senior roles:

> I need to be visible to junior women. When you ask women why they leave, they know all about the trade-offs that women have to make between families and work. They know what the job entails, they are smart people, but they need to feel that getting to the top is achievable. If they do not have women in numbers above them, they get disillusioned because then they feel that the sacrifices are not worth it. They also need to see that I'm a 'normal' person with a life and outside interests.

Change

Marisa has been proactive in trying to bring about change for women in finance:

> I am generally optimistic about women's progress although things are difficult in this volatile market for everyone. On a positive note, I feel that there has been a marked change in attitudes in the last 8–9

years. There is naming and shaming of companies where there are no women on the Boards of Directors and there are legislative initiatives happening across Europe to mandate change.

She has been active in setting up a 'Diversity Forum' with seven competing firms, all of which have sent a senior woman to try and bring about change for women in investment banking (see Chapter 7, pp. 165–166).

Key points

Marisa has met gender stereotyping, but believes that she has benefited from being a woman in a generally masculine world. She credits mentoring as having an important role in her success and is aware of the role played by her own qualities, including following her own instincts in building her career. She is committed to the work that she loves and has a partner who is totally supportive. She sees mentoring and having plenty of women role models as the main agents of change for women and has been active in supporting younger women.

Helen Fernandes

Helen Fernandes was appointed as Consultant Neurosurgeon at Addenbrookes Hospital in Cambridge in 2002, the first female surgeon to be appointed there. She specializes in the treatment of both adult and paediatric patients with brain and spinal problems.

Helen also has a commitment to both undergraduate and postgraduate medical education. She is Associate Director of Postgraduate Medical Education in Addenbrookes responsible for the supervision, teaching and assessment of over 80 junior doctors. She also chairs the national body WinS (Women in Surgery), part of the Royal College of Surgeons of England. This organization has over 3,000 members and works to promote surgery as a career for women.

Challenge

Helen is one of the younger interviewees who came into the male world of surgery at a time when things were starting to change for women. However, she is still aware of stereotypes that patients and others hold about women:

> It does not bother me, but on a ward round with a male trainee, I can see the patients' eyes look over my shoulder to him. People don't take

information in under these circumstances [i.e. who is the consultant] and what they do is just a reflection of society.

She was a pioneer as a woman in the field of surgery:

> Once I was in a consultant post I just had this feeling that you were viewed slightly differently, as slightly weaker, by everyone, patients and doctors.
>
> When you become a consultant it is up to you to develop your career and organise training time. You can sit back or develop both your surgical skills and enhance the reputation of your department. You can be included in committee work and in training. No one says, 'Would you like to do it?' You have to seek it out as an individual. I found this stage more difficult. The people you have to deal with tend to be very middle-aged, male and stale. When you are competing it can be quite intimidating. You may be the only female in the room, 10–15 years younger, quite small and in my case I have got some ethnicity in my background. But then I would think, 'Get over it. I would not be here if I was not capable.'

She has been aware of being viewed and treated differently as a woman surgeon, for example when using new techniques:

> There have been two or three instances when I've come across criticism and felt that if I had been male I would not have received that criticism. One example was when an older man was brought back in to help. He was unaware of new techniques, and I was told [by him] that I was taking on a case I was not ready for. If a chap did that [used new techniques] he will be thought of as well trained and doing things that were good for the department. That was two or three years ago. I say nothing and carry on and do the work and eventually people look at the quality of the work, not at you as a young slip of a thing.

Responding to the challenges

Helen felt that she met the challenges through:

> Having a talent, ambition, drive, wanting the end result has always been important. Enjoying what I do. My life would not be as rich if

I did not have the career I wanted. [It has been important that I was] able to do my chosen speciality, neurosurgery.

Choices

Helen was a pioneer in her field as a woman consultant surgeon with children:

> I went back to work after the first child and it was the first time that unit had experienced that process. It was good and positive, but I had to be fairly resolute about the child needing picking up at a certain time. I asked for one regular night on call to be fixed. The person who did the rota said it was impossible and I had to seek help to get that sorted. It was daunting and a bit scary. I had lots of positive mentoring from seniors in that department and I had a supportive husband.

She commented on structural changes in the life of doctors which give women the opportunity to work hard and get fully qualified in their 20s and have children once they have reached that stage:

> With training so structured, you are qualified at 23/24 years old, and have eight years of training. People used to spend longer in training. The European Work Directive means it will be possible to condense the working week, and for people having children later this is good. It might be possible to condense the working week into two long shifts. As a consultant it is easier to organise your own time than when you are a trainee. People now wait till they are 30 and have a baby.

Change

Helen has seen rapid change in the stereotype of women surgeons:

> Lady consultants when I was a trainee were generally strong, single and slightly unpleasant. They gave an image of tweed skirts and hairy legs. They made lots of sacrifices and that changed them, shaped them and embittered them. The surgical profession has got to shake that impression off for the public and for young medical students.

Helen chairs the network Women in Surgery, which seeks to change the current situation where around 7 per cent (Halliday et al., 2005) of consultant surgeons are women. She stated that:

I would hope that in 5–10 years' time WinS is redundant, its job done.

When asked if this was realistic, she said:

Probably not, I think it will get the proportion up to 20 per cent and it would settle at that. I think that is acceptable. Hopefully that will reflect other specialities.

When asked, why not 50 per cent?

You can't get away from genetics. Surgery will attract strong-minded ambitious females and there are only a proportion of these amongst women, although looking at teenagers today, girls are much more confident.

Helen was aware of the importance of changing the perceptions of girls and boys and of the wider public through research and the media:

We also wanted in this organisation to understand why girls were not choosing surgery or leaving surgery. Once we know the issues we can look to see what you can do to change. Changing perceptions in the media forms part of that. There are TV programmes planned about surgery, and we are working with them to ensure they represent a diverse group of surgeons.

She currently acts as a role model to young women, including her own daughters and work experience students:

It is important to change the perceptions that it is difficult to have a senior position in surgery and a life. My daughters don't have a problem. They see it as perfectly possible, nice and enjoyable. I have quite a few female work experience people, from local schools.

Key points

Helen is aware of stereotypes held about women surgeons and that as a relative rarity she is likely to be treated somewhat differently from her male colleagues. She feels that her success is due to her own drive, determination and love of her job. Changes in the ways that consultants are trained have been helpful to her in planning and having her family and she is committed to changing the public perception of women in surgery to encourage more women to become surgeons.

Carol Peace

From being a probationary teacher and the only biologist in a brand new comprehensive school in Nottinghamshire, head of biology, senior mistress and deputy head at secondary schools in Leeds, to being head teacher of a mixed 11–18 comprehensive school in North Yorkshire, Carol's career in education has spanned over 35 years. 'Achievement for All' was her motto throughout. She was one of the founders of the women's network Senior Women in Secondary Schools (SWISS). After taking early retirement, Carol worked part-time as a Trainer and Assessor for the National Professional Qualification for Headship (NPQH) but is now enjoying spending more time with family and friends.

Challenges

Carol talked about the initial difficulties she faced when seeking headship:

> At my interviews for headships I was asked sexist questions: men on panels asking about my domestic arrangements and how I would cope with my young children and doing the necessary work as a head teacher or how I would manage the older men on the staff. After one interview, where I was not successful, one half of the panel was saying I would be too soft and the other half that I would be too hard. Improper questions were asked at other interviews too. All of this fuelled my ambition even more.

She also recalled how as a woman deputy head she knew she could do as well as many heads that she had encountered over the years:

> As a deputy head I was taking school assemblies, leading staff meetings, chairing committees and writing reports for governors and the LEA – just as the Head did. As a member of the Senior Management Team I felt separated from the rest of the staff and I decided to cross the bridge completely and try for headship. I had worked with several heads and I just thought: 'I could do it.'

Responding to the challenges

Her ambition was vital to her progress:

> Basically, I am a very ambitious person. If there is a career path with obvious progression I always wanted to go to the next highest level. For example, when I started as a biology teacher I wanted to be head of department. I was in a brand new school and I got a lot of opportunities early on. The school had a female head, she was not a particularly strong role model for me, but after two years in post I was made head of biology. I wanted to organise a school camp and she let me do it even though I was young and inexperienced. So, the things that helped my career progress were ambition and being given opportunities and wanting to go on to promoted posts.

Carol tried a different career route going back to university to do scientific research but knew what she really wanted:

> I did not enjoy it very much because I missed the people. I am not a pure research person so I was there for nine months and then pulled out. It probably put my teaching career back by a year. After it I got a Scale 1 post and also taught part-time. Then I married and came to Leeds and got a Scale 3 post. The experience made me all the more determined to drive on. I did another jump from Scale 3 to senior mistress. There were people who had confidence in me. For example in one of my references it said 'if anyone can do it Carol can'.

Among the factors that helped her in her progress were her excellent qualifications and planning her career and also an element of being in the right place at the right time:

> I got a good degree, a first, and a distinction for my post-graduate certificate in education; that makes a good basis. I think also a bit of planning. The schools I have applied for have all been good ones with Sixth Forms. Also I have been in two new schools where it was a blank canvas and we were starting something fresh. There was everything there to play for. At one school, that was brilliant, the school was filling up and I was the first starting A levels and the sixth form. Going into a church school as a senior mistress was helpful...I have been in good schools that had good reputations and had a good CV building up.

She was also conscious of the importance of support from her male mentors and her husband.

She was a founder member of the active network for women SWISS (see Chapter 4) and has been an advocate for women, running professional development courses and championing the case for women as head teachers.

Choice

Carol was unusual at the time in choosing to progress to headship while having young children:

> I had young children but I got a deputy headship. They actually delayed the interviews for a few days because I was in hospital having a baby. There were these two male heads, one I worked for and one in the school where the vacancy was, who did not mind having a woman with a family in a senior post. I had proved I could work and do the job with a baby and nanny at home. I went to the interview the day after I came out of hospital. I remember I could not put on my suit as the skirt was too tight so I had to wear a dress and jacket! Being a mother did not get in the way of the interview and these two male heads had not held the fact that I had just had a baby against me at all.

Personal and later practical support at home was important for the choice that she made:

> On a personal front I had a supportive husband. He's never interfered. He knew I was ambitious and did not stand in my way. The one thing was I did not look for jobs all over the country. I always managed to find schools within a half-hour commute from home. My husband and I researched childcare and he did not mind whether we had nannies and I went to work, or if I thought I could not leave the children and stayed at home. He didn't make any demands. I suppose his job and our financial situation meant I didn't have to go out to work. I was working at a career because I wanted to. It helped me to know he was at home some of the time as he was doing shift work so the children were seeing Daddy during the day when I was not around.

Having the 'right' childcare was important:

> I thought about childminder, nursery or nanny and having the best, the nanny or a live-in nanny felt right in the early days. If you are

top of your career you can afford that. Having a live-in nanny took much of my salary, but it was a good investment as it gave me peace of mind. It didn't feel right to leave my children in a group of 30 at a nursery.

Change

Carol thought broadly about changes for women in the world of work:

> The 1980s generation of women were the ones who tried to have it all and in the 1990s it was not so normal to do that, when high-flying women started to give up careers and stay at home with their children. Now we are back in a dilemma with more choice. With the recession and job situation, the luxury of choice in the 1990s has gone. There is more flexible working now with more part-time working and portfolio careers. Information Technology has provided more opportunities for working at home and combining a career and family. The choice is not so black and white to stick to a career or to have children; now there are more mix and match options.

However, she appreciated that there were differences between professions and that education provides a career that is more compatible with having children than most:

> Ultimately in some professions it isn't possible and is still as cut-throat where women have to make hard choices and be dedicated to their career: young women who are training to be lawyers, accountants or business executives and so on. I often wonder how they will manage, working exceedingly long hours and being expected to travel abroad at short notice, for example. Teachers have the luxury of the holidays and this makes work more compatible with having children. This is the future. It is so demanding to compete with the men on male terms. It is difficult to think about marrying let alone having children. Whether they can take a gap in their career I don't know, but it is going to be more difficult for them.

Carol drew out the implications of trying to have a family while trying to fit in with a 'male' pattern of career:

> Last week I met with women from SWISS for lunch. We were discussing whether it is better to have your children when you are young. Perhaps it is best to get your degree, have a family and then build

your career. Having children when you are much older could be a problem. It does not seem healthy for future generations. Our society is pushing it.

Finally Carol commented on the important statutory changes that have taken place:

> Pay and conditions and maternity rights have come on by leaps and bounds. Now your partner can share the time off. You feel better if you can leave your baby with your partner. At least the baby is with one parent. A lot has changed in the last 20 years.

Key points

In the early part of her career Carol was aware of sexism. She was ambitious and clear that she wanted to both build a career and have children. She credits her own qualifications, judgement and planning and the support of mentors and her husband as contributing to her success. Carol sees more opportunities now for women to combine work and motherhood through flexible working aided by IT and statutory changes relating to maternity rights and childcare, but is aware that there are some careers that are as difficult as ever to combine with having a family. She has been active in supporting women who are, or aspire to be, senior leaders in education.

Judith Hanratty

Judith Hanratty is currently a non-executive director of PatnerRe Ltd, a leading international reinsurance company listed on the New York Stock Exchange, and was a senior executive for British Petroleum plc until she retired in 2003. Currently, she is also a non-executive director of Charles Taylor Consulting plc and Chairman of the Commonwealth Education Trust. She has held a number of non-executive directorships of major enterprises both in New Zealand and the UK, and central government appointments such as the Competition Commission and the Gas and Electricity Markets Authority in the UK. She is also an Honorary Fellow and former trustee of Lucy Cavendish College, Cambridge University, and a fellow of the Royal Society for the Encouragement of Arts, Manufacture and Commerce. She received an Honorary LLD from her New Zealand university in 2005, was awarded the Order of the British Empire in 2002, and was made a Commander of the Royal Victorian Order in 2007.

Challenges and responding to the challenges

Judith came from New Zealand and was relatively unusual as a young woman in being qualified in law in the 1960s. Although aware of the challenges faced by women in work, she was perhaps uniquely equipped to handle working in a male-dominated environment, as she realized that her prowess as a sportswoman gave her an entrée to levels of male power that few women could access at the time:

> I was very at good at sports and represented New Zealand in golf. What that taught me was how to succeed and to be comfortable with success and with publicity, both negative and positive. My situation was made easy socially because of golf and because the game was popular with business and professional men. I was a member of a club that had as members senior practitioners from the professions, members of the judiciary and government ministers. It, unusually, had a long tradition of women and men playing often together. This gave me immediate access to senior male networks. I remained in New Zealand until I was 42 but I was still playing golf at that time on a 1 handicap. By then I had a number of prominent public and private sector appointments.

Judith attended university in Wellington while pursuing her golfing career, remaining at the university after completing a postgraduate degree in law before moving into private commercial practice. She came to the UK in 1986 to take up a position by invitation – initially not intending to stay more than three years. This was an advantage, and she felt that a further advantage for her at the time was that she came from outside the UK. This meant that 'They did not have a box to put you in'. She was, from the time she arrived, the most senior woman in the organization. A little later two other women from abroad joined the senior ranks but both left after relatively short periods. It took until the late 1990s before more women began to penetrate the senior echelons.

> When I arrived I found it rather surprising that in the late 1980s/ early 1990s in the UK there were so few women in the City or in the big companies. Starting in a senior position was relatively rare in an established organisation, for men as well at that time. The way I came in provided an explanation as an exception to the prevailing situation.

Her background and talents continued to be helpful:

> I had a good knowledge about things; many of them were comfortable talking about in a social setting, for example golf and rugby as well as the arts generally. I had to do a fair share of entertaining which was an important aspect of networking, but it was unusual then for the woman to be a host. This was a great ice-breaker. I was also respected for my golfing ability and that helped a very great deal. It provided immediate small talk. Also I was not 'of them'; I had come in and they could make the excuse that I had come from elsewhere and they did not have to feel guilty that there were no other women operating at that level. Having had a depth of experience in a very male-dominated profession in New Zealand I was also very comfortable myself working and socialising with men. These were I think advantages at that time that many other women may not have had.

Referring to the lack of women in senior posts in the earlier part of her career:

> Eventually of course the question came up 'what about women?' In the late 1980s/early 1990s in the UK I felt that there was nothing I could do by getting on a soapbox other than doing what I did as well as I could professionally. I was conscious that the most important contribution I could make to the acceptance of more women in the future was to succeed, to set an example in a matter of fact way. There were two women who came into the organisation later, both from abroad, but they 'opted out' fairly quickly and returned home.

When asked why that was, Judith commented on the male and class culture that was predominant in the UK at the time, seeking to unravel the intersections of class and gender that contributed to the culture:

> Men will trade with each other and also compete fiercely. You have to recognise this; how much is a mob thing. They were a relatively cohesive group. They came from a male-oriented predominately public or old grammar school and Oxbridge or major university background and sometimes with a regimental link as well as a legacy from national service. They were a very particular sort of man of that time – things have changed so radically now this may be incomprehensible to the young today.

They tended to choose themselves. People tended to be more comfortable choosing people in their own image. Rebelliousness and grittiness was avoided. That has faded. The very people who had been recruiting, all those chaps, had largely spent their whole life in a predominantly male-only environment from the age of about nine till they got to work.

When they got there most of the women were people who were serving them in one way or another as secretaries or tea ladies. They did not have the experience of a woman colleague, and certainly not a woman boss. Also very few had wives, however able, who had careers or even worked.

When I went to the City branch of a UK national banking network in 1986 with an introduction from the company so that I could open an account to receive my salary, the manager told me that they could only open an account for me if my husband would guarantee it. So I continued to maintain an account with the very small London branch of my New Zealand bank.

Judith then commented on the difficulties in trying to change a work culture, coming to the conclusion that it is better to try and change things gently from the inside and that any attempt to force change head-on is likely to fail or at least slow progress:

If you want to get to the top you do need to understand the context and culture you are operating in. If you are uncomfortable about it you have to be careful to get into a position to counter that. Rebelling against it does not always have results. You have to be a bit more subtle – it may be a case of either being able to move into a position of control and influence or move out to a position where you can effect change. Fizzing around in a rage inside is counterproductive to the situation and counterproductive to you.

Choices

Although Judith did not have children she was well aware of the impact of children on a woman's working life. In making her choices, she was able to follow the rare example of a mother who worked professionally in a male-dominated field:

Instinctively if I had had children I would have adjusted my working career for at least the first ten years. After that children can understand better how important work is for any individual and can learn a great deal from their parents. In our family there was a tradition of educated women and my parents were very supportive.

Commenting on bringing up children today, Judith spoke in favour of both parents working and of the possibility of role reversal or parents taking equal shares in nurturing children:

> It is good for children to have parents engaged in the real world. I don't think it is wrong to hire the right skilled people to help.
>
> There is no reason at all why men should not participate in the home. It is a personal thing to be worked out between couples.

Change

Moving on to questions of change, Judith remained aware of the difficulties for women combining childcare and work but was optimistic about the impact of technology on enabling women to at least partially work from home:

> It can be difficult for women to take too long a career break but that too has improved. There are many ways now, through IT for example, that you don't have to take a complete break. I know women lawyers who stay at home but keep a core practice going. Technology is to the benefit of the equalisation process that we are in the middle of.

In regard to more structural change, Judith remembered that:

> There were three women out of 100 in the class when I started [to study law]. In the period from then which was 1962 until 2005 when I received my honorary doctorate there was an increase from three per cent to 60 per cent women. It was an extraordinary period of change. There were very few women practitioners, and then from the late 1980s there was a sort of avalanche. Some of it was through the baby boom, but it got picked up in New Zealand in a determined effort at that time when the government formed a Ministry of Women's Affairs, and promoted a culture which embraced the idea that women could do anything. The society was receptive to it and it has achieved significant results.

Although things have improved for women, she recognized that the odds are still stacked in favour of men:

Since 1986 things have changed enormously. A meritocracy has developed and for men that has been far more productive proportionately than for women. Men may react more instinctively to competition. But generalities are difficult and the entrepreneurial climate that has emerged since the 1980s has particularly given women opportunities in the small and medium-sized companies, but in big companies it has been more of a hard slog to get recognition.

She felt that things had changed more for women in New Zealand than the UK:

I think progress is being made a little more slowly here but it is catching up. I feel it is relatively much better in New Zealand but then it is a smaller society. There will be bullying of all sorts in any environment where you have people of that kind, but my impression is that male on female bullying in New Zealand would be set on, not just by women but by men as well. Processes would tend to eliminate it more quickly than here. It has got a lot to do with the way the society has developed.

Although change has been beneficial to women who want careers, she felt that there have been losses compared to when she started work. Then:

People were more polite. They did have the veneer of the respectable English gentleman. The Bar in those days was also very courteous if competitive. What has changed is grace and courtesy. Those attributes go a long way to solving problems although they can be distracting too. There is a greater tension, a tendency to take matters to the 'edge', a loss of principles; a tendency to try to work the rules and ignore the spirit. What's happening at the moment may temper that [referring to the economic downturn].

Key points

Judith's prowess as a sportswoman gave her an entrée into a masculine world of work. As she also came from outside the UK she was seen as an exception in work where the culture was male and upper class. She recognizes the importance of women as role models but was aware of the difficulties of trying to change the work culture single-handedly. She understands the tensions that arise for women combining work and motherhood and is appreciative of the changes in society that make this more acceptable, although she regrets the loss of 'grace and courtesy' in today's workplace.

Common themes

The accounts of how six successful women have met challenges, made choices and envisage change are of course very individual, and it would be invidious to generalize from such a small number. However, there are some commonalities between the 'stories'. Some recall overt sexism, but all of them recognize the difficulties such as stereotyping that are faced by women at work. Each of the women has been reflective about the development of her career and in some cases has exercised intuition about career choices, sometimes rejecting what might seem to be the better option. Throughout their careers they appear to have a conviction about what is right for them and are prepared to work extremely hard, sometimes taking on extra responsibilities beyond their normal workload. They are respectful of others, but not deferential, and they revel in their enjoyment of their work. Most of them mention mentoring as having been important in their success and most belong to a women's network.

All of them are aware that women face career barriers additional to those faced by men, and that having children adds enormous responsibilities and tensions for parents, mothers in particular. In different ways they are advocates for other women although most stop short of fully endorsing feminism. They are realistic about the difficulties of combining motherhood and a demanding job both as women and as employers. They are pragmatic about gender discrimination, preferring to deal with it constructively and collaboratively rather than fight it head-on, while supporting younger women and welcoming and endorsing changes that benefit women.

All of these themes also appear in the interviews of the other women.

In Chapter 7 the focus will be on change for women leaders at work, taking in the views of all the women interviewed, including the six featured in this chapter.

7
Change for Women at Work

The headline from me about women in business is that we have come a long way since we got the vote etc., but the workplace is still a difficult place. It is not just hierarchical, but gendered. We can never escape that. It's a fundamental part of human nature.

Working motherhood is the number one challenge for the next generation.

Technology makes it easier and easier for women with children to manage. They get home at a reasonable time and then continue to work after the children are in bed. It makes a big difference.

(views of three interviewed women)

Throughout the lives of those interviewed, there have been changes in attitudes towards, and perceptions of, the role of women. The interviewed women were aware that attitudes to women at work and the place of the family have changed and were continuing to change. However, across the age range they were broadly in agreement that gender had been a factor that had impacted on their career. They recognized that there were continuing stereotypes which disadvantaged women and that combining a demanding job with being a mother, although more possible than previously, was still stressful if rewarding.

The women were all in responsible positions as leaders at work. A sample of 60 may be insufficient for generalizations about all women at work, but their views are indicative of opinions of 'top' women in an age range of 40–70, with a median age in the 50s. The opinions offered in the book are not representative of the younger generation of women leaders now in their 20s and 30s whose experiences may well differ. These younger women come from a generation where girls and women have been acknowledged to be academically superior and where they appear to be more successful than their predecessors in accessing the lower and middle levels of management (Scott et al., 2008). However, as White (2000) found, it is in their late 30s, when women have children, that they tend to step off the career ladder and lose out to their male colleagues both in status and pay.

Some of the women who were interviewed started work in the 1960s and 1970s at a time when gender discrimination was not illegal, there was no maternity leave and the culture was tolerant of sexual harassment, intolerant of women working when their children were young, and women leaders were very rare. Even as recently as the early 1990s one woman recalled: 'I remember that when I first told my then boss that I was going to carry on working and have childcare he said: "No wonder there are so many problems in the world."'

Among the older women in particular, there was a realization that things have changed for the better for women. However, some discrimination remains and some women felt that the subtlety of current discrimination made it more difficult to deal with. The following comment from a woman who was in broadcasting encapsulated the opinions of many of the women interviewed.

> Things are still tough for women, but more under the surface than in the open. I still think it is not easy. I don't know how we help ourselves. The obvious discrimination was easier to deal with in some ways. I do think there are particular difficulties for women.

The particular challenges that women face can be grouped broadly into the gender stereotypes that we examined in Chapter 2, and the family responsibilities that we considered in Chapter 5. In this concluding chapter we first consider the stance of the interviewed women in relation to change in these two areas. Then the focus will be on current and future practice and the expectation of further positive changes for women in the workplace. These changes will affect not only them but also their male colleagues and their families. The changes include technological development and societal trends, including the fact that most, and a growing proportion of, employable women will be in paid work and that younger men wish to play a larger part in family life (Gratton, 2010). The chapter ends with recommendations for individual women and for employers, drawn from the distilled experience of the interviewed women.

The stance of the 'top' women towards change

The career challenges faced by women will only reduce through continuing cultural change bringing about a society where men and women are sensitized to subtle discrimination, and caring duties are seen as the responsibility of both women and men. The twin challenges of dealing with a male culture and decisions about family still remain.

A male work culture

The culture is changing, but the stereotype which casts men as leaders and women as supporters lingers (Schein, 2007), so that women can be caught in the 'no win' situation of the 'femininity/competence bind' (Still, 2006, p. 187). This means that if a woman appears as very feminine she is not perceived as leadership material, but if she comes across as competent and authoritative she is seen as not being feminine. This dissonance makes it difficult for her to be accepted as a leader. In general the male culture of work identified through the interviews is slowly diminishing, although still strong in some areas. Aspects of the male culture include: exclusive male networking, particularly through sport; a generally 'macho' culture; and the bullying and manipulation by men of women. There are a range of potentially negative gender stereotypes about women which can be applied to women whether they are single, married, with children, without children and of any age, and they affect the way in which women as individuals negotiate the workplace. For example, one of the youngest women interviewed explained:

> In the dynamics of working with your colleagues and at senior levels, if you want to sell your ideas to men you have to choose the way in which you operate. They may treat you like they are your father, or they may flirt with you. If they are flirting you may have to choose whether to fall in with the role. You have to choose when to battle and when to give in. In the media world this is key.

It seems that women appear to be judged differently to men when it comes to age, particularly in the media, with a danger of being written off over the age of 50.

A new form of sexism may be found in its very denial and the assertion that it is now out of date and irrelevant. This argument is even used in relation to board membership where the proportion of women is so low (Thomson and Graham, 2005). Women may be told that they cannot take a joke if they respond to a sexist comment. This serves to put them in the wrong, making it difficult to react in a way that does not diminish them.

Internationally, there has been a change in attitudes towards styles of leadership with more general approval of a transformational, collaborative, nurturing approach (Bass and Avolio, 1994) which is typical of the 'feminine' archetype. Many of the women talked about having adopted this style which was derived from their values and beliefs. Without adopting an 'essentialist' approach to women and men it appears that there is a greater tendency for women than men to adopt this generally approved style (Eagly and Johannesen-Schmidt, 2007). However, the expectation that it is natural for women to act in this way may mitigate against any advantage that this offers.

Despite a slowly changing attitude to work/family responsibilities, gender stereotypes persist. Although the interviews revealed that some areas such as education, medicine and the media are tending to be more family-friendly, these areas were not necessarily free of gender bias and stereotypes. In particular, there was concern among the women working in higher education, and to some extent in schools, that there was a growing trend towards a managerialist culture that tends to favour men and makes it less likely that women will be appointed to leadership roles.

For the women, gender stereotypes are generally handled through a pragmatic, individualistic approach. The young woman working in the media quoted above went on to say: 'As a woman in business you just have to get on with it. You have to take responsibility for yourself and go for it.' The emphasis on the agency of the individual is typical of the views of most of the interviewed women. It was clearly stated by one of the women surgeons who said that: 'surgeons tend to have an "I'm just going to do it" attitude. They have to be extremely self-reliant as a surgeon and very decisive'. This attitude may be typical of surgeons, but it could be applied to many of the successful women in other professions.

The interviewed women recognize the changes that are occurring but in general they appear realistic and pragmatic, working within the system and accepting that, at least in the medium term, business motives may have to be prioritized over equity. One CEO stated it clearly:

> Business has to succeed. You have to play by the rules until you can change the rules. You have to win the race there is and then change the race. It is now a bit easier to win the race.

Gradually more women are 'winning the race' but changing the rules involves dealing both with a culture inimical to women at the top and practical and cultural changes to how we view families and who takes responsibility for them

Maternity leave, childcare and work/family balance

Having a child and taking maternity leave were once seen as complete anathema to a successful career for a woman. Talking about her son, one senior woman recalled just how difficult it had been:

> I had him at the height of my career when I was an executive vice president – they were horrified! There was no maternity policy, it was an interesting time. There was quite a lot of pressure, a feeling that if I screw this up no one else will be able to do it. There was barely any maternity leave. I took two and a half to three weeks. I was the first person who had a remote computer, the first to have access to the mainframe, it was unprecedented. Maternity leave in the USA was called disability and it was six weeks or eight weeks with a C-section, it was paid as disability, but they had never had a senior executive ask for this. Legally they could just end your employment. We have come a long way!

This illustrates the importance of the right to maternity leave as well as illustrating a work culture that has hopefully all but disappeared. Only the older women in the UK had experienced a time when maternity leave was unavailable, but they, like their younger colleagues, fully accepted the reality of women combining work and motherhood. As senior women, they sometimes adopted the perspective of the employer although this stance was informed by their own experience. To some extent women and children are obliged to fit round the needs of employers: this much is accepted by the women interviewed. One woman talking about the changes that have occurred ended by saying: 'There comes a point where the generosity of companies with women and children will come to an end.' When asked about change, one woman in the media identified both the duties of women as employees and the fact that there are some jobs that do not lend themselves to flexible working:

> I think it has got a lot better. There will be a challenge for some women in middle management who want to have it all but who are not prepared to give as well. There are now fantastic examples of flexibility and job share out there, but some women take it as a right.

There has to be a quid pro quo. There are some jobs that simply can't be done in three days a week. Just because something is available it does not mean women have a right to it.

As employers themselves, some were aware of the difficulties of handling maternity leave:

I appointed a woman to be managing director when she was pregnant. When she was on maternity leave it was hard on me personally. I had to step in to do some of her work, so appointing her was a personal decision for me. She is now pregnant for the third time. I can understand why male executives think twice about employing women of childbearing age. In a big organization they can manage, but in a smaller company I can see why men stumble over the appointment of women.

They were also realistic about needing to ensure that childcare was fully covered:

If you have to observe office hours you need home care that you can rely on, or a partner who is not in this industry. A nanny who lives in is expensive but a key thing. People find a way round it, but it is a massive issue.

To some extent these views were shared across all the work sectors from which the women were drawn, but there were some differences between sectors. Those working in education, the health service and the media appear to experience a more tolerant attitude towards the needs of families in contrast to other areas, such as finance and retail. For example a woman CEO in media explained that:

My career was fantastically interesting and having a child just got pushed aside. I encourage women not to delay. Take six months off, or a year off and don't worry about it. I did not feel that was possible in the 1980s. I really believe that has changed.

Her view was that once babyhood was passed both parents should have an equal part to play:

I believe we need children as a society and need to be able to bring them up well. Inevitably women are mainly responsible for the first two years. Then after that it is equal. It is sad for dads if they don't get to take children to the dentist or go to a school play. It is better if we are even handed about it.

In schools and in higher education, women perceive a continuing, or in some cases growing, preference for men in leadership and the continuing domination of leadership by men (Bagilhole, 2002). However, attitudes to families and a work/family balance were more positive, with the head teachers keen to ensure that young mothers and fathers were able to combine work with family responsibilities and some of those in higher education determined to set good examples for work/family balance. One head teacher remarked how when she was a young teacher her head had set the example that she then followed with her staff of letting her teachers go to their children's nativity plays. She went on to say that she had worked in schools where women teachers had to pretend that they were ill rather than say they wanted time off for their children. She wanted people to know that they could be honest.

In medicine, it appears that change relating to family/work balance is happening quite fast, aided by EU working time directives that limit the number of hours that doctors can work. One of the surgeons commented:

> The old school don't see the need for different hours. The younger trainees, women are more aware and the men too. They want a life outside surgery. This is a difficult perceptual barrier for older members. We have the benefit of the working time directives. That should make it easier for women and men to have a better balance.

A woman in broadcasting pointed out that caring responsibilities are not exclusively the province of women:

> I don't see having families as an issue. Everyone has domestic issues of some sort. A man could have an elderly parent to consider. I find it a bit bizarre that women with children are regarded as more difficult. If anything I think they go to more trouble to jump through hoops not to interfere with their work.

There were examples quoted by those who worked in media, for flexibility in special cases, for example: 'We enabled a woman with a sick mother to work part of the time from the mother's home.'

It was generally felt that the culture had changed somewhat regarding men and their attitudes to their young families:

> I think men are now allowed to show a softer side, and they do help out, and some do flexible hours and help with the childcare, but women still do the bulk.

Although there is a general recognition that men might take a share of family responsibilities, men are rarely the main carer, and examples of flexibility over childcare were limited to the public sector and the area of media. A report on modern parents (Ellison et al., 2009), which focused on work in general, indicated that three-quarters of mothers said they took the lead in childcare, fathers tended to work longer hours than mothers and only 5 per cent of men worked part-time compared to over a third of mothers. Although men are more likely than previous generations to play an active part in childcare, change is slow.

One of the ways in which change is brought about in the culture is by the state taking the lead and introducing legislation which may be controversial but which points the way to a fairer society.

The individual and the state

However determined an individual might be, society plays a part in shaping the lives of women. Legislation is a necessary but not sufficient condition to bring about change. For example, most of the women interviewed at least had the option of taking paid maternity leave. The equality legislation of the 1970s has been extended by The Equality Act of 2006 which imposes a positive duty on public bodies to promote gender equality. Although this only applies to the public sector, the fact that public authorities will need to consider gender equality in all their functions is likely to have a gradual impact on society in general. Other legislation, such as the Right to Request, and Duty to Consider, Flexible Working, has implications for the work/family balance of men and women and will have an impact on the labour market, although so far the rights have been taken up by women rather than men (Hegewisch, 2009). Although legislation provides some protection for women in the workplace, at the higher levels of some types of work, e.g. finance, where jobs are prestigious and highly paid, there appears to be no alternative but to prioritize work at the expense of other aspects of life. One woman in broadcasting stated:

> Legislation coming through in recent years such as family-friendly policies can be enabling so that women can combine career and

family and straddle both sides but I don't see things changing. It is the same battles.

The women recognized that legislation had improved the opportunities for women to combine a career with motherhood. They also saw that there had been a change in attitudes to fathers, sanctioning an increased role for them in family life. However, they were not particularly optimistic about further or radical change, seeing women as generally continuing to take major responsibility for the family.

As the general feeling was that the individual woman has to take responsibility for her own career and future, there was limited support for a feminist interpretation of society or for positive discrimination.

Attitudes to feminism and affirmative action

The women interviewed were very likely to be supporting other, younger women, sometimes mentoring informally, and other times offering more formal support, including for example through the organization Opportunity Now. When asked about support for women, many stated that they offered support equally to younger women and men. There were mixed feelings about positive action to benefit women. Antipathy to women-only courses was expressed by one woman in the financial world:

> We provide a lot of coaching, and leadership training, but it is not separate for women. I believe that the more you segregate women the more unrealistic it is. It is not what the workplace is like. I have sent two women on a women-only programme but they did not enjoy it. They felt that it was feminist-oriented.

This view was not shared by all, with the all-women networks offering or having offered training courses and networking opportunities for younger women (see Chapter 4).

Feminism or feminist ideas were rarely mentioned and affirmative action met disapproval. There is some evidence from research (Banyard, 2010; Woodfield, 2007; Howard and Tibballs, 2002) that there is a backlash against feminism, with younger women in particular feeling that their fate is in their own hands. A study of women teachers, students and firefighters found:

> strong evidence that feminism did not 'speak' to the participants to anything like the degree that individualism did, nor the degree to which we might hope or expect given some of the experiences they

related. There was a conspicuous lack of feminist discourse in the education group and in the fire fighter group although there was some evidence among teacher participants. (Woodfield, 2007, p. 227)

Among the interviewed women, the clearest identification with feminism came from some of those in higher education. One stated:

As a feminist I think women should get up there and show we can do it, be role models to younger women. Being a woman it is mostly a matter of what you have to overcome, but I have learned how to celebrate and be proud of being a woman and of being confident in it.

Such an overtly feminist statement was rare. Despite the women being aware of the challenges that women face in their careers and the benefits of getting more women onto boards of directors, most of the women would hesitate to call themselves feminists and tended to regard feminism somewhat negatively. A very senior woman in media commented:

With active role models we will stimulate more women to aspire up. It is so necessary now, especially in this climate. We've got to help graduates get jobs, go into the schools and talk about work, let them shadow us. We must all commit to the goal of improving that 12 per cent [of women in FTSE company directorships]. We need senior women talking about their experience in accessible terms rather than trotting out theories and feminist nonsense.

When asked: 'What do you mean by "feminist nonsense"?' she said: 'when women start going into "we are better than men" speak'. It appears that the term 'feminism' has gathered negative connotations of essentialist cultural feminism that cause some women to reject the label.

Although none of the women were believers in strong cultural feminism, that is valuing the qualities of women more than those of men, most were supporters of weak cultural feminism (Gilligan, 1982) in that they identified certain qualities as more likely to be found in women while recognizing that an androgynous mixture of both feminine and masculine qualities might be found in leaders:

All I would say is that I do believe men and women are different, but I am wary of generalizations. However, I sort of think that modern business values that have been practised by generations of women: openness, dialogue, collaboration and multi-skilling are now recognized. But other key qualities like drive and ambition which are male remain very important.

One of the younger women in media gave a vivid example of how she sees that gender still plays out at work:

> Women are great in the workplace. In the game I work in women are better than men. Maybe it is the subject matter; maybe it is intuition. There are lots of male creatives here, but we had a session for all the account management people and it was obvious it was all women around who were doing account management. Women look after clients, keep everyone happy, make sure that things are happening on time. I wonder if it is the softness, the creative nature of the subject matter. It is funny here, production and planning and the boss, all are male and the rest mainly women. It has changed since I came here. There are two key women, myself and xxx. She is fantastic. She has been here two years or less. Having her on the management team is a real bonus.

The women interviewed were in favour of weak equality of opportunity (Evans, 1995), that is the desire for the 'race' to be equal, but they stopped short of strong equality of opportunity (ibid.) where positive efforts are made to engineer the conditions in favour of those who might be suffering discrimination. Despite this, there was considerable support among those who belonged to women-only networks for such networks. The idea of the 'queen bee' actively discouraging other women from climbing the career ladder to rival them (Rindfleish, 2000; Mavin, 2006) was not present in any of the interviews. The feeling among the women was that things were slowly improving and the glass ceiling still exists, but might have moved upwards to board level. As one remarked:

> I think things have changed but not completely changed. There is still something about the very top jobs.

Although the women might all be within the 20 per cent of women that Hakim (2004) considers are work-centred, they are fully cognizant of the difficulties that might minimize an individual woman's chances of reaching the top in any profession. Becoming a board director is an extreme example of this.

The business case for women on boards

There is a strong business case for limiting the waste of talented women who have much to offer in the workplace, and this principle is particularly appropriate to the level of board director (Branson, 2007; Hewlett, 2007) which is recognized by all the women as being beyond the glass ceiling. As pragmatists, the women were well aware that there were good business reasons for women to be involved at the highest level. One of the women who had worked at a very senior level but was now retired commented:

> I think that teams greatly benefit from having diversity of gender, age and ethnicity. It reflects the true composition of your customer base. It is a mistake to have teams comprising totally of alpha males. The world population is configured very differently.

The research of Grattan et al. (2007) shows that mixed teams perform more successfully than single-sex teams. Thomson and Graham (2005, p. 7) quote research in the US and in the UK that shows that women make or influence the vast majority of consumer decisions of all types, concluding that: 'companies that wish to be market-driven, therefore, effectively wish to be women-driven'. It makes good business sense to include women at the heart of such companies. In addition there is evidence that women on boards, particularly where there is more than a token one or two, add to the quality of governance and the qualities of decisions taken (Kramer et al., 2006). There appears to be a strong relationship between having women on boards and good financial performance (Thomson and Graham, 2005). One of the women interviewed drew on this research:

> Studies show that women have enormous economic influence, making something like 80 per cent of consumer decisions. The FTSE data [on women board directors] shows the scale of work to be done in addressing the number of women in leadership positions.

There is awareness that at the highest levels of business there are still large and persistent obstacles to overcome in relation to the appointment of women:

> We are living with a heritage of women being overlooked. People have said about boards or senior positions: 'We have got one women and

we can't have another one'. There is a mentality of tokenism. At the thought of a complete board of women people are horrified. Why?

Research undertaken for *The Independent* (Arnott, 2010) showed that there are only 120 individual women out of a total of 1,100 directors on the boards of the FTSE top 100 companies, that only five of the companies have female chief executives and that there are only 20 who are executive directors compared to 309 men.

Thomson and Graham (2005) identified the perceptions of male CEOs relating to the absence of women as board members. They recognize that some industries are seen as 'male', where there is a more macho culture inimical to women. They see that international assignments and travel are often regarded as necessary experience for board membership and as discussed in Chapter 5 this is a particular problem for women with families. The male chairs of companies thought that a third reason for the small number of women board directors was the absence of women suitable for appointment from the level that Thomson and Graham have termed the 'marzipan' layer as it is just below the 'icing' of the top layer. However, they recognized that women might bring valuable qualities to the boardroom.

Several of the women interviewed talked about their wish to become board directors, both executive and non-executive. One who was planning longer term said that she was: 'Elbowing my way into the next level up', but that she would also like:

> a non-executive role as a lever to move in five years' time into a portfolio of activities. In 7–8 years' time I would like one or two corporate non-executive roles, a charity and possibly a government role.

Another said: 'I see an upward trajectory. I see myself as having a portfolio of boards.' A woman who was aware that attitudes to women board members might be changing at least in some industries said:

> I will want board-level work...I think that there will be boards that want women. I think it will be helpful to be a woman. There are some kinds of jobs that you go for where women are less wanted.

In a review of women on corporate boards of directors in 12 countries (Burke and Vinnicombe, 2008, p. 3) they note that there are a number of forces for and against including more women on boards. On the positive side there is the approach taken by Norway, Sweden and Spain of legislating to achieve a quota of women on all boards. Other positive approaches are through corporate governance frameworks which require more independent directors; there is public opinion influenced by the media and the: 'visibility/prestige attributed to companies with increasing numbers of women on their boards'. The negative forces against the appointment of more women to boards are seen to be common to many countries and include the conservative nature of many CEOs and chairmen who tend to appoint other males, the reluctance of consultants and head hunters to put women forward, and stereotypes about women at work and their family commitments. In addition it is thought that women are insufficiently likely to put themselves forward for the role. One of the interviewed women brought experience from the USA and felt that this failure to put themselves forward was endemic for women at work, not just at the level of board membership:

> in the UK women would not participate; they would not decide for themselves. There is a reluctance to push, to say I deserve this, I'm going to take charge of my career. I have to coach women to say what they contribute and blow their own trumpet a bit. I tell them to send a memo about the achievement of the team if they don't want to talk about their own achievement. They need to put themselves on the radar screen. They have a fear of being a sycophant, but you can't expect that you will put your head down and work and get noticed.

However, some of the interviewed women actively seeking board positions found difficulties in doing so, for example being told that they did not network sufficiently or meeting resolute 'gatekeepers'. One woman described how:

> I have been going through a saga, getting a non-executive role on a PLC. It was interesting that when I was going through that process, the chairman...did not want to see me, when my name was put forward by the head hunter...The head hunter pushed it and the guy still said that it was a waste of time, but when I walked out after talking to him, he said I was the best person he could possibly have had.

Despite the benefits that women appear to offer as board members, change is slow, with EHRC (2009) estimating that at the present rate of change it would take 73 years to achieve equal numbers of men and women on the boards of FTSE 100 companies.

Actions for change at work

In attempting to change the proportion of women in top jobs, both the interviewees and the relevant literature stress the importance of mentoring and coaching (see Chapter 3) and networking both of mixed and all-women groups (see Chapter 4). These are ways in which women can manipulate difficult work cultures and help to boost their careers. Practical ways in which change might be brought about for women in the workplace now and in the future are through flexible working, including job shares, working from home and working hours different from the norm. The use of technology is particularly important in facilitating working from home.

Many of the interviewed women were conscious of how powerful the provision of strong and varied female role models might be in encouraging younger women. In addition, the women were very conscious of their own individual power and determination. It has already been mentioned that they were agentic and pragmatic in the ways that they approached their working life, and at the end of this chapter we will revisit some of the advice that the women would offer to their younger sisters who are trying to achieve their career ambitions, before reviewing best practice for employers and raising some final questions for the future.

Mentoring and coaching

The extensive support that the women had received from male and female mentors was documented in Chapter 3. The women generally benefited from long-term mentoring with individuals where the relationship was organic rather than being imposed. In contrast they found that the short-term use of a formally appointed expert coach for a specific purpose was extremely useful. Both mentoring and coaching can be used specifically to help women overcome career challenges, including those relating to gendered attitudes. In one case, coaching was used in an innovative way to help smooth the absence of a very senior woman from her organization for maternity leave. Coaching was used to help the woman herself, but also to help her board of directors adjust to the idea that she was going to be away:

> I got a coach in when I was concerned about maternity leave. She did some work with every member of the board about what it was essential that I was involved in and what was not. She interviewed the editor and group chief executive who told her what was worrying them. She then ran a session on who was going to cover for me for what,

identifying what were the important things. It all worked brilliantly. I took three months maternity leave and worked with the coach to help us with this. I scoped it and it worked very well. When I had my twins, who were unplanned, they [the board] were reassured [about maternity leave] as we had done it before. It was the same, and things worked really well. We found ways of working, for example, people would come to the house. I attended all the board meetings and did emails and calls throughout.

Planning for maternity leave involving a board is unusual, as this woman was in a particularly senior role, but the use of coaches to discuss how to handle maternity leave can be useful in terms of career planning for the individual woman who has choices to make, and for her team who will need to plan for her temporary absence.

Mentoring can also be used for the specific purpose of helping women achieve their desired senior role, for example, the FTSE 100 Cross-Company Mentoring Scheme set up by Thomson and Graham (2005), whereby chairmen and CEOs of some of the largest companies in the UK set out to mentor women in the 'marzipan' layer with the aim of increasing the proportion of women on the FTSE 100 boards. Mentoring appears to be one of the most positive and enabling forces to bring about change for women at work although there may still be limitations on the types of mentoring that women receive compared with their male peers. Ibarra et al. (2010) have recently shown that although women may now receive more mentoring than men in some work situations, the men are more likely to be promoted than the women. It is possible that men coaching other men may be more likely to actively champion them than women in progressing up the career ladder.

Role models

It is difficult to be a pioneer as was the case with some of the women interviewed, particularly in the very 'male' industries, for example, engineering or power, or in the male-dominated world of surgery. Among the many pioneers interviewed, one had been the first woman to spend a night on an oil rig. For younger women following on, having the example of a role model who has already broken through particular barriers is immensely helpful. This was particularly true where women had combined having a family with their career, as one interviewee stated:

I chaired Opportunity Now for four years. I went to the media, banks, insurance, retail and manufacturing sectors speaking at their women's networks. I have mentored women either as a NED [non-executive director] or in the industry. It is really important to me to do this. Wherever I have spoken, the question I always get from women is: How do you do it? These are women in middle management who want to get into senior roles. They want to know how I manage with my job and with three children. They want to hear about it so that they can visualize how they could do it. They want to see a role model.

The same sentiment was expressed by one of the secondary head teachers who had been a head while her two children were very young. She commented: 'Some of the women who attended [the courses] wanted to discuss the practicalities of how to manage with children and work. Women on courses were fascinated by my situation.'

Another of the interviewed women summed up the situation: 'they [younger women] need to see that getting to the top is achievable'. In their review of women's progress in the FTSE 100 boardrooms, Sealy et al. (2008, p. 45) found that 80 per cent of senior women agreed that having senior women as role models made them more optimistic, while the lack of such role models was 'a significant deterrent'.

However, Rindfleish and Sheridan (2003) found that women in senior management, in this case in Australia, do not directly challenge the gendered nature of senior management, raising the possibility that it may be wrong to think that change will come about simply through increasing numbers of women in senior roles.

Networking

Networks have been useful to the interviewed women for expressive and instrumental purposes, and joining networks was recommended as a means of development and support by many of the women, particularly those working in the higher levels of business, where contacts across firms are so important in the building of social capital (Tharenou, 2005). The interviews have revealed a patchwork of interrelated networks, both mixed and women-only that range from formalized 'top-down' prescribed networks, through the formally established but emergent networks, to the informal groups of work colleagues and friends who provide emotional support. Access to most of the women interviewed was via their network and most then belonged to one of the five all-women networks discussed in Chapter 4. Some of those interviewed were approached through different means as individuals.

Four of the five networks were about 20 years old and all had been successful in supporting women, but not all appeared likely to continue. Of the two in education, one has now formally ceased to exist and the other is diminished in its functions and membership (for further details, see Coleman, 2010). In both cases the membership was ageing with a proportion moving on to retirement. The numbers leaving were not equalled by new recruits. In addition, there was a perception that life had become more demanding in schools, colleges and universities leaving less flexibility and time for activities deemed non-essential. A member of Through the Glass Ceiling commented:

> We have tried to attract younger women, e.g. by suggesting that we each bring along a younger colleague, and we have sent out flyers. We had a few who came and liked it but did not have time, funds or energy to keep it going. Changes in HE and in the times generally have led to this.

The members were conscious that the age profile of the organization was changing:

> A lot of people in TTGC are retiring. I was talking to others who have not yet retired and seem to be thinking of retiring, for example a couple of women who have felt it is all getting too much now. With grandchildren coming along these women have felt there is more to life than this now.

In the case of Senior Women in Secondary Schools the same was true, but they also found that their earlier role of training women in leadership was no longer as necessary since more courses were now offered locally and nationally. Their function was somewhat reduced and mainly expressive:

> I am not sure about training. I think it is more about support. One-to-one sessions really seem to help people…I think that support mechanisms are very valuable, more for women who need role models. That's the role I could see with SWISS. Maybe it's an anachronism, but I don't think it is. I see a role but not sure how possible it is. Who will provide it? People doing headship just don't have time.

The future role of WinS is set to counter the stereotype that surgery is male and to provide information and role models for younger women and students to become surgeons: 'We are trying to show people surgery is a place for women. Now you don't have to work long hours.'

Forum UK and Women in Advertising and Communications in London are continuing networks that cater only for senior women and who appear to have a dual role which is both instrumental and expressive. The value that women obtain from membership of Forum UK means it is set to continue on its current successful course. However, members are aware of the need to check on the age profile and representation from different sectors.

> We need to keep a balance between people like me who are basically retired but active and younger women, and also do new things, new events. There are so many things going on we need to be fresh and innovative.

WACL combines networking events for its members with an educational function for younger women in the industry: 'We try to equip younger women with the skills and training that they need. The senior women are generous with their experience.'

The five all-women networks mentioned here are a tiny sample that cannot be representative of the many local, national and international networks that exist to help individual women in their careers and employers who want to support women and reap the benefits of the business case for employing women (Opportunity Now, 2010). More detailed lists are available, e.g. Coleman (2008b) and McCarthy (2004).

One of the women interviewed had been instrumental in starting up a new specialized women's network within her industry that acted to mentor, coach and champion younger women. The following long extract from her interview describes how she helped set up this interesting development:

> I have set up the 'Competitors Diversity Forum'. We asked seven member firms to participate and send one woman from each firm. They had to be senior women who could try to force change. They can also share best practices within the firms in regard to women's recruitment. We got together and agreed to do what we could to help things along. It is a good network, with nine member firms now. We are starting to pass the baton to women below us. The originals are people who faced the same issues in day-to-day business and can trust each other. We have had to face issues and use creative ingenuity. We wanted to hold a CEO dinner to move things on. It was hard just getting the diaries together. Eventually the CEOs showed

up, and it was 'group think'; each claimed that gender equality was important to their firm. As they were there, we were able to ask, 'What are you going to do about it?'

Each year we take on an issue at a particular level. One year we wanted to raise the profile of young women, to get investment banking on the radar. Guidance counsellors will tell young women it is not a career for them, that it's all lap-dancing and sexism in the City. We focused on the young for an 'Invest in your future' day, a non-branded event, and invited young undergraduate women. The first year we had 100, the second 200 the third 400; it was a big success and raised the visibility of the career.

Another year we worked on the vice-president level which is the level where you take on client responsibility and it also tends to be at a time when women are thinking about having families.

This type of initiative has enormous potential in engaging people at the highest levels to become actively involved in the question of women's career advancement as well as setting role models and showing younger women the potential in what is generally seen as a male career area. There are a number of networks set up for women within a specific firm or industry with potential for changing the work culture and providing particular support for women (see for example, Coleman, 2008b; Mays et al., 2005).

Whether all-women networks are set up within a specific workplace or specific industry or bridge across industries they appear to have a useful role in facilitating instrumental connections between women that can be useful to them in building social capital. Perhaps most importantly they provide expressive support that cannot be obtained through a mixed network but sustains women in countering the particular difficulties that women meet at work. However, most of the women interviewed belonged to other networks that were mixed as well as relying of the support of informal friendship groups.

Flexible working

Although practice varies, there are many young women who do not continue with their careers because their employers are unable or unwilling to accommodate their needs, for example to work part-time or more flexibly. Research on graduates of the previous ten years (Purcell and Elias, 2008, p. 46) indicated just how varied experience can be with:

Examples of good practice: high-quality part-time work, with part-time workers valued and promoted and provided with opportunities for career development [were found], in the same sectors where employees in other organisations had met with obstacles more related to company culture than commercial imperatives.

Thus flexible working may carry a cost for women and men despite the comment of one of the interviewed women: 'We invest so much time in training people and then let it all go to waste.'

The difficulties of working part-time or flexible hours have been rehearsed in Chapter 5. However, there are indications that, in all but the most intransigent environments, more flexible ways of working can be offered to senior women returning to work after having children. For example, there are specialist head hunters who broker jobs for women and men who wish to work flexibly in senior roles and who adopt the business case argument for the employment of women who might otherwise be lost to the economy (see, for example, Sapphire Partners www.sapphirepartners.co.uk/). In relation to a similar agency a woman media CEO commented on senior women who choose to be mothers working shorter hours at work but extra hours at home in order to fit into the school day:

> There is plenty of business that can be done in those hours. People get so much out of them and it allows the women to use their brains. There is a future model there. People can pick up their emails in the evening, take telephone calls.

This flexibility is seen positively by the women, but does nothing to reduce the overall demands made of their time, as it enables them to contribute to the 24/7 culture.

One of the women interviewed who worked in broadcasting gave an example of job sharing which, although in some ways successful, suffered from the sort of 'scope creep' discussed in Chapter 5. If a job has not been sufficiently well scoped before hours are curtailed it is unlikely to fit into less than full-time hours. In this case:

> At the time it was one of the most senior job shares ever sanctioned. People came to us for advice to see how it worked. We actually overlapped one day a week. However, we both worked at home on our days off. We could not share the overseeing of a complicated project. There was so much detail to immerse ourselves in. I was the operational one and tended to still do all the project work and run them on location; she tended more to do the people management and internal administration. In fact it became quite exhausting. Work would bleed into everything. My gratitude to work became quite infected

over time. We were always shattered by it...I have now moved on, and work Monday to Wednesday long days in the office, and half-days on Thursday and Friday at home. I work in the evenings too, and sometimes at weekends.

Although the difficulties in establishing new and flexible ways of working are apparent, such experience can be harnessed and used to improve further trials. One CEO in media was particularly optimistic:

People are working more flexibly. Some of my friends in other industries have jobs where they can work term-time or take the whole of August off. We have clients who live elsewhere and come to London to work in the week. There are new structures and new systems being tried out. We are more experimental. Bosses are willing to let people try things out.

In another case:

The company is slightly more female than male and is pretty equal at every level. Where people, men or women, want flexible working we give it. One of the male managers worked one day a week from home and the other female director does a four day week.

Although such flexibility is not necessarily open to all, most senior people will now take advantage of the greater flexibility made possible through technology, in particular the use of email and conference calls. Many of the interviewed women, especially those with children, were appreciative of the benefits of such technology in making their lives more manageable and saw further development and change in this area as likely to benefit them further.

The potential of technology

The increased use of technology does not mean that women necessarily work fewer hours, but it does mean that they can work with a laptop and mobile phone from somewhere other than their office. It therefore means that they can adapt their lives round seeing children at the end of a normal working day, even if that then means a return to work (at home) in the evening. One stated:

Technological change has definitely helped. Without that I might have struggled. When I had my first child things were changing.

Before that you had a secretary who typed up reports and that meant that you had to stay at the office. Once I had a child, if we had not had laptops and been able to do stuff at home it would have made things difficult. I am not sure I could have coped without that change. It came just at the right time and meant that I did not have to put in such long hours at the office as it was possible to do some work at home.

This example shows how technology has allowed a woman with children flexibility, but that nevertheless emails and telephone calls have the potential to infiltrate home life with possible negative consequences for family/life balance.

The women were aware of the potential of technology to change the ways that we work in a way that would be particularly significant for women, although there was still much to learn and develop:

What will life hold for my friends' daughters? Working remotely will happen more. But how do you manage the work flow?

Although technology may have particular significance in empowering women in the workplace through more flexible forms of working, gender issues also arise in electronic communications. Just as gender influences language and communication in face-to-face encounters, it is also shown to influence the ways in which we write and receive emails and other forms of online communication such as conferencing. Although senior women may be protected by their known status, they may need to be aware that: 'the way text-based messages are constructed often conveys the social cues that are traditionally used to determine gender difference in organizations' (Panteli and Seeley, 2006). Technology is not gender-free and women may need to be aware that, just as in face-to-face communication, tentativeness can be mistaken for weakness and such contributions can then be overlooked.

That change has occurred, albeit slowly in some sectors, is recognized by the interviewed women. Within the workplace, the women rate mentoring, coaching and networking along with the provision of strong and varied female role models as important instruments of change. Change in some work sectors has included recognition of the importance of family life for men as well as women, and flexible working has been employed to bring about some marginal changes, although working less than full-time hours is generally seen as disadvantageous for the ambitious. However, women feel that they have benefited from the flexibility that technology, particularly mobile phones and laptop computers, has enabled.

The main issues

The women who were interviewed shared a positive approach in the sense that they believed in taking control of their lives and pushing determinedly for what they wanted as a career. Although generally supportive of other women they were able to see the difficulties that employers faced when women were absent for maternity leave and then requested flexible working. Those in the public sector, i.e. education and medicine, and those in the world of media and advertising, although not free of gendered attitudes, were experiencing a more 'family-friendly' environment than women in other areas. In these work areas it appears that there has been more of a change in culture that meant that both parents and individuals with other caring obligations, such as for older relatives, might have their needs accommodated through adjustments to their work. However, there was recognition that in some types of work this was not yet possible. Indeed they could not envisage that flexible working including part-time work could ever be the case where individuals had to be available on an international basis at all times.

The individualistic attitudes of many of the women meant that generally they did not identify with feminism, although they were supportive of women and many had taken part in training or mentoring younger women. They respected the business case for diversity with the implication that there should be a better balance of individuals including many more women on boards. In some cases they felt that they had benefited from being a woman in an environment where senior women were rare.

The actions that support change for women at work include targeted mentoring and coaching and the provision of role models, taking full advantage of the instrumental and expressive functions of networks to expand social capital, and the provision of flexible working patterns for women and men, supported by growth in the use of electronic communications and technology.

The interviewed women operate and are successful within the status quo, but are aware of the challenges that women continue to face. They endorse gradual rather than radical change. Within this context, recommendations for women and their employers emerge from the experiences recounted in this book.

Recommendations for individual women

The following recommendations and advice are distilled from the women interviewed for this book who tended to rate their own agency and determination as vital in achieving success at work. The recommendations do not therefore set out to be comprehensive although they are certainly informed. There is detailed and focused advice in other literature for women who are ambitious (see, for example, Thomson and Graham, 2008) for advice for women who want to find their place in the boardroom.

The advice and recommendations are grouped under the headings:

Early years
Establishing a career
Work/family balance

Early years

Very few of the women had started with a clear career plan, but once they fixed on a path, they were determined and had faith in themselves. In some cases they were fighting low expectations either at school or at work. They felt that as women who would be competing in a male world it was advantageous to get the best possible qualifications and to be as informed as possible in their specialist area.

- Have faith in yourself;
- Fight low expectations;
- Try to adopt a 'gender neutral' approach to choices about career and qualifications;
- Obtain the best possible relevant qualifications and experience.

Establishing a career

The women interviewed were determined and not afraid to stick to their intuition about what might be good for them, sometimes making career decisions that were considered unwise by others. They recognized gendered attitudes and dealt with them pragmatically, finding ways round them rather than meeting them head-on. They had benefited from joining an appropriate all-women network for support and advice. Networking of all kinds is considered vital to building social capital, establishing useful contacts and 'weak links' across and within business. Many of them had ongoing relationships with more experienced mentors, who might be male or female, but had benefited from observing women who were good role models. They had used coaching to good effect for short-term problems and for taking stock. Some advised taking on additional responsibilities at work to get known, although there is the possibility of being too good an organizational citizen with the attendant risk of being exploited. Although it might be difficult to play a political game, they had tried to ensure that people knew of their successes. They had found that working internationally was good experience but that might need to be traded off against family needs. With a continuing pay gap between men and women they felt it was important, if difficult, to be prepared to speak openly about salary and other work requirements.

- Trust your intuition;
- Be determined;
- Be aware of gendered attitudes, e.g. the femininity/competence bind;
- Join networks, both mixed and all-women, ensuring that both your affective and instrumental needs are met;
- Establish one or more good mentoring relationships;
- Take note of female role models;
- Make use of coaching for specific short-term purposes;
- Consider taking on 'extra' work within your organization that might get you known;
- Consider taking on external responsibilities or secondments that might enhance your social and human capital;
- Make sure that your successes are known and noted;
- Work internationally if possible;
- Be prepared to negotiate about your salary being objective about your true worth;
- Be aware that you are acting as a role model to younger women.

Work/family balance

Approximately half of the women interviewed had a child or children. There was understanding among all of them that combining a demanding job and having children was difficult to manage, and that some compromises had to be made. These successful women who had children had them either before their career was established or once they were well established. Alternatively they worked and had children but relied on good support from family or paid highly for professional help. Only in a small number of cases was their husband/partner the main carer. They were generally working within a 'male' career model and had to be prepared to handle or avoid long working hours and the possibility of international travel. None of them worked part-time but some of those who were more senior were able to organize their work life to some extent, often aided by new technology, in order to spend more time with their family.

- If possible, plan when might be the best stage of your career to have your children;
- Be prepared to make compromises;
- Negotiate with your partner about sharing childcare;
- Plan ahead for the most suitable childcare for your family;
- Seek work which does not involve regular international travel;
- Have boundaries around client work that is likely to involve constant availability and/or out of office hours entertaining;
- Be proactive in suggesting ways to combine work and family responsibilities;
- If appropriate seek out specialist agencies which may be able to arrange flexible working;
- If you opt to work part-time, ensure that your workload is properly scoped to fit the hours.
- Be aware that you are acting as a role model to younger women.

Although the women rated their own determination as an important factor in their success they were also aware of the part played by sympathetic employers. If the workplace is to change further for women, action on the part of employers to facilitate change is vital.

Recommendations for employers

These suggestions of positive actions for employers who want to support women at work arise from the interviews. In addition, comprehensive lists can be found elsewhere (see, for example, Vinnicombe et al., 2008; Burke and Mattis, 2005).

Some of the interviewees referred to careful auditing for diversity and training for equal opportunities for those who make appointments. All were in favour of mentoring and coaching with some particularly strong examples of effective coaching schemes benefiting both those who coach and those who are coached. They were aware of the waste of resources when well-trained women leave work when they have children and when suitable women find difficulty in accessing boards. Some had been involved in establishing in-house support groups for younger women. They endorsed flexible working, including the use of technology.

Employers are therefore recommended to:

- Audit and monitor the diversity of the workforce by levels;
- Ensure that there is an equal opportunities policy;
- Provide equal opportunities training for those who interview and appoint staff;
- Consider supporting an in-house development group for women;
- Set up mentoring and coaching schemes;
- Be aware of the business case for women at the top, e.g. mixed teams/boards;
- Allow flexibility and working at home;
- Make use of technology to assist flexible working;
- Ensure access for women to the very top;
- Take steps to create a work culture that is supportive to women.

The future

It seems likely that the trend towards greater gender equity at work will continue, but, as noted in Chapter 1, the pace of that change is painfully slow. There are countervailing forces. Gendered attitudes that subtly discriminate against women linger to some extent in all professions and workplaces. There is a general indifference or even antipathy to feminism and a tendency to believe that the fate of each individual is their own responsibility. However, on the positive side, there are many organizations and networks which aim to support women and a growing realization that boards of directors should be representative of all the population. In addition the growing number of women in senior leadership positions in business and politics provides role models to younger women. Changes in technology and a greater acceptance of more flexible ways of working are helpful to women and men, and there is some indication that younger men want to be more involved in family life than previous generations of men.

Some of the women questioned what the effect of the recession might be on the employment of women in senior roles, but they took opposite stances. One felt that the effect would be negative:

> The really sad thing is that it [progress for women] seems to go forward a bit then back. I don't see pace at all. The recession will make

it harder, it will put progress back. Companies will take less risk. The job of non-executive director will become more onerous and that will disadvantage women.

However, another considered that the upheaval and re-evaluation might prove beneficial for women:

Up to now I would have said there was bedrock of attitudes about women and families that wasn't going to change. The difference now is the economic circumstances. It could be a different world. Maybe the jobs that are left will be 'women's jobs'.

A very practical reaction to the cutbacks was that:

With this recession all the girls have gone off and had babies. They felt they might as well. I don't know what impact that will have.

The variety of interpretations of the impact of the current economic climate is indicative of the difficulty of being too definite about the future for women leading in the workplace. However, the changes that have occurred during the lifetimes of the interviewed women seem to indicate that further positive changes for women will continue. The business case for employing women at senior levels may be more persuasive than the social justice argument, but from either point of view the dominance of one sex in positions of power seems untenable in the long run.

References

Adam, R. (2000) *A Woman's Place: 1910–1975*, London, Persephone Books.

Altman, Y., Simpson, R., Baruch, Y. and Burke, R. (2005) Reframing the 'Glass Ceiling' Debate in R. Burke (ed.) *Supporting Women's Career Advancement*, Cheltenham, Edward Elgar.

Arnott, S. (2010) Revealed: The gender gap in British business, in *The Independent*, August 14.

Bagilhole, B. (2002) Challenging Equal Opportunities: Changing and Adapting Male Hegemony in Academia, in *British Journal of Sociology of Education*, Vol. 23, No. 1, pp. 19–33.

Banyard, K. (2010) *The Equality Illusion: The Truth about Men and Women Today*, London, Faber and Faber.

Barrett, M. and Davidson, M.J. (2006) (eds) *Gender and Communication at Work*, Aldershot, Ashgate.

Bass, B.M. and Avolio, B.J. (1994) *Improving Organizational Effectiveness through Transformational Leadership*, London, Sage Publications.

Becker, G. (1981) *A Treatise on the Family*, Cambridge, MA: Harvard University Press.

Bem, S.L. (1974) The Measurement of Psychological Androgyny, in *Journal of Consulting and Clinical Psychology*, Vol. 42, No. 2, pp. 155–162.

Bendl, R. and Schmidt, A. (2010) From 'Glass Ceilings' to 'Firewalls' – Different Metaphors for Describing Discrimination, in *Gender – Work and Organization*, Vol. 17, No. 5, p. 612.

Blackmore, J. (1999) *Troubling Women: Feminism, Leadership and Educational Change*, Buckingham, Open University.

Bligh, M.C. and Kohles, J.C. (2008) Negotiating Gender Role Expectations: Rhetorical Leadership and Women in the US Senate, in *Leadership*, Vol. 4, No. 4, pp. 381–402.

Boseley, S. (2008) Equality watchdog fears progress has stalled as number of women in top jobs declines, in *The Guardian*, September 4, p. 4.

Bradbury, L. and Gunter, H. (2006) Dialogic Identities: The Experiences of Women who Are Head Teachers and Mothers in English Primary Schools, in *School Leadership and Management*, Vol. 26, No. 5, pp. 489–504.

Brick, S. (2009) High flyers and low blows, in *The Guardian*, 17 August, p. 3.

Broadbridge, A. (2008) Senior Careers in Retailing: An Exploration of Male and Female Executives' Career Facilitators and Barriers, in *Gender in Management*, Vol. 23, No. 1, pp. 11–35.

Brooks, R. (2010) War of the women at the BBC, in *The Sunday Times*, 4 April.

Brunner, C. (2002) Professing Educational leadership: Conceptions of Power, in *Journal of School Leadership*, Vol. 12, No. 2, pp. 693–720.

Burke, R.J. (2005) Women's Advancement in Management: What is Known and Future Areas to Address, in Burke, R.J. and Mattis, M.C. (eds) *Supporting Women's Career Advancement: Challenges and Opportunities*, Cheltenham, Edward Elgar.

Burke, R.J. and Mattis, M.C. (eds) (2005) *Supporting Women's Career Advancement: Challenges and Opportunities*, Cheltenham, Edward Elgar.

Burke, R.J. and Vinnicombe, S. (2008) Women on Corporate Boards of Directors: International Issues and Opportunities, in Vinnicombe, S., Singh, V., Burke, R.J., Bilmoria, D. and Huse, M. (eds) *Women on Corporate Boards of Directors: International Research and Practice*, Cheltenham, Edward Elgar Publishing Ltd.

Bush, T. and Coleman, M. (1995) Professional Development for Heads: The Role of Mentoring, in *Journal of Educational Administration*, Vol. 33, No. 5, pp. 60–73.

Carli, L. (2006) Gender Issues in Workplace Groups: Effects of Gender and Communication Style on Social Influence, in Barrett, M. and Davidson, M.J. (eds) *Gender and Communication at Work*, Aldershot, Ashgate.

Carnell, E., MacDonald, J. and Askew, S. (2006) *Coaching and Mentoring in Higher Education: A Learning Centred Approach*, London, Institute of Education.

Carvel, J. (2008) Two into one won't go: Cambridge survey shows new doubts over working mothers, in *The Guardian*, 6 August, p. 9.

Chittenden, M. (2009) Too much maternity leave hurts career, in *The Sunday Times*, 29 November, p. 11.

Clutterbuck, D. (1992) *Mentoring*, Henley: Henley Distance Learning.

Clutterbuck, D. and Ragins, B.R. (eds) (2002) *Mentoring and Diversity*, Oxford, Butterworth, Heinemann.

Coleman, M. (2002) *Women as Head Teachers: Striking the Balance*, Stoke on Trent, Trentham Books.

Coleman, M. (2005) *Gender and Headship in the Twenty-first Century*, Project Report. eprints.ioe.ac.uk/4164/ - Cached

Coleman, M. (2007) Gender and Educational Leadership in England: A Comparison of Secondary Head Teachers' Views Over Time, in *School Leadership and Management*, Vol. 27, No. 5, pp. 383–399.

Coleman, M. (2008a) *Annotated Bibliography: Support and Development of Women Senior Leaders at Work*. http://www.wlecentre.ac.uk/cms/files/projectreports/annotated_bibliography_support_and_development_for_women_senior_leaders_at_work.pdf

Coleman, M. (2008b) *Digest of Groups and Organizations Supporting Women in Work*. http://www.wlecentre.ac.uk/cms/files/projectreports/digest_of_groups_and_organizations_supporting_women_in_work.pdf

Coleman, M. (2010) Women-only (Homophilous) Networks Supporting Women Leaders in Education, in *Journal of Educational Administration*, Vol. 48, No. 6, pp. 769–781.

Collins, J. and Singh, V. (2006) Exploring Gendered Leadership, in McTavish, D. and Miller, K. (eds) (2006) *Women in Leadership and Management*, Cheltenham, Edward Elgar.

Connell, R.W. (2002) *Gender*, Cambridge, Polity Press.

Czarniawska, B. and Guje, S. (2008) The Thin End of the Wedge: Foreign Women Professors as Double Strangers, in *Gender Work and Organization*, Vol. 15, No. 3, p. 235.

Davidson, A. (2009) Fanfare for city's ice queen, in *The Sunday Times, Business section*, 17 May, p. 8.

Davies, C. (2009) Poor pay, worse jobs and terrible bonuses too – sexism in the city lives on, says study, in *The Guardian*, 7 September.

Davison, K.G. and Frank, B.W. (2006) Masculinities and Femininities and Secondary Schooling: The Case for a Gender Analysis in the Postmodern Condition, in C. Skelton, B. Francis and L. Smulyan (eds) *The Sage Handbook of Gender and Education*, London, Sage Publications.

DCSF (2010) http://www.dcsf.gov.uk/rsgateway/DB/SFR/s000927/sfr11–2010-index.pdf (accessed November 2010).

Driscoll, M. (2010) Women doctors: the waste of money you'll be glad to see, in *The Sunday Times*, 9 May.

Dunn-Jensen, L.M. and Stroh, L.K. (2007) Myths in the Media: How the News Media Portray Women in the Workforce, in Bilimoria, D. and Piderit, S. K. (eds) *Handbook on Women in Business and Management*, Cheltenham, Edward Elgar.

Duxbury, L. and Higgins, C. (2005) Work-life Challenges Professional Women Face in Pursuing Careers, in Burke, R.J., and Mattis, M.C. (eds) *Supporting Women's Career Advancement: Challenges and Opportunities*, Cheltenham, Edward Elgar.

Eagly, A.H. (1987) *Sex Differences in Social Behaviour: A Social-Role Interpretation* Hillsdale, NJ, Lawrence Erlbaum Associates.

Eagly, A. and Carli, L. (2007) *Through the Labyrinth*, Boston, Harvard Business School Press.

Eagly, A.H. and Johannesen-Schmidt (2007) Leadership Style Matters: The Small, but Important, Style Differences between Male and Female Leaders, in Bilimoria, D. and Piderit, S.K. (eds) *Handbook on Women in Business and Management*, Cheltenham, Edward Elgar.

EHRC (Equality and Human Rights Commission) (2009) *Sex and Power 2008 Index*, Manchester, Equality and Human Rights Commission.

EHRC (2010) *How Fair is Britain? The First Triennial Review Executive Summary*, Manchester, Equality and Human Rights Commission.

Elliott, F. (2009) Labour imposes women-only lists in half of seats left by retiring MPs, in *The Sunday Times*, 5 August, p. 7.

Ellison, G., Barker, A. and Kulasuriya, T. (2009) *Work and Care: A Study of Modern Parents*, Research Report: 15, Manchester, Equality and Human Rights Commission.

Embry, A., Padget, M.Y. and Caldwell, C.B. (2008) 'Can Leaders Step Outside of the Gender Box? An Examination of Leadership and Gender Role Stereotypes' in *Journal of Leadership and Organizational Studies*, Vol. 15, No. 1. pp. 30–45.

Erkut, S., Kramer, V.W. and Konrad, A.M. (2008) Critical Mass: Does the Number of Women on a Corporate Board Make a Difference?, in Vinnicombe, S., Singh, V. Burke, R. Bilimoria, D., Huse, M. (eds) *Women on Corporate Boards of Directors: International Research and Practice*, Cheltenham, Edward Elgar.

Evans, J. (1995) *Feminist Theory Today: An Introduction to Second-Wave Feminism*, London, Sage Publications.

Fernandez-Mateo, I. (2009) The Glass Pay Cheque, in *American Journal of Sociology*, Vol. 114, No. 4, pp. 871–923.

Fiske, S.T. and Lee, T.L. (2008) Stereotypes and Prejudice Create Workplace Discrimination, in Brief, A.P. (ed.), *Diversity at Work*, Cambridge, Cambridge University Press.

Fletcher, C., Boden, R., Kent, J. and Tinson, J. (2007) Performing Women: The Gendered Dimensions of the UK New Research Economy, in *Gender Work and Organization*, Vol. 14, No. 5, Sept., pp. 434–453.

Ford, R. (2009) Fifth of women childless as careers take precedence, study shows, in *Timesonline*, 26 June.

Fuller, K. (2009) Women Secondary Head Teachers: Alive and Well in Birmingham at the Beginning of the Twenty-first Century, in *Management in Education*, Vol. 23, No. 1, pp. 19–31.

Gaskell, J. and Taylor, S. (2003) The Women's Movement in Canadian and Australian Education: From Liberation and Sexism to Boys and Social Justice, in *Gender and Education*, Vol. 15, No. 2, pp. 151–168.

Gatrell, C. (2006) Managing Maternity, in McTavish, D. and Miller, K. (eds) *Women in Leadership and Management*, Cheltenham, Edward Elgar.

Gentleman, A. (2009) Having it all: working fathers want more time with their children too, says report, in *The Guardian*, 20 October, p. 17.

Gilligan, C. (1982) *In a Different Voice*, Cambridge, MA, Harvard University Press.

Government Equalities Office (2010) *Working towards Equality: A Framework for Action*, London, GEO.

Granovetter, M.S. (1973) The Strength of Weak Ties, in *The American Journal of Sociology*, Vol. 78, No. 6, pp. 1360–1380.

Gratton, L., Keland, E., Voigt, A., Walker, L. and Wolfram H-J. (2007) *Innovative Potential: Men and Women in Teams*, London, London Business School.

Gratton, L. (2010) The Future of Work, in *Business Strategy Review*, Q3, pp. 16–23. London, London Business School.

Groskop, V. (2008) Back in business, in *The Guardian*, 1 September, pp. 6–9.

Grummell, B., Devine, D. and Lynch, K. (2009) The Care-less Manager: Gender, Care and New Managerialism in Higher Education, in *Gender in Education*, Vol. 21, No. 2, pp. 191–208.

Guardian (2009) Call yourself a feminist? *The Guardian*, 9 September.

Guillaume, C. and Pochic, S. (2009) What would you Sacrifice? Access to Top Management and the Work-Life Balance, in *Gender, Work and Organization*, Vol. 16, No. 1, pp. 14–36.

Hakim, C. (2004) *Key Issues in Women's Work: Female Diversity and the Polarisation of Women's Employment*, London, The Glasshouse Press.

Halliday, A., de Souza, B., Nitkunan, T., Ragawan, S. Odumenya, M., Wynn-McKenzie, C., Garvey, J. and Roberts, J. (2005) After the FRCS: Is Career Progression a Level Playing Field?, in *Bulletin of the Royal College of Surgeons of England*, Vol. 87, No. 6, pp. 194–196.

Harkness, S. (2008) The Household Division of Labour: Changes in Families' Allocation of Paid and Unpaid Work, in Scott, J., Dex, S. and Joshi, H. (eds) *Women and Employment: Changing Lives and New Challenges*, Cheltenham, Edward Elgar.

Hegewisch, A. (2009) *Flexible working policies: a comparative review*, Research report 16, Manchester, Equality and Human Rights Commission.

Hewlett, S.A. and Luce, C.B., (2005) Off-Ramps and On-Ramps: Keeping Talented Women on the Road to Success, in *Harvard Business Review on Women in Business*, Harvard Business School Publishing Corporation.

Holden, J. and McCarthy, H. (2007) *Women at the Top: A Provocation Piece*, London, City University.

Hofstede, G. (1980), *Culture's Consequences: International Differences in Work Related Values*, 1st edn. Newbury Park, CA, Sage.

House of Commons Treasury Committee (2009) *Women in the City*, http://www. publications.parliament.uk/pa/cm200809/cmselect/cmtreasy/uc967-i/uc96 (accessed 28.10.2009).

Howard, M. and Tibballs, S. (2002) *Talking Inequality*, London, Future Foundation.

Ibarra, H. (1992) Homophily and Differential Returns: Sex Differences in Network Structure and Access in an Advertising Firm, in *Administrative Science Quarterly*, Vol. 37, No. 3, pp. 422–447.

Ibarra, H. (1993) Personal Networks of Women and Minorities in Management: A Conceptual Framework, in *Academy of Management*, Vol. 18, No. 1. pp. 56–87.

Ibarra, H., Carter, N.M. and Silva, C. (2010) Why Men Still Get More Promotions Than Women, in *Harvard Business Review*.

Isaac, C., Behar-Horenstein, L. and Koro-Ljungberg, M. (2009) Women Deans: Leadership Becoming, in *International Journal of Leadership in Education*, electronic journal.

Judiciary of England and Wales (2007) *Annual Diversity Statistics*.

Karau, S.J. and Eagly, A.H. (1999) Invited Reaction: Gender, Social Roles and the Emergence of Leaders, in *Human Resource Development Quarterly*, Vol. 10, No. 4, pp. 321–327.

Kemp. S. and Squires, J. (1997) (eds) *Feminisms*, Oxford, Oxford University Press.

Klein, D. (2000) *Women in advertising: 10 years on* London, Institute of Practitioners in Advertising.

Kram, K.E. (1983) Phases of the mentor relationship, in *Academy of Management Journal*, Vol. 26, pp. 608–625.

Kramer, V.W., Konrad, A.M. and Erkut, S. (2006) *Critical Mass on Corporate Boards: Why Three or More Women Enhance Governance*. Wellesley Centers for Women's Publication Office.

Kumra, S., (2010) Exploring Career 'Choices' of Work-centred Women in a Professional Service Firm, in *Gender in Management: An International Journal*, Vol. 25, No. 3, pp. 227–243.

Line Germain, M. and Scandura, T.A. (2005) Mentoring and identity development: the role of self-determination, in Burke, R.J. and Mattis, M.C. (eds), *Supporting Women's Career Advancement: Challenges and Opportunities*, Cheltenham, Edward Elgar.

Lumby, J. with Coleman, M. (2008) *Leadership and Diversity*, London Sage Publications.

Martin, L.M., Warren-Smith, I., Scott, J. and Roper, S. (2008) Boards of Directors and Gender Diversity in UK Companies, in *Gender in Management: An International Journal*, Vol. 21, No. 5, pp. 349–364.

Mavin, S. (2006) Venus Envy 2: Sisterhood, Queen Bees and Female Misogyny in Management, in *Women in Management Review*, Vol. 21, No. 5, pp. 349–364.

Mays, L., Graham, J. and Vinnicombe, S. (2005) Shell Oil Company US: The 2004 Catalyst Award Winner for Diversity Initiatives in Burke, R.J., and Mattis, M.C. (eds) *Supporting Women's Career Advancement: Challenges and Opportunities*, Cheltenham, Edward Elgar.

McCarthy, H. (2004) *Girlfriends in High Places*, London, Demos.

McTavish, D. and Miller, K. (eds) (2006) *Women in Leadership and Management*, Cheltenham, Edward Elgar.

McVeigh, T. and Asthana, A. (2010) Babies don't suffer when mothers return to work, study reveals, in *The Observer*, 1 August.

Miller, J. (1996) *School for Women*, London, Virago Press.

Miller, K. (2006) Introduction: Women in Leadership and Management: Progress Thus Far? in McTavish, D. and Miller, K. (eds) *Women in Leadership and Management*, Cheltenham, Edward Elgar.

Moreau, M-P, Osgood, J. and Halsall, A. (2005) *Final Report of the Women Teachers' Careers and Progression Project*, IPSE London Metropolitan University, and Leicester SHA.

Morgan, C., Hall, V. and Mackay, H. (1983) *The Selection of Secondary Headteachers*, Milton Keynes, Open University Press.

Morley, L. (2000) The Micropolitics of Gender in the Learning Society, in *Higher Education in Europe*, Vol. XXV, No. 2, pp. 229–235.

Myers, K. and Taylor, H. with Adler, S. and Leonard, D. (2007) *Genderwatch: Still Watching*, Stoke on Trent, Trentham Books.

Ogden, S. M., McTavish, D. and McKean, L., (2006) Clearing the Way for Gender Balance in the Management of the UK Financial Services Industry: Enablers and Barriers, in *Women in Management Review*, Vol. 21, No. 1, pp. 40–53.

Olsson, S. (2006) We Don't Need Another Hero!: Organizational Storytelling As a Vehicle for Communicating a Female Archetype of Workplace Leadership, in Barrett, M., Davidson, M.J. (eds) *Gender and Communication at Work*, Aldershot, Ashgate.

Olsson, S. and Walker, R. (2004) The Wo-men and the Boys: Patterns of Identification and Differentiation in Senior Women Executives' representations of career identity, in *Women in Management Review*, Vol. 19, No. 5, pp. 244–251.

O'Neill, K.S., Hansen, C.D. and May, G.L. (2006) The Effect of Gender on the transfer of Interpersonal Communication Skills Training to the Workplace in Barrett, M., Davidson, M.J.(eds) *Gender and Communication at Work*, Aldershot, Ashgate.

ONS (Office of National Statistics) (2007) *Labour Force Survey*.

Opportunity Now (2010) website http://www.opportunitynow.org.uk/ (accessed 25.08.10)

Oxford, E. (2008) Last women standing, in *THES*, 31 January, pp. 38–39.

Panteli, N. and Seeley, M. (2006) The Email Gender Gap, in Barrett, M., Davidson, M.J. (eds) *Gender and Communication at Work*, Aldershot, Ashgate.

Partington, G. (1976) *Women Teachers in the 20th Century in England and Wales*, Slough, NFER.

Peck, J. (2006) Women and Promotion: The Influence of Communication Style in Barrett, M. and Davidson, M.J. (eds) *Gender and Communication at Work*, Aldershot, Ashgate.

Perkins, A. (2009) How Harriet lit up August, in *The Guardian*, 6 August.

Perriton, L. (2006) Does Woman + Network = Career Progression?, in *Leadership*, Vol. 2, No. 1, pp. 101–113.

Pidd, H. (2009) 'He served me up like a piece of meat' ex-sales executive claims in *The Guardian*, 18 November, p. 7.

Pini, B., Brown, K. and Ryan C. (2004) Women-only Networks As a Strategy for Change? A Case Study from Local Government, in *Women in Management Review*, Vol. 19, No. 6, pp. 286–292.

Portanti, S. and Whitworth, S. (2009) *A comparison of the characteristics of childless women and mothers in the ONS Longitudinal Study*, ONS, www.statistics.gov.uk/articles/population_trends/PT136MothersAndChildlessWomenArticle.pdf · Cached page · PDF file, accessed 14 November 2010.

Pounder, J. and Coleman, M. (2002) Women - better leaders than men? In general and educational management it still 'all depends', in *Leadership and Organisational Development*, Vol. 23, No. 3, pp. 122–133.

Powell, A., Bagilhole, B. and Dainty, A. (2009) How Women Engineers Do and Undo Gender: Consequences for Gender Equality, in *Gender, Work and Organization*, Vol. 16, No. 4, pp. 411–428.

Purcell, K. (2000) Changing boundaries in employment and organisations, in Purcell, K. (ed.), *Changing Boundaries in Employment*, Bristol, Academic Press.

Purcell, K. and Elias, P. (2008) Achieving Equality in the Knowledge Economy, in Scott, J., Dex, S. and Joshi, H. (eds) *Women and Employment: Changing Lives and New Challenges*, Cheltenham, Edward Elgar.

Rindfleish J. (2000) Senior Management Women in Australia: Diverse Perspectives, in *Women in Management Review*, Vol. 15, No. 4, pp. 172–180.

Rindfleish J. and Sheridan A. (2003) No Change from Within: Senior Women Managers' Response to Gendered Organizational Structures, in *Women in Management Review*, Vol. 18, No. 6, pp. 299–310.

Roberts, J. (undated, c. 1995) *Didn't I Just Say that?: The Gender Dynamics of Decision Making. Research Paper 1*, Australian Government Publishing Service.

Roberts, Y. (2005) Afterword in Adam, R. (2000) *A Woman's Place: 1910–1975*, London, Persephone Books.

Ross-Smith, A. and Huppatz, K. (2010) Management, Women and Gender Capital in, *Gender – Work and Organization*, Vol. 17, No. 5, p. 547.

Ruderman, M.N. and Ohlott, P.J. (2002) *Standing at the Crossroads: Next Steps for High-Achieving Women*, San Francisco, CA: Jossey-Bass.

Runte, M. and Milles, A.J. (2006) Cold War, Chilly Climate: Exploring the Roots of Gendered Discourse in Organization and Management Theory, in *Human Relations*, Vol. 59, No. 5, pp. 695–720.

Ryan, M.K. and Haslam, S.A. (2005) The Glass Cliff: Evidence that Women are Over-Represented in Precarious Leadership Positions in *British Journal of Management*, Vol. 16, pp. 81–90.

Ryan, M. and Haslam, S.A., (2006) Beyond the Glass Ceiling: The Glass Cliff and the Precariousness of Women in Leadership in T. Jefferson, L. Lord, N. Nelson and A. Preston (eds) *Proceedings from the Inaugural International Women and Leadership Conference*, Fremantle 16 and 17 November 2006.

http://www.sapphirepartners.co.uk/ (accessed 25.08.10)

Schein, V.E. (2001) A Global Look at Psychological Barriers to Women's Progress in Management, in *Journal of Social Issues*, Vol. 67, pp. 675–688.

Schein, V. (2007) Women in Management: Reflections and Projections, in *Women in Management Review,* Vol. 22, No. 1, pp. 6–18.

Schick-Case, S. (1994) Gender Differences in Communication and Behaviour in Organizations, in Davidson, M.J. and Burke, R.J. (eds) *Women in Management: Current Research Issues,* London, Paul Chapman Publishing.

Scott, J., Dex, S., Joshi, H., Purcell, K. and Elias, P. (2008) Introduction: Changing Lives and New Challenges, in Scott, J., Dex, S. and Joshi, H. (eds) *Women and Employment: Changing Lives and New Challenges,* Cheltenham, Edward Elgar.

Sealy, R., Vinnicombe, S. and Singh, V. (2008) The Pipeline to the Board Finally Opens: Women's Progress on FTSE 100 Boards in the UK, in Vinnicombe, S., Singh, V. Burke, R. Bilimoria, D. and Huse, M. (eds) *Women on Corporate Boards of Directors: International Research and Practice,* Cheltenham, Edward Elgar.

Sealy, R. Vinnicombe, S. and Singh, V. (2008) *A Decade of Delay, Female FTSE Report, 2008,* International Centre for Women Leaders Cranfield School of Management.

Shakeshaft, C. (1986) *Women in Educational Administration,* Newbury Park, Sage.

Singh, A., Vinnicombe, S. and Kumra, S. (2006) Women in Formal Corporate Networks: An Organizational Citizenship Perspective, *Women in Management Review,* Vol. 21, No. 6, pp. 458–482.

Smithson, J. and Stokoe E. (2005) Discourses of Work-Life Balance: Negotiating 'Genderblind' Terms in Organizations, in *Gender, Work and Organization,* Vol. 12, No. 2, pp. 147–168.

Spanier, G. (2009) Rise of the capital's golden skirts, in *London Evening Standard,* 2 July.

Still, L. (2006) Gender, Leadership and Communication, in Barrett, M. and Davidson, M.J. (eds) *Gender and Communication at Work,* Aldershot, Ashgate.

Stuhlmacher, A.F. and Winkler, R.B. (2006) Negotiating while Female: Research and Implications, in Barrett, M. and Davidson, M.J. (eds) *Gender and Communication at Work,* Aldershot, Ashgate.

Suseno, Y., Pinnington, A.H. and Gardner, J. (2007) Gender and the Network Structures of Social Capital in Professional-Client Relationships, in *Advancing Women in Leadership Online Journal,* Vol. 23 Spring, pp. 251–260.

Sunderland, R. (2009) Revealed: Failure of Top UK Firms to Get Women on Board, in *The Observer, Business and Media section,* 23 August, pp. 3–5.

Tharenou, P. (2005) Women's Advancement in Management: What is Known and Future Areas to Address, in Burke, R.J. and Mattis, M.C. (eds) *Supporting Women's Career Advancement: Challenges and Opportunities,* Cheltenham, Edward Elgar.

Thomson, P. and Graham, J. with Lloyd, T. (2005) *A Woman's Place is in the Boardroom,* Basingstoke, Palgrave Macmillan.

Thomson, P. and Graham, J. with Lloyd, T. (2008) *A Woman's Place is in the Boardroom: The Roadmap,* Basingstoke, Palgrave Macmillan.

Tomas, M., Lavie, J., Duran, M. Del M, and Guillamon, C. (2010) Women in Academic Administration at the University, in *Educational Management Administration and Leadership,* Vol. 38, No. 4, pp. 487–498.

Tonge, J. (2008) Barriers to Networking for Women in a UK Professional Service, in *Gender in Management*, Vol. 23, No. 7, pp. 484–505.

Vinkenburg, C.J. and van Engen, M.L. (2005) Perceptions of Gender, Leadership and Career Development in Burke, R.J., and Mattis, M.C. (eds) *Supporting Women's Career Advancement: Challenges and Opportunities*, Cheltenham, Edward Elgar.

Vinnicombe, S., Sealy, R., Graham, J. and Doldor, E. (2010) *The Female FTSE Report 2010: Opening up the Appointment Process*, Cranfield, International Centre for Women Leaders.

Vinnicombe, S., Singh, V. Burke, R. Bilimoria, D., Huse, M. (2008) *Women on Corporate Boards of Directors: International Research and Practice*, Cheltenham, Edward Elgar.

WACL (2008) *Eighty five years of women in advertising*, WACL, www.wacl.info.

Walsh, K. and Hastings, C. (2009) Hedge heroines outdo men in City, in *The Sunday Times*, 11 September, p. 11.

Walter, N. (2010) *Living Dolls: The Return of Sexism*, London, Virago Press.

Ward, L. and Carvel, J. (2007) Best ideas come from work teams mixing men and women, in *The Guardian*, 1 November, p. 18.

Ward, R.M., Popson, H.C. and DiPaolo, D.G. (2010) Defining the Alpha Female: A Female Leadership Measure, in *Journal of Leadership and Organizational Studies*, Vol. 17, No. 3, pp. 309–320, http://jlo.sagepub.com/content/17/3/309.abstract.

Weyer, B. (2007) Twenty Years Later: Explaining the Persistence of the Glass Ceiling for Women Leaders, in *Women in Management Review*, Vol. 22, no. 6, pp. 482–496.

White, B. (2000) Lessons from Successful Women, in Davidson, M.J. and Burke, R.J. (eds) *Women in Management: Current Research Issues Volume II*, London, Sage Publications.

Wilson, J.Z., Marks, G., Noone, L, and Hamilton-Mackenzie, J. (2010) Retaining a Foothold on the Slippery Paths of Academia: University Women, Indirect Discrimination, and the Academic Marketplace, in *Gender and Education*, Vol. 22, No. 5, pp. 535–545.

Woodfield, R. (2007) *What Women Want from Work: Gender and Occupational Choice in the 21st Century*, York Studies on Women and Men, Basingstoke, Palgrave MacMillan.

Wray, R. (2009) Former head of Economist is first female CBE president, in *The Guardian*, 18 May, p. 25.

Younge, G. (2009) US conservatives are fighting for the rights of a minority – white men, in *The Guardian*, 8 June, p. 27.

Annotated Bibliography: Women Senior Leaders at Work

Focus of the bibliography

Although there is general but slow progress for women in accessing leadership roles at work, it is generally believed that there is a 'glass ceiling'. There is only a limited literature on women who have broken through the 'ceiling'. Most literature about women, work and career progress does not differentiate between senior women leaders who might be regarded as above the glass ceiling and women who aspire to such senior roles. This bibliography therefore includes literature that relates to senior women leaders and then widens out to include literature relating more generally to the challenges that women face and the support and development of women's career progress. The necessarily brief comments on books, chapters and papers cannot do justice to the content, but identify issues that were useful to me in writing this book.

The year 2000 has been taken as an arbitrary cut-off point for the literature included which cannot claim to be comprehensive.

Structure and organization of annotated bibliography

Entries have been organized in sections according to what appears to be the most dominant theme of the work, but other themes may also be present and in some cases are cross-referenced.

Within sections 1–4 and their sub-sections, entries are alphabetical according to the first named author's surname.

Section 1: Women in senior leadership roles at work.
Section 2: The career progress of women in general (mainly edited books with some chapters on the forms of support and development discussed in section 3).
Section 3: The most common forms of support and development for women's career progress (mainly journal articles).

Section 3 is divided into two main sub-sections.
The first sub-section relates to the *individual* and their actions accessing:

- networking; and
- mentoring, coaching and/or role models.

The second sub-section focuses on the *organization* and includes the impact of gender on:

- teams and meetings;
- the existence and impact of gender equity policies including affirmative action.

Section 4: The contextual and structural barriers to career progress for women.

This section includes sub-sections on:

- general background including gendered occupations and the pay gap;
- barriers to progress: the glass ceiling; gender stereotypes and gendered leadership discourses;
- backlash to feminism;
- identities;
- work/family balance;
- barriers created by other women: the 'queen bee' syndrome.

Section 1: Women in senior leadership roles at work

This section includes books, reports and articles that relate to women in leadership positions.

Branson, D.M. (2007) *No Seat at the Table: How Corporate Governance and Law Keep Women Out of the Boardroom,* New York, New York University Press.

Focuses on corporate governance and the poor representation of women on boards. Gives advice to women and boards.

Equality and Human Rights Commission (2008) *Sex and Power 2008,* www.equalityhumanrights.com.

Gives data for the proportion of women leaders in 25 categories over the previous five years. In 2008 there were fewer women holding top posts in 12 of the 25 categories. In another five categories the proportion remained unchanged

EOC (2006) *Sex and power: who runs Britain? 2006,* Manchester, Equal Opportunities Commission.

Gives the proportions of women in powerful positions in politics (28 per cent), business (12 per cent), media and culture (17 per cent) and public and voluntary sectors (23 per cent). Compares with the past and the international situation and looks at ethnic minority women in 'top jobs'.

Elliott, C. and Stead, V. (2008) Learning from Leading Women's Experience: Towards a Sociological Understanding, in *Leadership,* Vol. 5, No. 2, pp. 159–180.

The authors have interviewed six notable women outside business, Shami Chakrabati, Betty Boothroyd, May Blood, Tanni Gray-Thompson, Rebecca Stephens and Fiona Stanley, taking a narrative approach and focusing on their upbringing, environment, focus and networks and alliances.

Grattan, L., Kelan, E. and Walker L. (2007) *Inspiring Women: Corporate Best Practice in Europe,* London, London Business School, The Lehman Brothers Centre for Women in Business.

A study of gendered practice in 61 organizations in Europe. Makes recommendations.

Hewlett, S.A. (2007) *Off-Ramps and On-Ramps: Keeping Talented Women on the Road to Success*, Boston, Harvard Business School Press.

Makes the business case for a different model of career for women and men employees and their employers and discusses actual models as practiced by larger employers.

Huse, M., Solberg, A. G. (2006) Gender-related Boardroom Dynamics: How Scandinavian Women Make and Can Make Contributions on Corporate Boards, in *Women in Management Review*, Vol. 21, No. 2, pp. 113–130.

[Also relevant for sub-section on 'gender and teams' and sub-section on 'barriers to progress']

The objective of this article is to examine and conceptualize gender-related boardroom dynamics that affect how women can make contributions on corporate boards.

Kramer, V.W., Konrad, A.M. and Erkut, S. (2006) Critical mass on Corporate Boards: Why Three or More Women Enhance Governance. Executive summary. Wellesley Centers for Women's Publication Office.

[Also relevant for sub-section 'gender and teams']

Based on interviews and discussions with 50 women directors, 12 CEOs and seven corporate secretaries from Fortune 1000 companies, they show that a critical mass of three or more women can cause a fundamental change in the boardroom and enhance corporate governance.

Martin, L.M., Warren-Smith, I., Scott, J.M. and Roper, S. (2008) Boards of Directors and Gender Diversity in UK Companies, *Gender in Management*, Vol. 23, No. 3, pp. 194–208.

A quantitative analysis which aims to map the incidence of female directors in UK companies against types of firms finds that male dominance continues. Although female directors are one in four of all UK directors, they tend to be found in the smaller firms with the service sector having most female directors.

Parkhouse, S. (2001) *Powerful Women: Dancing on the Glass Ceiling*, Chichester, John Wiley and sons.

Covers the successes of 26 individual women.

Ruderman, M.N. and Ohlott, P.J. (2002), *Standing at the Crossroads: Next Steps for High-Achieving Women*, San Francisco, Jossey-Bass.

Research with 61 high-achieving women plus questionnaires with 276 others led to the identification of five interconnected themes in their journeys. They are authenticity, connection, controlling your destiny, wholeness and self-clarity.

Female FTSE reports

These annual reports are available online from 2001 onwards. Comments on the last three reports below.

Sealy, R. Vinnicombe, S. and Doldor, E. (2009) *The Female FTSE Report 2009*, Cranfield University.

Norway and Spain where the new laws have a positive impact have joined the census. While there has been a small increase in the percentage of women on the boards of the top 100 FTSE companies (up to 12.2 per cent) and a growth in the number of women in the pipeline, there has been a decline in the number of companies with female executive directors (from 16 to 15), a decline in the number of boards with multiple women directors (from 39 to 37) and a decline in the overall number of companies with women on boards. One in four companies has an exclusively male board.

Sealy, R., Vinnicombe, S. and Singh, V. (2008) *The Female FTSE Report 2008: A Decade of Delay,* Cranfield University.

This report indicates a slight increase in directorships held by women on the FTSE 100 corporate boards (11.7 per cent). Thirty-nine companies each have two or more women on their boards; 22 companies have all-male boards, ethnic minorities are under-represented and of the 149 new appointees only 15 (10.7 per cent) were women. A survey of 217 women from FTSE 350 executive committees, and interviews with 20, indicate that they are ambitious for board directorships but are pessimistic about the future of women on corporate boards. The report makes recommendations.

Sealy, R., Singh, V. and Vinnicombe, S. (2007) *The Female FTSE Report, 2007: A Year of Encouraging Progress,* Cranfield University.

There were 100 women holding 123 directorships on the FTSE 100 boards, 11 per cent of the total. Women accounted for 20 per cent of new director appointments in the year. There were 122 women (16 per cent) sitting on the FTSE 100 executive committee representing an increase of 40 per cent over 2006. The number of executive directorships and the total number of directorships were at their lowest level for nine years, but the number of non-executive directorships was at its highest for nine years.

Shakeshaft, C. (2006) Gender and Educational Management, in Skelton, C., Francis, B. and Smulyan, L. (eds) *The Sage Handbook of Gender and Education,* London, Sage.

Provides a short analysis of the international scene in relation to women in educational management, focusing mainly on barriers and leadership styles.

Singh V., and Vinnicombe S. (2002) The 2002 Female FTSE Index and Women Directors, in *Women in Management Review,* Vol. 18, No. 7, pp. 349–358.

Reports the slow change in the position of female directorships in the UK's FTSE 100 companies and the statistics on women directors in the top 100 listed companies. Comments on the findings regarding companies with women directors and the women holding those directorships, reviewing their background and experience.

Thomas, P. and Graham, J. with Tom Lloyd (2005) *A Woman's Place is in the Boardroom,* Basingstoke, Palgrave Macmillan.

The book is predicated on a business case for there being more women in directorships because of their power as customers, the potential loss of up to half the talent pool and the fact that women bring distinctive qualities to management. The book argues that businesses that employ more women in senior roles will perform better and make more profit. The book identifies the 'marzipan' layer of women who are just below the board level and also reports on the FTSE 100 Cross-Company Mentoring Programme which brings together the male board members and the marzipan layer. The authors conclude that institutional culture change is necessary so that women do not have to play by male rules.

Thomas, P. and Graham, J. with Tom Lloyd (2008) *A Woman's Place is in the Boardroom: The Roadmap*, Basingstoke, Palgrave Macmillan.

Follows up on 'how to' from the 2005 book. Continues on the basis of there being both things that women can do to improve their career prospects and things that companies should do to ensure that there are more women on their boards. However, the book deals predominantly with the things that women can do. These things constitute the 'roadmap', which has eight main challenges that women confront in trying to become board members.

Vinnicombe, S. and Bank, J. (2003) *Women with Attitude: Lessons for Career Management*, London Routledge.

Draws lessons about women and leadership from the stories of women who have won the Veuve Cliquot Business Woman of the Year award.

Wittenburg-Cox, A. and Maitland, A. (2009) *Why Women Mean Business*, Chichester, John Wiley and sons Ltd.

Makes the business case for women at the top and argues for a more feminized way of working.

Section 2: The career progress of women in general

Section 2 includes mainly edited books, and particularly relevant chapters are picked out. Some of the chapters refer to mentoring, networking and work/family balance which are also relevant to sections 3 and 4.

Bilimoria, D. and Piderit, S.K. (eds) (2007) *Handbook on Women in Business and Management*, Cheltenham, Edward Elgar.

Written by academics in the UK, USA, Canada and Australia. Part 1 deals with societal roles and contexts of women in business and management, part 2 with career and work/life issues, part 3 with organizational processes affecting women in business and management and part 4 with women as leaders in business and management. Particularly relevant chapters are:

Chapter 1. Dunn-Jensen, L.M. and Stroh, L.K. 'Myths in the media: how the news media portray women in the workforce'. The authors state that stories about women opting out are a myth and not based on scholarly research.

Chapter 5. Burke, R.J. 'Career development of managerial women: attracting and managing talent'. Recommends family-friendly and flexible policies. Takes the view that a supportive environment is vital and hard work is key.

Chapter 6. Hopkins M.M. and O'Neil, D.A. 'Women and success: dilemmas and opportunities'. Considers factors impacting women and success – gender stereotypes and discrimination, work/family considerations, access to developmental opportunities.

Chapter 10. Graves, L.M. and Powell, G.M. 'Sex, sex similarity and sex diversity'. The chapter considers the importance of situational factors in teams. Recommends further research.

Chapter 11. Bilimoria, D., Godwin, L. and Zelechowski, D.D. 'Influence and Inclusion: a framework for researching women's advancement in organizations'. The chapter covers the usual barriers for women arguing that literature either focuses on (1) personal characteristics and behaviours of women leaders to explain the lack of women, or (2) the structural features of organizations that constrain women's rise but that there is a need to look at both 'influence' and 'inclusion'.

Chapter 12. Konrad, A.M. 'The effectiveness of human resource management practices for promoting women's careers'. Argues that there are four types of HRM practices with career outcomes for women and diversity.

1. Practices based on equity or equal opportunity including affirmative action;
2. Practices providing development opportunities – mentoring;
3. Practices that formalize the HRM system, e.g. requiring structured interviewing or having formal processes in place;
4. Work/life flexibility benefits.

Burke, R.J. and Mattis, M.C. (eds) (2005) *Supporting Women's Career Advancement: Challenges and Opportunities*, Cheltenham, Edward Elgar.

Many chapters are particularly relevant to the theme of support and development of senior women. Academics who have contributed are drawn from the UK, USA, Canada, Australia and the Netherlands. Particularly interesting chapters are:

Chapter 2. Burke, R.J. 'High-achieving women: progress and challenges'. This is an introductory chapter setting out the context and issues and covering some of the initiatives of large companies.

Chapter 3. Tharenou, P. 'Women's advancement in management: what is known, and future areas to address'. Review of literature indicates that women advance more by working in high-level male occupations but working in large organizations with long promotion ladders does not help their advancement.

Chapter 4. Altman, Y., Simpson, R., Baruch, Y and Burke, R.J. 'Reframing the 'glass ceiling' debate'. Considers the barriers that women face as they move up the career ladder. Choices about family are key in their 30s. The glass ceiling may be relocated at a higher level.

Chapter 5. Vinkenburg, C.J. and van Engen, M.L. 'Perceptions of gender, leadership and career development'. Considers perceptions of leadership and concludes that they are still gendered.

Chapter 6. Germain, M.L. and Scandura, T.A. 'Mentoring and identity development: the role of self-determination'. Reviews literature on mentoring, putting particular emphasis on the role of the mentee.

Chapter 7. Gordon, J.R. and Whelan-Berry, K.S. 'Women at midlife: changes challenges and contributions'. Suggests that organizations can implement career development that considers the unique features of midlife, to encourage and support family friendliness and appreciate increasing equality in the careers of couples.

Chapter 9. Duxbury, L. and Higgins, C. 'Work-life challenges professional women face in pursuing careers'. Canadian context based on two studies; in both studies parents reported higher role overload, interference from work to family, and vice versa, and more job stress than non-parents. Motherhood remains more stressful than fatherhood.

Chapter 11. Mattis, M.C. 'Best practices for supporting women engineers' career and development in US corporations'. Best practice for women utilized by a range of companies is outlined.

Chapter 12. Giscombe, K. 'Best practices for women of color in corporate America'. Covers issues and ways of tackling them, with some case study examples. Points to the key role of middle managers, as commitment to diversity strategies often does not filter down below senior levels.

Chapter 13. Levin, L. 'Marketing diversity in the corporate workplace'. Presents the economic and business case for diversity and the demographic case for gender diversity. Draws a parallel between a marketing framework and the development of a diversity programme.

Chapter 14. Mays, L., Graham, J. and Vinnicombe, S. Shell Oil Company US: the 2004 Catalyst Award winner for diversity initiatives. Covers Shell initiatives.

Chapter 15. Rutherford, S. 'Different yet equal'. Reports on Joint Catalyst and Opportunity Now survey (2000) on senior women managers in the UK.

Burke, R.J. and Nelson, D.L. (eds) (2002) *Advancing Women's Careers*, Oxford, Blackwell Publishers.

Particularly interesting chapters are:

Chapter 4. Davidson, M.J. 'Black and Ethnic Minority Women Managers'. Covers role conflict in a bicultural world, tokenism and occupational stress.

Chapter 7. Tharenou, P. 'Gender Differences in Explanations for Relocating or Changing Organizations for Advancement'. Women change occupations more often than men when they are in hostile environments and when able to be mobile.

Chapter 8. Holton, V. 'Training and Development: Creating the Right Environment to Help Women Succeed in Corporate Management'. Sign-posting is considered important to help them progress, and also women-only programmes.

Chapter 9. Burke, R.J. 'Career Development of Managerial Women'. Recommends developing challenging assignments and making good relationships with men in a male environment.

Chapter 10. Scandura, T.A. and Baugh, S.G. 'Mentoring and developmental relationships'. Chapter is based on use of role theory in mentoring relationships. Considers how the roles of women are evaluated, negotiated and sanctioned.

Chapter 11. Lee, M.D., Engler, L., Wright, L. 'Exploring the Boundaries in Professional Careers: Reduced load work arrangements in law, medicine and accounting'.

Chapter 12. Vinnicombe, S. and Singh, V. 'Developing Tomorrow's Women Business Leaders'.
The authors advocate women-only programmes or electives as part of mainstream management programmes.
Chapter 13. Spinks, N.L. and Tombain, L. 'Flexible work arrangements: A successful strategy for the advancement of women at the Royal Bank Financial Group'.
Chapter 14. Moore, D.P. 'Boundaryless Transitions: Global entrepreneurial women challenge career concepts'. Rise in female entrepreneurship seen as an important alternative for women.
Chapter 17. Burke, R.J. 'Organizational Culture: A key to the success of work and family programmes'.
Chapter 18. Mattis, M.C. 'Best Practices for Retaining and Advancing Women Professionals and Managers.' Makes a business case for this and advocates monitoring through benchmarking.
Chapter 19. Hammond, V. 'Advancing Women's Executive Leadership'. Challenges organizations to make the necessary changes to encourage talented women and men to work for them who also want a good family/work balance.

Cleveland, J.N., Stockdale, M. and Murphy, K.R. (2000) *Women and Men in Organizations: Sex and Gender Issues at Work*, Lawrence Erlbaum Associates (New Jersey and London).

A psychological approach. Deals with stereotypes, perceptions, power, discrimination, legal context, sexual harassment, gender and leadership, stress, health and gender.

Chapter 13. 'Managing Diversity: Research and Interventions', looks at various theories including intergroup conflict, social identity theory, mentoring and culture change.

Davidson M.J. and Burke, R.J. (eds) (2004) *Women in Management Worldwide: Facts, Figures and Analysis*, Aldershot, Ashgate.

Overview of 20 individual countries looking at the status of women in management, discrepancies and policies. Chapters are in a common format to allow comparisons between countries.

Davidson, M.J. and Burke, R.J. (eds) (2000) *Women in Management: Current Research Issues Volume II*, London, Sage Publications.

There is a preceding volume I published in 1994.

This book is in four sections. Part 1 takes an international view of women managers in Europe and entrepreneurs in New Zealand, the USA and Norway. Part 2 focuses on career development issues for women management, networking leadership and overseas assignments. Part 3 considers two issues, occupational stress and race and gender issues for BME women managers in the USA and the UK. Part 4 looks to future organizational and government initiatives.

Particularly relevant chapters are in Part 2.

Chapter 7. Travers, C. and Pemberton, C. 'Think Career Global, but Act Local: Understanding Networking as a Culturally Differentiated Career Skill'. Reviews the nature of networking and differences between men's and women's networks. Also indicates that networking may be experienced differently in different countries.

Chapter 10. Bilimoria, D. and Wheeler, J.V. 'Women Corporate Directors: Current Research and Future Directions.' Reviews past research (now rather dated) and points to future research which may itself have a transformative impact.

Chapter 11. White B. 'Lessons from the Careers of Successful Women.' Looks in-depth at the stages of successful women's lives and their family and career sub-identities.

Eagly, A.J. and Carli, L.L. (2007) *Through the Labyrinth: The Truth about How Women Become Leaders*, Harvard, Harvard Business School Publishing Corporation

The authors replace the metaphor of the glass ceiling with that of a labyrinth which is potentially less difficult. Deals with gender stereotypes and family responsibilities, and also asks whether women and men lead in different ways. Considers how some women find their way through the labyrinth and suggests strategies including building social capital through networks.

Hayward, S. (2005) *Women Leading*, Basingstoke, Palgrave MacMillan.

Focuses on women as taking control of their own destiny, creating their own leadership styles, employing different skills to men.

McTavish, D. and Miller, K. (eds) (2006) *Women in Leadership and Management*, Cheltenham, Edward Elgar.

The book is based on empirical research. Part 1 deals with issues, debates and perspectives. Part 2 deals with business and public sector dimensions. Particularly interesting chapters are:

Chapter 1. Collins, J. and Singh, V. 'Exploring gendered leadership'. The authors found that some female CEOs believed they had broken into male networks. Some thought women were excluded. All believed that developing female connections informally was important at CEO level. They saw themselves as role models.

Chapter 2. Mavin, S., Bryans, P. and Waring T. 'Challenging gendered leadership and management education'. The chapter refers to the gender blindness of UK business and management schools and the marginalization of women academics.

Chapter 3. Swan, E. 'Gendered leadership and management development: therapeutic cultures at work'. The focus of this chapter is the self rather than society. Men will be advantaged in adding new qualities, women punished for taking on more masculine qualities.

Chapter 4. Mavin, S. 'Expectations of women in leadership and management – advancement through solidarity?' Discusses solidarity and competitiveness in the 'queen bee' role. Research showed that more are keen to be visible in supporting women in management, but do not want to be labelled as feminist.

Chapter 5. Gatrell, C. 'Managing maternity'. States that employment is an essential part of social identity, but there is a 'maternal wall' and discrimination. There is an assumption of there being either a home or a career orientation and part-timers find that their career is blocked.

Chapter 6. Singh, V. and Vinnicombe, S. 'Opening the boardroom doors to women directors'. The Higgs Review (2003) found that only 4 per cent of new directors were interviewed; the rest were already known to those who appointed. The chapter uses social identity theory (Tajfel, 1982). Individuals are categorized by social identification, e.g. sex, race, age and job level, class.

Chapter 8. Ogden, S.M. and Maxwell, G.A. 'The smaller business context: a conducive environment for women in management'.

Chapter 9. Fidden, S. and Hunt, C. 'Female entrepreneurship: challenge and opportunities – the case for online coaching'. Women are increasingly becoming entrepreneurs but they are only half as likely as male counterparts to be involved in entrepreneurial activity. Women do not access support because of lack of confidence and childcare issues.

Chapter 10. McTavish, D. Miller, K. and Pyper, R. 'Gender and public management: education and health sectors'. The chapter is written in the context of gender and modernization in UK public management, e.g. the 2006 Equality Act. The organizational culture of both higher education and the health sector remains highly masculine despite there being a female workforce.

Section 3: The most common forms of support and development for women's career progress

This section includes mainly journal articles but some books. The references have been divided into two sub-sections according to whether their focus is on the individual or the organization. The references are then further sub-divided and presented alphabetically according to the surname of the first named author.

Individual chapters in books included in section 2 also consider types of support and development for women but are not cross-referenced in this section.

Sub-section 1: Individual actions

General advice

Ferreira, M.M. (2006) Succeeding in Academia: Practical Strategies for Achieving Tenure and Promotion at Research Universities, in *Advancing Women in Leadership Online Journal*, Vol. 21, Fall, http://www.advancingwomen.com/awl/fall2006/ferreira.htm

The author recognizes that women and ethnic minorities face more problems than men in obtaining promotion. Offers recommendations based on experience for mentoring, networking, keeping records and practising good time management and prioritizing writing and re-energizing.

Networking

Blass, F.R., Brouer, R., Perrewe, P.L. and Ferris, G.R. (2007) Politics Understanding and Networking Ability as a Function of Mentoring, in *Journal of Leadership and Organizational Studies*, Vol. 14, No. 2, pp. 93–105.

[Full details under 'mentoring']

Coleman,M. (2010) Women-only (homophilous) Networks Supporting Women Leaders in Education, in *Journal of Educational Administration*, Vol. 48, No. 6, pp. 769–781.

Applies network theory to two all-women networks in education and concludes that the potential support they offer has implications for women leaders in education.

Devos, A. (2004) Women, Research and the Politics of Professional Development, in *Studies in Higher Education*, Vol. 29, No. 5, pp. 591–604.

Gives an example of an institutional network offering professional development to support women academics who felt 'outsiders' as researchers.

Emmerik. I.J., Euwema, M.C., Geschiere, M. and Schouten, M.F.A.G. (2006) Networking your Way through the Organization: Gender Differences in the Relationship between Network Participation and Career Satisfaction', *Women in Management Review*, Vol. 21, No. 1. pp. 54–66.

The focus is on formal and informal networking and the relationship with career satisfaction. Although the female employees in this study engage more in networking than the men, they profit less from it in terms of career satisfaction.

Fletcher, C., Boden, R., Kent, J. and Tinson, J. (2007) Performing Women: The Gendered Dimensions of the UK New Research Economy, in *Gender, Work and Organization*, Vol. 14, No. 5, pp. 434–453.

[Also relevant for 'mentoring', 'organization wide structures and initiatives' and 'gendered leadership discourse']

Relates to gendered patterns of work in HE in a managerial context. Interviews showed that networking and mentoring were seen as important but the managerial culture of the university was inimical to mentoring. Lack of confidence and time pressure were also issues for women. Gender mainstreaming recommended.

Greener, I. (2007) The Politics of Gender in the NHS: Impression Management and 'Getting things done, in *Gender, Work and Organization*, Vol. 14, No. 3, pp. 281–299.

The article is based on interviews with 16 men and 15 women senior NHS managers examining interactions between senior men and women managers and senior male doctors. Seems to indicate that male managers gain surprisingly little from their privileged contact with doctors outside work, in apparent contradiction of expectations.

Hackney, C.E. and Runnestrand, D. (2003) Struggling for Authentic Human Synergy and a Robust Democratic Culture: The Wellspring Community for Women in Educational Leadership, in *Advancing women in Leadership*, Spring, No. 2, pp. 113–130.

Feeling isolated, women leaders in education grouped together to support each other. This is a good example of a women-only network that provides support.

McCarthy, H. (2004) *Girlfriends in High Places*, London, Demos.

This report draws on interviews with 24 network leaders and diversity experts and three case studies and a questionnaire. The report examines formal organized women's networks in the UK. Networks are seen as particularly important in overcoming career barriers for women. Finishes with recommendations. Also includes a directory of women's networks in the UK.

Ogden, S.M., McTavish, D. and McKean, L. (2006) Clearing the Way for Gender Balance in the Management of the UK Financial Services Industry: Enablers and Barriers, in *Women in Management Review*, Vol. 21, No. 1, pp. 40–53.

[Full details in sub-section on 'organization-wide actions']

Padavic, I. and Reskin, B. (2002) *Women and Men at Work*, (second edition) London, Sage Publications.

An American examination of gender and occupation, reviewing the barriers and difficulties and providing occupational statistics. A section on management and leadership refers to the importance of networking.

Perriton, L. (2006) Does Woman + Network = Career Progression?, in *Leadership*, Vol. 2, No. 1, pp. 101–113.

Considers theory and research on networks, but indicates that even when included in networks women do not benefit as much as men. Women may receive social support from other women, probably in informal networks, and instrumental support from mainly male networks. Networks are differentiated by density and homophily but tend to reflect existing norms.

Pini, B., Brown, K. and Ryan C. (2004) Women-only Networks as a Strategy for Change?' A Case Study from Local Government, in *Women in Management Review*, Vol. 19, No. 6, pp. 286–292.

Examines a case study of a women's leadership group – the Australian Local Government Women's Association. Data were drawn from interviews with the 19 female mayors in the Australian state of Queensland. Concludes that women-only networks have a valuable role to play in securing greater equity for women in management.

Singh, A., Vinnicombe, S. and Kumra, S. (2006) Women in Formal Corporate Networks: An Organizational Citizenship Perspective, in *Women in Management Review*, Vol. 21, No. 6, pp. 458–482.

Investigates women's corporate networks in the UK, and the reported benefits for the women and their employers. The data suggest that employers benefit from internal women's networks which exhibit beneficial citizenship behaviour.

Suseno, Y., Pinnington, A.H. and Gardner, J. (2007) Gender and the Network Structures of Social Capital in Professional-Client Relationships, in *Advancing Women in Leadership Online Journal*, Vol. 23, Spring.

Uses social capital theory to examine the influence of gender in professional service firms. To counter disadvantages women should ensure that they participate in a range of networks inside and outside their business, focusing on their firm's clients to increase social capital.

Tonge, J. (2008) Barriers to Networking for Women in a UK Professional Service, in *Gender in Management*, Vol. 23, No. 7, pp. 484–505.

Set in the UK PR sector and based mainly on interviews. Barriers to networking that emerged are psychological, situational and social. Women identified 17 barriers and men seven. Women, particularly young women, appear to be excluded from powerful networks.

Walby, S. (2007) *Gender (In)equality and the Future of Work*, Manchester, Equal Opportunities Commission. Executive summary.

Relates to the wider issues of the transformation of work and how gender will impact on this. Briefly refers to networks, but points out that they do not necessarily produce opportunities for women and minority groups.

Waldstram C. and Madsen, H. (2007) Social Relations Among Managers: Old Boys and Young Women's Networks, in *Women in Management Review*, Vol. 22, No. 2, pp. 136–147.

A large-scale survey of managers in Denmark found that male managers tend to see their colleagues more as friends the older they are, but the reverse is true of female managers. The paper identifies the role of age in the gender differences in perception of social support.

Mentoring, coaching and role models

Blass, F.R., Brouer, R., Perrewe, P.L. and Ferris, G.R. (2007) Politics Understanding and Networking Ability as a Function of Mentoring, in *Journal of Leadership and Organizational Studies*, Vol. 14, No. 2, pp. 93–105.

[Relates also to sub-section on 'networking']

Based on a study of recent business school graduates which found that mentoring appears to be the most important way of learning about politics in organizations, particularly for men. There is support for the argument that political skill is in part learned.

Bower, G., Hums, M.A. and Keedy, J.L. (2006) Factors Influencing the Willingness to Mentor Females in Leadership Positions within Campus Recreation: A Historical Perspective, in *Advancing Women in Leadership Journal*, Spring.

Identified through their life histories that senior managers saw later 1950s, 1960s and early 1970s as a time when barriers to women were important and mentoring to protect them was vital. Since the early 1970s they do not see any difference between mentoring men and women.

Carnell, E., MacDonald, J. and Askew, S. (2006) *Coaching and Mentoring in Higher Education: A Learning Centred Approach*, London, Institute of Education.

Examines theory and practice of mentoring in a university setting.

Clutterbuck, D. and Ragins, B.R. (2002) (eds) *Mentoring and Diversity*, Oxford, Butterworth, Heinemann.

Particularly interesting chapters are:

Chapter 1. O'Neill, R.M. 'Gender and race in mentoring relationships: a review of the literature'. Looks at types of mentoring and how gender and race influence outcomes and types, also the composition of mentoring relationships.

Chapter 2. Ragins, B.R. 'Understanding diversified mentoring relationships: Challenges in diversified mentoring programmes'. Discusses challenges and strategies, such as role modelling, use of stereotypes, restricted comfort zones. States that clarifying ground rules is a key strategy. The book then develops these themes and includes many case studies.

Ehrich, L.C. (2008) Mentoring and Women Managers: Another Look at the Field, in *Gender in Management*, Vol. 23, No. 7, pp. 469–483.

A literature review exploring issues relating to mentoring for women managers in the UK, USA, Canada and Australia. The three main areas discussed are: the nature and focus of the relationship, managing cross-gender mentoring and negotiating the power dimension.

Singh, V., Vinnicombe, S. and James, K. (2006) Constructing a Professional Identity: How Young Female Managers Use Role Models, in *Women in Management Review*, Vol. 21, No. 1, pp. 67–81.

The purpose of this paper is to explore how young career-minded women use role models. The paper is based on in-depth interviews with ten young professional women who revealed that they actively draw on role models from different domains. The women revealed that they preferred learning from external role models rather than focusing on individual women from the top of their own professions.

Organizational support and development

General issues

Burke, R.J., Burgess, Z. and Fallon, B. (2006) Organizational Practices Supporting Women and their Satisfaction and Well-being', in *Women in Management Review*, Vol. 21, No. 5, pp. 416–425.

An exploratory study in Australia examined how women perceive the organizational practices designed to support women's career advancement. Women report higher levels of job and career satisfaction where there are more organizational practices supportive of women.

Fletcher, C., Boden, R., Kent, J. and Tinson, J. (2007) Performing Women: The Gendered Dimensions of the UK New Research Economy, in *Gender, Work and Organization*, Vol. 14, No. 5, pp. 434–453.

[For details see section on 'networking']

Kark, R. and Waismel-Manor, R. (2005) Organizational Citizenship Behaviour: What's Gender Got to Do With It?, in *Organization*, Vol. 12, No. 6, pp. 889–917.

Presents a feminist reading of the concept of organizational citizenship behaviour (OCB). Shows that although OCB is presented as being gender neutral it does have gendered connotations and it can negatively affect both men and women. Different aspects of good citizenship are identified as being 'male' or 'female'.

Lamsa, A-M. and Hillos, M. (2008) Career Counselling for Women Managers at Mid-career: Developing an Autobiographical Approach', in *Gender in Management*, Vol. 23, No. 6, pp. 395–408.

Argues for the need to change the dominant understanding of a 'normal' career in management based on the career autobiographies of mid-career women which do not follow a straightforward trajectory.

Maxwell, G.A., Ogden, S.M. and McTavish, D. (2007) Enabling the Career Development of Female Managers in Finance and Retail, in *Women in Management Review*, Vol. 22, No. 5, pp. 353–370.

Reports on case studies in seven organizations. The factors that foster the career development of women are recognition of the business case for a managerial gender mix, a transformational leadership style and supportive organizational culture, also flexible working arrangements and training and development opportunities.

Ogden, S.M., McTavish, D., McKean, L., (2006) Clearing the Way for Gender Balance in the Management of the UK Financial Services Industry: Enablers and Barriers, in *Women in Management Review*, Vol. 21, No. 1, pp. 40–53.

[Relates also to 'networking']

Females make-up just over half of the workforce in the UK financial services sector. Despite progress, men and women agree that females encounter more barriers to career progression than men, relating primarily to a long-hours culture and networking. The long-hours aspect of the industry culture tends to leak through into areas of the industry where it is less important for fostering client relationships.

Wentling, R.M. (2003) The Career Development and Aspirations of Women in Middle Management – Revisited, in *Women in Management Review*, Vol. 18, No. 6, pp. 311–324(14).

[Relates also to 'barriers']

Reports the results of the second phase of a research study on the career development and aspirations of women in middle management in business firms in the USA. Women first interviewed in 1995 had not attained the positions to which they aspired and believe they are not progressing as rapidly as they think they should. However, they still believe that it is realistic that they will attain these positions.

Wirth, L. (2001) *Breaking through the Glass Ceiling: Women in Management*, Geneva, International Labour Organization.

Analyses gender inequalities in the labour market and in society and considers career development and policies for promoting women in management including international action such as mainstreaming. Considers the importance of training and networking.

Women and Work Commission (2006) *Shaping a Fairer Future*, London, DTI.

A review from the Women and Work Commission focusing on the need to change our culture to maximize potential; the difficulties of combining work and family life; opportunities for women; and improving workplace practice. Gives recommendations.

Gender and teams

Court, M. (2007) Changing and/or Reinscribing Gendered Discourses of Team Leadership in Education?, in *Gender and Education*, Vol. 19, No. 5, pp. 607–626.

Shows how feminist ways of working contribute to team leadership and shows how individuals can impact on dominant discourses. A contrast is drawn with gendered team relationships.

Gratton, L., Keland, E., Voigt, A., Walker, L. and Wolfram, H-J. (2007) *Innovative Potential: Men and Women in Teams*, London, London Business School, The Lehman Brothers Centre for Women in Business.

Survey results indicate that women still carry the burden of domestic work. Men are expected to work long hours and are working under great pressure. Tokenism for women on teams has a detrimental effect. Innovation through teams is greatest when the gender balance is 50/50.

Grisoni, L. and Beeby, M. (2007) Leadership, Gender and Sense-making, in *Gender Work and Organizations*, Vol. 14, No. 3, pp. 192–209.

Looks at the impact of gender (one team of men, one team of women, one mixed) and found little difference between them and suggests that male ways of working are embedded.

Huse, M. and Solberg, A.G. (2006) Gender-related Boardroom Dynamics: How Scandinavian Women Make and Can Make Contributions on Corporate Boards', in *Women in Management Review*, Vol. 21, No. 2, pp. 113–130(18).

[For details see Section 1]

Kramer, V.W., Konrad, A.M. and Erkut, S. (2006) *Critical mass on Corporate Boards: Why Three or More Women Enhance Governance*. Executive summary. Wellesley Centers for Women's Publication Office.

[For details see Section 1]

Kruger, M. L. (2008) School Leadership, Sex and Gender: Welcome to Difference, in *International Journal of Leadership in Education*, Vol. 11, No. 2, pp. 155–168.

Argues that leadership that combines masculine and feminine elements and mixed teams is likely to be better able to produce effective schools.

Ollilainen, M. and Calasanti, T. (2007) Metaphors at Work: Maintaining the Salience of Gender in Self-Managing Teams, in *Gender and Society*, Vol. 21, No. 5, pp. 5–27.

A study of four teams indicated that cultural aspects of teamwork still work against women's full participation; for example, mothering behaviour furthered the interests of the young men and older males are seen as father. Men showed reluctance to answer phones or take on clerical tasks and expected that the women would do this. Women are seen to make the men more 'civilized'.

Gender policies including equal opportunities and affirmative action

Ainsworth, S., Knox, A. and O'Flynn, J. (2010) 'A Blinding Lack of Progress': Management Rhetoric and Affirmative Action, in *Gender, Work and Organization*, Vol. 17, No. 6, pp. 658–678.

Despite the obligation in Australia for private organizations employing 100 or more to report on their affirmative action programmes, in an examination of the hospitality sector over 14 years the researchers found that employers tended to 'blame' women and absolve themselves from the need for action.

Bagilhole, B. (2002) Challenging Equal Opportunities: Changing and Adapting Male Hegemony in Academia, in *British Journal of Sociology of Education*, Vol. 23, No. 1, pp. 19–33.

Categorizes the responses of pre-1992 universities to equal opportunities policies in the light of continued male domination of management. Four responses were observed: confusion, collusion and cynicism, while the fourth, contrariness, was overt resistance. There is an implicit comparison with the older universities which are resistant to change.

Chinkin, C.M. (2001) *Gender Mainstreaming in Legal and Constitutional Affairs: A Reference Manual for Governments and Other Stakeholders*, London, Commonwealth Secretariat.

Analyses the key gender issues in the legal and constitutional sector and offers recommendations at the national and international level.

Deem, R., Morley, L. and Tlili, A. (2005) *Negotiating equity in higher education institutions*. Report to HEFCE, SHEFC, HEFCW.

Reports on a research project using interviews and focus groups in six HEIs to explore staff experiences of equity issues and equity policies and the views of senior managers. Found a gulf between views of staff and senior managers, and that equity for students was perceived as being more important for students than staff.

Deem. R. and Morley, L. (2006) Diversity in the Academy: Staff Perceptions of Equity Policies in Six Contemporary Higher Education Institutions, in *Policy Futures in Education*, Vol. 4, No. 2, pp. 185–202.

Based on research outlined above using findings to consider how HE employees understood 'equality' and 'diversity'. Concludes that there may have been a relative depoliticization of staff equality in HE. Equality policies are uneven, with staff not as well covered as students. Gender and ethnicity are better understood than other aspects of diversity.

Hearn, J. (2005) Gendered Leaderships and Leaderships on Gender Policy: National Context, Corporate Structures and Chief Human Resources Managers in Transnational Corporations, in *Leadership*, Vol. 1, No. 4, pp. 429–454.

Finland, like the other Nordic countries, leads the world in terms of women's empowerment but there is persistence of gender inequalities in the private sector. Although the law requires at least 40 per cent membership for women and men on state and municipal bodies, only two-thirds of the 100 largest companies had gender equality plans and the dominant attitude was 'individualist'.

Marshall, C. (2000) Policy Discourse Analysis: Negotiating Gender Equity', in *Journal of Education Policy*, Vol. 155, No. 2, pp. 125–156.

A study of gender equity policy in the context of the Australian experience based on participant observation, document analysis and elite interviewing including 'femocrats'. Identified strategies for taking gender equity policies further.

Mukhopadhyay, M., Steehouwer, G. and Wong, F. (2006) *Politics of the Possible*, The Hague, Oxfam Novib.

Concerns using a toolkit to bring about gender mainstreaming in seven organizations (NGOs) in the Middle East and South Asia who were committed to promoting gender equality. Shows how organizational change is necessary.

Noble C. and Mears J. (2000) The Impact of Affirmative Action Legislation on Working in Higher Education in Australia: Progress or Procrastination?, in *Women in Management Review*, Vol. 15, No. 8, pp. 404–414.

Focuses on the impact of the Australian Affirmative Action (Equal Employment Opportunity) legislation (1986), on women's employment in the higher education sector. There has been a general growth in women's employment but there is still a glass ceiling preventing women in both academic and administrative positions from moving into management structures.

Prentice, S. (2000) The Conceptual Politics of Chilly Climate Controversies, in *Gender and Education*, Vol. 12, No. 2, pp. 195–207.

Set in Canadian HE, this article presents the difficult struggle over the meaning of equity initiatives, showing how meanings are political and value-laden.

Still, L.V. (2006) Where are the Women in Leadership in Australia?, in *Women in Management Review*, Vol. 21, No. 3, pp. 180–194.

Reviews the current representation of women in leadership in Australia with data drawn from official government statistics. Despite 30 years of legislative, policy and social change in the equity area, women have not attained leadership positions in any significant numbers. Suggested reasons include a lack of line management and profit centre experience and Australia's 'macho' culture.

Tienari, J., Holgersson, C., Merilainen, S. and Hook P. (2009) Gender, Management and Market Discourse: The Case of Gender Quotas in the Swedish and Finnish Media, in *Gender, Work and Organization*, Vol. 16, No. 4, pp. 501–521.

Argues that the situations in the two countries are different, with differing discourses and potentially different criticisms.

Woodward, R. and Winter, P. (2006) Gender and the Limits to Diversity in the Contemporary British Army, in *Gender, Work and Organization*, Vol. 13, No. 1, pp. 46–67.

Discusses the Army's attitude to equal opportunities and gender (problematic) and identifies the limitations of the move to diversity management.

Section 4: The contextual and structural barriers to career progress
This section includes books, articles and reports on:

- General background, including explanations for gendered occupations and the pay gap;
- Barriers to career progress: the glass ceiling, gender stereotypes and gendered leadership discourses;
- Backlash to feminism and advances for women;
- Identities;
- Work/family balance;
- Barriers created by other women: The 'queen bee' syndrome.

General background, including explanations for gendered occupations and the pay gap

Breakwell, G.M. and Tytherleigh, M.Y. (2007) UK University Leaders at the Turn of the 21st Century: Changing Patterns in their Socio-Demographic Characteristics, in *Higher Education*, Vol. 56, No. 1, pp. 109–127.

> Mainly about the changing role of vice-chancellors but does show that there was an increase in the numbers of women and social scientists, and an increase in the age at which appointments are made during the period 1997–2006.

Broadbridge, A. (2010) Choice or Constraint? Tensions in Female Retail Executives' Career Narratives, in *Gender in Management: An International Journal*, Vol. 25, No. 3, pp. 244–260.

> Challenges Hakim's preference theory indicating through qualitative interviews that women's choices are constrained.

Gatrell, C. and Swan, E. (2008) *Gender and Diversity in Management: A Concise Introduction*, London, Sage.

> An introduction to the background and current issues relating to gender and diversity issues in organizations including the argument that gender issues are no longer relevant. They couple gender and diversity because issues of intersectionality mean that the situation is too complex to just focus on one aspect of diversity.

Hakim, C. (2004) *Key Issues in Women's Work: Female Diversity and the Polarisation of Women's Employment*, London, The Glasshouse Press.

> The author puts forward her preference theory to argue that women can choose in relation to work and have the best of both worlds, deciding whether to be centred on the home or on the workplace. The book represents an argument that claims to disprove feminist claims about discrimination and the pay gap.

Kumra, S. (2010) Exploring Career 'Choices' of Work-centred Women in a Professional Service Firm, in *Gender in Management: An International Journal*, Vol. 25, No. 3, pp. 227–243.

> Similar to Broadbridge (above) in challenging Hakim's preference theory.

Metcalf, H. (2009) *Pay gaps across the equality strands: a review Research Report 14*, Manchester, Equality and Human Rights Commission.

Examines the pay gap from the point of view of gender, sexual orientation and ethnicity.

Metcalf, H. and Rolfe, H. (2009) *Employment and earnings in the finance sector: A gender analysis. Research Report 17.* Manchester, Equality and Human Rights Commission.

Examines the impact of gender on employment patterns, earnings and recruitment in the finance sector.

McNamara, O., Howson, J., Gunter, H., Sprigade, A. and Onat-Steima, Z. (2008) *Women Teachers' Careers: Report for the NASUWT.* NASUWT.

Research carried out between 2006 and 2007 that examined the nature of women teachers' careers including factors that assist or impede. One section devoted to gender and leadership confirms that men are still over-represented in leadership.

Scott, J., Dex, S. and Joshi, H. (eds) (2008) *Women and Employment: Changing Lives and New Challenges*, Cheltenham, Edward Elgar.

[Also relevant to 'work/family balance' section]

Analyses the changes in women's lives over the past 25 years, focusing on changes in the labour market and relating them to demography, diversity, equality and work/family balance drawing on quantitative and qualitative research.

Particularly interesting chapters are:

Chapter 1. Purcell, K. and Elias, P. 'Achieving equality in the knowledge economy'. Considers how gender impacts on the careers of graduates, including pay differentials and the impact of having a family.

Chapter 2. Dex, S., Ward, K. and Joshi, H. 'Changes in women's occupations and occupational mobility over 25 years'. Examines changes in the impact of childbirth on women's careers.

Chapter 7. McRae, S. 'Working full-time after motherhood'. Examines the decisions taken by mothers about work, drawing on research following women over 11 years from birth of first child in 1988. Of these women, 14 per cent worked full-time.

Chapter 9. Crompton, R. And Lyonette, C. 'Mothers' employment, work-life conflict, careers and class'. Concludes that despite the importance of individualism, class and gender persist as structural constraints on the lives of women and men.

Chapter 13. Deakin, S. and McLaughlin, C. 'The regulation of women's pay: from individual rights to reflexive law'. Outlines relevant legislation and its impact.

Shackleton, J.R. (2008) *Should We Mind the Gap? Gender Pay Differentials and Public Policy*, London, Institute of Economic Affairs.

Argues that the gender pay gap is misleading and not necessarily related to discrimination which is often inferred. States that women may be compensated by greater job satisfaction and that attitudes and preferences as well as work experience and qualifications are the main reasons for the gap. Claims that the 'part-time penalty' applies only to a small proportion of occupation types.

Wilson, F.M. (2003) *Organizational Behaviour and Gender*, Aldershot, Ashgate.

Considers gender inequality looking at part-time work, low pay, vertical and horizontal job segregation and sexual harassment.

Gender barriers to career progress: the glass ceiling, gender stereotypes and gendered leadership discourses

Addi-Raccah, A. (2005) Gender, Ethnicity and School Principalship in Israel: Comparing Two Organizational Cultures, in *International Journal of Inclusive Education*, Vol. 9, No. 3, pp. 217–239.

Based on a large survey, different patterns of gender/ethnic stratification were found in the two Jewish education systems in Israel. Gender appears to have a stronger effect than ethnicity.

Addi-Raccah, A. and Ayalon, H. (2002) Gender Inequality in Leadership Positions of Teachers, in *British Journal of Sociology of Education*, Vol. 23, No. 2, pp. 157–177.

Based on a sample of over 10,000 teachers, the paper examines gender differences in appointment to leadership positions in school in the three different education sectors in Israel. Shows that gender has an independent influence on the probability of appointment, but that it is context-bound.

Barrett, M. and Davidson, M.J. (2006) *Gender and Communication at Work*, Aldershot, Ashgate.

Edited book which examines how gender interacts with communications of all types in the workplace. Particularly interesting chapters include:

Chapter 2. Buzzanell, P.M. and Meisenbach, R.J. 'Gendered Performance and Communication in the Employment Interview'. Examines the existing literature and further avenues for research.

Chapter 4. Peck, J.J. 'Women and Promotion: the influence of communication style'. Suggests that women's communication style is devalued and that might lead them to adopt a different more male style. However, women are expected to conform to sex role stereotypes. The 'new wave' style of management may be helpful to women, but may be rejected by men.

Chapter 5. Carli, L.L. 'Gender Issues in Workplace Groups: Effects of Gender and Communication Style on Social Influence'. Concludes that different social norms operate with regard to communication with men and with women. Women in powerful positions are in a double bind. As women they are regarded as less powerful and this is enhanced if they use a typically 'feminine' style, but if they use a more masculine style they are judged as not conforming to female patterns.

Chapter 11. Baxter J. 'Putting Gender in its Place: A case study on constructing speaker identities in a management meeting'.

[Relates also to 'identities']

This chapter takes a post-structuralist approach to a case study of a dotcom company with seven directors of which one was female. They identified four institutional 'discourses', competing specialisms (expertise), historical legacy, open dialogue and masculinization (stereotypically male speech patterns). There are shifting identities.

Chapter 13. Still, L.V. 'Gender, Leadership and Communication'. Reviews relevant literature and points out that there has been insufficient research on the part played by communication.

Chapter 14. Olsson, S. 'We don't need another hero!: Organizational storytelling as a vehicle for communicating a female archetype of workplace leadership'. Leaders are mainly male 'hero' archetypes and this chapter draws on narratives from female executives to show that in recent years things are changing. She outlines a female paradigm of leadership challenging the male norms and sees that women are providing better role models for younger women.

Chapter 15. Stuhlmacher, A.F. and Winkler, R.B., 'Negotiating while Female: Research and Implications'. Discusses how gender stereotypes contribute to negotiation differences contributing to pay differences and to promotion prospects but recognizes that the subtle negotiation situations means that more research is required.

Bendl, R. and Schmidt, A. (2010) From 'Glass Ceilings' to 'Firewalls' – Different Metaphors for Describing Discrimination, in *Gender – Work and Organization*, Vol. 17, No. 5, p. 612.

Introduces additional metaphor of 'firewall' and claims it may be more relevant than 'glass ceiling' because it is more complex, fluid and permeable.

Bligh, M.C. and Kohles, J.C. (2008) Negotiating Gender Role Expectations: Rhetorical Leadership and Women in the US Senate, in *Leadership*, Vol. 4, No. 4, pp. 381–402.

Their research indicated that women continue to experience the effects of gender stereotypes which have negative implications for their leadership.

Broadbridge, A. (2008) Senior Careers in Retailing: An Exploration of Male and Female Executives' Career Facilitators and Barriers, in *Gender in Management*, Vol. 23, No. 1, pp. 11–35.

[Also relevant to 'work/family balance']

Retailing is seen to be a strongly masculine culture but within this context women and men report similar facilitators and problems. Concludes that the senior women may have succeeded by ignoring their feminine characteristics and putting their career before family and personal life to adopt a male cultural norm.

Burke, R.J., Matthiesen, S.B., Einarsen, S., Fiskenbaurm, L. and Soiland, V. (2008) Gender Differences in Work Experiences and Satisfactions of Norwegian Oil Rig Workers, in *Gender in Management*, Vol. 23, No. 2, pp. 137–147.

Based on data collected from questionnaires to 1,022 men and women working in traditionally male occupations. Only a small number of women could be included. Women who survive in such jobs report very similar experiences to men after having faced challenges resulting from the gender culture of their work.

Byrd-Blake, M. (2004) Female Perspectives on Career Advancement, in *Advancing Women in Leadership Journal*, Spring.

African American, Hispanic and white women's perceptions of career barriers and strategies to overcome them. Family was the big difference. The majority of white (71 per cent) and African American female administrators (60 per cent) did not have a child at home, but 60 per cent of Hispanic women did. African Americans had more senior work experience and perceived the lack of a professional network, being excluded from informal socialization processes and considered they needed more training.

Chan, A.K-W. (2004) Gender, School Management and Educational Reforms: A Case Study of an Primary School in Hong Kong, in *Gender and Education*, Vol. 16, No. 4, pp. 491–510.

Based on a case study of a primary school in Hong Kong, showing how an increasingly managerialist culture in an entrepreneurial school has exploited young women and discriminated against motherhood.

Chisholm, L. (2001) Gender and Leadership in South African Educational Administration, in *Gender and Education*, Vol. 13, No. 4, pp 387–399.

[Also relevant to 'identities']

Article based on interviews with 16 educational decision-makers in the Gauteng Department of Education. Argues that the leadership discourse is masculine so that women find it difficult to hold leadership positions. Also discusses issues of race and intersectionality with gender.

Coleman, M. (2007) Gender and Educational Leadership in England: A Comparison of Secondary Head Teachers' Views Over Time, in *School Leadership and Management*, Vol. 27, No. 4, pp. 383–399.

A comparison of views of head teachers on the impact of gender on school leaders, based on two surveys, one in the mid-1990s the other in 2004. The perceptions of the heads are that there has been change in some areas but not in others, for example women still face discriminatory stereotypical views from governors.

Coleman, M. (2005) Gender and headship in the 21st century. Project Report. eprints.ioe.ac.uk/4164/ - Cached

Full report on comparison of surveys of head teachers undertaken in the mid-1990s and in 2004, showing changes and continuities.

Coleman, M. (2002) *Women as Head Teachers: Striking the Balance*, Stoke on Trent, Trentham Books.

Large-scale study of women and men secondary head teachers in England and Wales, reporting on the impact of gender on career progress and styles of leadership and management. Based on data from national surveys.

Coleman, M. (2001) Achievement Against the Odds: The Female Secondary Head Teachers in England and Wales, in *School Leadership and Management*, Vol. 21, No. 1, pp. 75–100.

Examines constraints on the promotion of women and concludes there is a continuing level of discrimination against women.

Coronel, J.M., Moreno, E. and Carrasco, M.J. (2010) Work-family Conflicts and the Organizational Work Culture as Barriers to Women Educational Managers, in *Gender, Work and Organization*, Vol. 17, No. 2, pp. 219–239.

[For details see 'identities' section]

Cushman, P. (2008) So What Exactly Do You Want? What Principals Mean When They Say 'Male Role Model', in *Gender and Education*, Vol. 20, No. 2, pp. 123–136.

Reports of survey of 250 New Zealand primary school principals finding that they favoured 'macho' men. Argues that boys need to be provided with male role models who allow them to visualize a range of different ways of being male.

Currie, J., Harris, P. and Thiele, B. (2000) Sacrifices in Greedy Universities: Are They Gendered?, in *Gender and Education*, Vol. 12, No. 3, pp. 269–291.

Study of two Australian public universities concluding that the uniformity of responses from staff indicate that there is a peak of masculinist discourse in HE.

Czarniawska, B. and Guje, S. (2008) The Thin End of the Wedge: Foreign Women Professors as Double Strangers, in *Gender Work and Organization*, Vol. 15. No. 3, p. 235.

Reports from life story standpoint that being a foreigner and a woman does not appear to give a double disadvantage to becoming a professor. They may have more success than their British sisters. The idea of 'wedge' is that they open the door but suffer from double pressure.

Duckin, A. and Ozga, J. (2007) Gender and Management in Further Education in Scotland: An Agenda for Research, in *Gender and Education*, Vol. 19, No. 5, pp. 627–646.

The authors argue that research on gender including masculinities may be particularly relevant in Scotland because of the cultural assumptions that make women so rare in leadership. The paper reports that there appears to be a gap between the equal opportunities policies of the colleges and the reality of life.

Embry, A., Padget, M.Y. and Caldwell, C.B. (2008) Can Leaders Step Outside of the Gender Box? An Examination of Leadership and Gender Role Stereotypes, in *Journal of Leadership and Organizational Studies*, Vol. 15, No. 30, pp. 30–45.

Uses vignettes to test how participants infer the gender of a leader. Results not always as hypothesized as women were more positive about gender inconsistent styles than men.

Fletcher, C., Boden, R., Kent, J. and Tinson, J. (2007) Performing Women: The Gendered Dimensions of the UK New Research Economy, in *Gender, Work and Organization*, Vol. 14, No. 5, pp. 434–453.

[For details see 'networking']

Ford, J. (2006) Discourses of Leadership: Gender, Identity and Contradiction in a UK Public Sector Organization, in *Leadership*, Vol. 2, No. 1, pp. 77–99.

Identifies macho-management discourse and post heroic (more feminine) leadership discourse as dominant. Concludes that charismatic and masculine models of leadership still feature heavily.

Grummell, B., Devine, D. and Lynch, K. (2010) The Care-less Manager: Gender, Care and New Managerialism in Higher Education, in *Gender in Education*, Vol. 21, No. 2, pp. 191–208.

Argues that identifying who does the caring is vital in understanding senior management roles in a managerialist higher education culture.

Haase, M. (2008) 'I Don't Do the Mothering Role that Lots of Female Teachers Do': Male Teachers, Gender, Power and Social Organisation, in *British Journal of Sociology of Education*, Vol. 29, No. 6, pp. 597–608.

The paper argues that male primary teachers continue to reproduce patriarchal gender power differentials.

Huse, M. and Solberg, A.G. (2006) Gender-related Boardroom Dynamics: How Scandinavian Women Make and Can Make Contributions on Corporate Boards, in *Women in Management*, Vol. 21, No. 2, pp. 113–130.

[For details see Section 1]

Isaac, C., Behar-Horenstein, L. and Koro-Ljungberg, M. (2009) Women Deans: Leadership Becoming, in *International Journal of Leadership in Education*, electronic journal.

Looks at the impact of gender on leadership of women deans and how women use power.

Kantola, J. (2008) 'Why Do All the Women Disappear?' Gendering Processes in a Political Science Department, in *Gender, Work and Organization*, Vol. 15, No. 2, pp. 202–225.

Research in Finland, where women have a very good representation in government and academia, explores why there are so few women in a political science department in the University of Helsinki. The author found no overt discrimination but she found women were likely to be teaching, men were seen as the norm as political scientists and women seen as difficult outsiders.

Kelan, E.K. (2008) Emotions in a Rational Profession: The Gendering of Skills in ICT World, in *Gender Work and Organization*, Vol. 15, No. 1, pp. 49–71.

Concludes that even workplaces associated with rationality and masculinity like the ICT industry are now valuing emotional and social competence at work. The interpretation of social and emotional competence in men identifies them with ideal worker skills, but the same identification in women is interpreted as normal and natural for women.

Kumra, S. and Vinnicombe, S. (2010) Impressing for Success: A Gendered Analysis of a Key Social Capital Accumulation Strategy, in *Gender – Work and Organization*, Vol. 17, No. 5, p. 521.

Identifies the importance of organizational norms and the difficulties women have in dealing with negative stereotypes that impact on their ability to accumulate social capital.

Lambert, C. (2007) New Labour, New Leaders? Gendering Transformational Leadership, in *British Journal of Sociology of Education*, Vol. 28, No. 2, pp. 149–163.

Identifies the discourses of leadership in educational speeches made by New Labour politicians showing how they are using a language leading to the 'masculinization' of education epitomized in the entrepreneurial school leader taking tough decisions.

Lyonette, C. and Crompton, R. (2005) The Only Way is Up?: An Examination of Women's 'Under-achievement' in the Accountancy Profession in the UK, in *Gender in Management: An International Journal*, Vol. 23, No. 7, pp. 506–521.

Women do not progress as well as men and earn considerably less. The main reason appears to be combining work with family responsibilities. Part-time and flexible working carry penalties of lower status and money. Concludes that although there are workplace barriers, the division of domestic labour is equally important.

Mavin, S., Bryans, P. and Waring, T. (2004) Gender on the Agenda 2: Unlearning Gender Blindness in Management Education, in *Women in Management Review*, Vol. 19, No. 6, pp. 293–303.

UK business and management schools continue to operate a gender blind approach to management education, research and the development of management theory. Argues that academic women are invisible in Schools of Business Management and that management research is the preserve of male academics. This tendency is reinforced by the RAE.

McLay, M. (2008) Head Teacher Career Paths in UK Independent Secondary Coeducational Schools, in *Educational Management Administration and Leadership*, Vol. 36, No. 3, pp. 353–372.

Examines the career paths of men and women head teachers in UK independent co-educational schools. Identifies factors which assisted or hindered career progress, and indicates what types of preparation were found most useful.

McTavish, C. and Miller, K. (2009) Gender Balance in Leadership? Reform and Modernization in the UK Further Education Sector, in *Educational Management, Administration and Leadership*, Vol. 37, No. 3, pp. 350–365.

Although many women are employed in the further education sector, relatively few are in leadership. Argues that the culture has become increasingly masculinized through managerialist practices.

Moreau, M-P, Osgood, J. and Halsall, A, (2007) Making Sense of the Glass Ceiling in Schools: An Exploration of Women Teachers' Discourses, in *Gender and Education*, Vol. 19, No. 2, pp. 237–253.

Based on empirical research in schools (Moreau, M-P, Osgood, J. and Halsall, A, (2005) *Final Report of the Women Teachers' Careers and Progression Project*, IPSE London Metropolitan University, Leicester, SHA). Draws on critical discourse analysis of 44 interviews, identifying that one of the main discourses is that of individual choice and there is a lack of awareness of gender issues.

Morley, L. (2000) The Micropolitics of Gender in the Learning Society, in *Higher Education in Europe*, Vol. XXV, No. 2, pp. 229–235.

Identifies gender issues played out in HE through subtle micro-political means that are sometimes difficult to pin down.

Morosi, P. (2010) South African Female Principals' Career Paths: Understanding the Gender Gap in Secondary School Management, in *Educational Management, Administration and Leadership*, Vol. 38, No. 5, pp. 547–562.

Identifies barriers to women principals throughout the stages of their career showing that the main one is the accepted male norm of leadership.

Oplatka, I. (2002) Women Principals and the Concept of Burnout: An Alternative Voice?, in *International Journal of Leadership in Education*, Vol. 5, No. 2, pp. 211–226.

Part of a wider Israeli study of psychological experiences of women principals in mid-career. Identifies the need to re-examine leadership in education as interpersonal and relationship-oriented.

Priola, V. (2007) Being Female Doing Gender. Narratives of Women in Education Management, in *Gender and Education*, Vol. 19, No. 1, pp. 21–40.

Based on the study of a business school of a British university where the majority of managerial roles were occupied by women. Most do not have children and those that do find role conflict. Women are more likely to apply for promotion but men tend to downgrade women's achievement. Women may adopt more masculine behaviours.

Runte, M. and Milles, A.J. (2006) Cold War, Chilly Climate: Exploring the Roots of Gendered Discourse in Organization and Management Theory, in *Human Relations*, Vol. 59, No. 5, pp. 695–720.

Argues that the absence of gender from theories of leadership and organization arises from the discourses of work and family that were endorsed throughout the Cold War period.

Ryan, M.K. and Haslam, S.A. (2005) The Glass Cliff: Evidence that Women are Over-Represented in Precarious Leadership Positions, in *British Journal of Management*, Vol. 16, No. 2, pp. 81–90.

Shows that during a time of stock-market decline, companies who appointed women to their boards had worse performance in the prior five months than those companies who appointed men.

Schein, V.E., (2007) Women in Management: Reflections and Projections, in *Women in Management Review*, Vol. 22, No. 1, pp. 6–18(13).

A major barrier to women's progress in management worldwide continues to be the gender stereotyping of managers. The paper examines how this 'think manager – think male' attitude has changed over the 30 years since the author's initial research. The overview reveals the strength and inflexibility of the attitude held by males across time and national borders.

Sinclair, A. (2004) Journey around Leadership, in *Discourse: Studies in the Cultural Politics of Education*, Vol. 25, No. 1, pp. 7–19.

Comments on leadership in education from her experience as a woman teacher of largely male management students.

Thompson, B. (2007) Working beyond the Glass Ceiling: Women Managers in Initial Teacher Training in England, in *Gender and Education*, Vol. 19, No. 3, pp. 339–352.

Although women are now successful in obtaining management responsibilities in teacher training this paper argues that changes in teacher education towards a more managerial style have left the management posts less fulfilling. Men are choosing not to take them.

Tomas, M., Lavie, J.M., Duran, M del M. and Guillamon, C. (2010) Women in Academic Administration at the University, in *Educational Management Administration and Leadership*, Vol. 38, No. 4, pp. 487–498.

Organizational culture is found to be the most important barrier to the appointment of women to senior posts.

Wilson, J.Z., Marks, G., Noone, L and Hamilton-Mackenzie, J. (2010) Retaining a Foothold on the Slippery Paths of Academia: University Women, Indirect Discrimination, and the Academic Marketplace, in *Gender and Education*, Vol. 22, No. 5, pp. 535–545.

Concludes that despite apparent reforms in Australia, career barriers for women remain and they are supported by the neo-liberal 'marketization' in higher education.

Wolfram, H-J., Mohr, G. and Schyns, B. (2007) Professional Respect for Female and Male Leaders: Influential Gender-relevant Factors, in *Women in Management Review*, Vol. 22, No. 1, pp. 19–32.

Shows that female leaders and males who follow female leaders are likely to receive less professional respect from their followers than male leaders and female followers of male leaders. Gender role discrepant female leaders (i.e. autocratic) got less respect than gender role discrepant male leaders (i.e. democratic).

Weyer, B. (2007) Twenty Years Later: Explaining the Persistence of the Glass Ceiling for Women Leaders, in *Women in Management Review,* Vol. 22, No. 6, pp. 482–495.

This conceptual paper uses social role theory and expectation states theory to explain the persistence of the glass ceiling for women leaders. States that the glass ceiling metaphor was introduced in 1986 in the *Wall Street Journal*. The glass ceiling will only disappear when women have greater social significance and there is a reduction in the power differential between men and women.

Wyn, J., Acker, S. and Richards, E. (2000) Making a Difference: Women in Management in Australian and Canadian Faculties of Education, in *Gender and Education*, Vol. 12, No. 4, pp. 435–447.

Concludes that the women have striven to make themselves different from the male norm but are conscious that they will not be fully assimilated into the university processes. They see themselves as forces for change. The new managerialism is identified with the challenge to feminist leaders.

Zorn, D. and Boler, M. (2007) Rethinking Emotions and Educational Leadership, in *International Journal of Leadership in Education*, Vol. 10, No. 2, pp. 137–151.

Summarizes research on emotions and educational leadership but uses feminist analysis, particularly relating to shame and gender, relating this to power and showing that shame is socially formed. Argues that emotion should be foregrounded in discussion of educational theory and practice.

Backlash to feminism and advances for women

Banyard, K. (2010) *The Equality Illusion: The Truth about Men and Women Today*, London, Faber and Faber.

The voice of the Fawcett Society, countering the public perception that women are now equal and there are no more battles to be won.

Burke, Ronald J. (2005) Backlash in the Workplace, in *Women in Management Review*, Vol. 20, No. 3, pp. 165–176.

This exploratory study examined backlash in the workplace. Backlash was considered in terms of employee views on how much their employer had done to support the advancement of four groups (women, disabled, aboriginal people, racial/visible minorities) and then whether it was too much, about right or too little.

Gaskell, J. and Taylor, S. (2003) The Women's Movement in Canadian and Australian Education: From Liberation and Sexism to Boys and Social Justice, in *Gender and Education*, Vol. 15, No. 2, pp. 151–168.

A comparative analysis of the ways in which the women's movement effected change in Australia and Canada 1970–2000. Shows that there has been a shift in the discourse away from women's liberation to boys as a problem and social justice for ethnic minorities.

Woodfield, R. (2007) *What Women Want from Work: Gender and Occupational Choice in the 21st Century*, York Studies on Women and Men, Basingstoke, Palgrave MacMillan.

Analyses occupational segregation, horizontal and vertical. Points out that if we take into account the overall diverse effects of occupational segregation women could be seen to be advantaged as they are concentrated in the middle to lower ranks but not often in the lowest occupational categories. Men's occupations are more polarized. Narrative accounts from women firefighters and teachers found that feminism did not 'speak' to them but that they felt they were individually responsible for their lives.

Young, M.D. (2005) Shifting Away from Women's Issues in Educational Leadership in the US: Evidence of a Backlash, in *International Studies in Educational Administration*, Vol. 33, No. 2, pp. 31–42.

Considers that we are experiencing a backlash and slippage in women's equality overall and in the field of education.

Identities

[Many of the articles in this sub-section are also relevant to 'barriers to progress']

Barrett, M. and Davidson, M.J. (2006) *Gender and Communication at Work*, Aldershot, Ashgate. Chapter 11 Baxter J. 'Putting Gender in its place: A Case Study on Constructing Speaker Identities in a Management Meeting'.

[For details see 'leadership and gender stereotypes' and 'gendered leadership discourses']

Bradbury, L. and Gunter, H. (2006) Dialogic Identities: The Experiences of Women who Are Head Teachers and Mothers in English Primary Schools, in *School Leadership and Management*, Vol. 26, No. 5, pp. 489–504.

An interview-based study with 20 women head teachers showing how their dual identities as mothers and head teachers are in constant negotiation. Guilt is a key feature of their lives as they live within contradictory settings.

Davey, K.M. (2008) Women's Accounts of Organizational Politics as a Gendering Process, in *Gender Work and Organization*, Vol. 15, No. 6, pp. 650–671.

Aims to explore changes in identity described by women joining male-dominated organizations.

Gill, J., Mills, J., Franzway, S. and Sharp, R. (2008) 'Oh You Must be very Clever!' High-Achieving Women, Professional Power and the Ongoing Negotiation of Workplace Identity, in *Gender and Education*, Vol. 20, No. 3, pp. 223–236.

Of 41 women engineers, most were uncomfortable in the masculine domain of engineering but women were aware of the advantage connected with their minority position.

Powell, A., Bagilhole, B. and Dainty, A. (2009) How Women Engineers Do and Undo Gender: Consequences for Gender Equality, in *Gender, Work and Organization*, Vol. 16, No. 4, pp. 411–428.

Found that women engineers 'perform' gender in a way that does not challenge the male image of engineering.

Pullen, A. and Rhodes, C. (2008) 'It's All About Me!': Gendered Narcissism and Leaders' Identity Work, in *Leadership*, Vol. 4, No. 1, pp. 5–25.

Applies theory of narcissism to identify four ideal types illustrated by research data from a project investigating managerial identity work at times of organizational change including masculine stereotypical qualities (narcissistic in a traditional masculine form) and a feminine type (feminine/defensive Echo).

Olsson, S. and Walker, R. (2004) 'The Wo-men and the Boys': Patterns of Identification and Differentiation in Senior Women Executives' Representations of Career Identity, in *Women in Management Review*, Vol. 19, No. 5, pp. 244–251.

Research into 'corporate masculinity' suggests that executive men position their difference, status and power through discourses by which they differentiate themselves from women. Findings suggest that women engage in comparable processes of identification often asserting female difference that includes distinctions between 'the wo-men and the boys'.

Priola, V. (2004) Gender and Feminine Identities - Women as Managers in a UK Academic Institution, in *Women in Management Review*, Vol. 19, No. 8, pp. 421–430.

Considers gender identities in higher education in a school that was unusual because women held the majority of senior managerial posts. It appeared that the construction of femininities is mainly around four (stereo)typical aspects generally associated with feminine management practices (multi-tasking, supporting and nurturing, people and communication skills, and teamwork).

Schnurr, S. (2008) Surviving in a Man's World with a Sense of Humour: An Analysis of Women Leaders' Use of Humour at Work, in *Leadership*, Vol. 4, No. 3, pp. 299–319.

Draws on discourse data in two New Zealand organizations to show how women leaders skilfully employ humour to portray themselves as leaders while also performing their gender identities.

Sinclair, A. (2005) Body Possibilities in Leadership, in *Leadership*, Vol. 1, No. 4, pp. 387–406.

Stresses the importance of the body in leadership, taking two case examples: a white woman police chief and an Aboriginal man head teacher. She feels that males are regarded as 'bodiless'.

Wilkinson, J. and Blackmore, J. (2008) Re-presenting Women and Leadership: A Methodological Journey, in *International Journal of Qualitative Studies in Education*, Vol. 21, No. 2, pp. 123–136.

Concludes that it is necessary to draw on different methodological per-spectives to understand the ways in which women's leadership identity is formed.

Young, P. (2004) Leadership and Gender in Higher Education: A Case Study, in *Journal of Further and Higher Education*, Vol. 28, No. 1, pp. 95–106.

Reports on triangulated leadership styles exhibited by leaders in HE. Showed that women exhibited attitudes in keeping with male gender paradigms (Gray, 1993; Coleman, 2002) while men showed female paradigm identification.

Work/family balance

Coronel, J.M., Moreno, E. and Carrasco, M.J. (2010) Work-family Conflicts and the Organizational Work Culture as Barriers to Women Educational Managers, in *Gender, Work and Organization*, Vol. 17, No. 2, pp. 219–239.

[Also relevant to section on 'barriers to progress']

Barriers to women educational managers in Spain are seen to be lack of sup-port, role conflict through family responsibilities and organizational work culture.

Ellison, G., Barkder, A. and Kulasuriya, T. (2009) *Work and Care: A Study of Modern Parents, Research Report 15*, Manchester, Equality and Human Rights Commission.

Reports on research conducted in relation to work and parenthood.

Guillaume, C. and Pochic, S. (2009) What would You Sacrifice? Access to Top Management and the Work-life Balance, in *Gender, Work and Organization*, Vol. 16, No. 1, pp. 14–36.

Issues of work/life balance are addressed from the points of view of the individual and the firm.

Hegewisch, A. (2009) *Flexible working policies: a comparative review. Research Report 16*. Manchester, Equality and Human Rights Commission.

Reports on flexible working practices in the UK, Netherlands, Germany and New South Wales.

Oplatka, I. and Tamis, V. (2009) I Don't Want to be a School Head, in *Educational Management, Administration and Leadership*, Vol. 37, No. 2, pp. 216–238.

Traces the stories of 25 Israeli women deputy heads teachers who do not aspire to headship.

Scott, J., Dex, S. and Joshi, H. (eds) (2008) *Women and Employment: Changing Lives and New Challenges*, Cheltenham, Edward Elgar.

[For details see earlier section on general background]

Seay, S. (2010) A Comparison of Family Care Responsibilities of First-generation and Non-first-generation Female Administrators in the Academy, in *Educational Management, Administration and Leadership* Vol. 38, No. 5, pp. 563–577.

[Also relevant for 'impact of gender equity policies']

Concludes that family-friendly workplace policies that include consideration of coverage for elderly parents are helpful for first generation women in senior roles.

Smithson, J. and Stockoe, E.H. (2005) Discourses of Work-Life Balance: Negotiating 'Genderblind' terms in Organizations, in *Gender Work and Organizations*, Vol. 12, No. 2, pp. 147–168.

Interesting study of the use of language in discussing work life balance in banking and finance, showing how the apparent acceptance of equality for men and women in terms of childcare and maternity leave is not really the case. Introduces the concept of 'macho maternity', when women take off only two or three weeks for maternity leave.

Wood, G.J. and Newton, J. (2006) Childlessness and Women Managers: 'Choice', Context and Discourses, in *Gender, Work and Organization*. Vol. 13, No. 4. pp. 338–358.

Discusses issues of agency in relation to childlessness of female managers in Australia. There is a recognition of the difficulties caused by the long work hours culture but that there are many aspects of the decision to be childless.

Barriers created by other women: the 'queen bee' syndrome

Mavin, S. (2006) Venus Envy 2: Sisterhood, Queen Bees and Female Misogyny in Management, in *Women in Management Review,* Vol. 21, No. 5, pp. 349–364.

Challenges assumptions of solidarity and aims to analyse empirical data to explore negative relations between women in management. Senior women recognize barriers facing women in management but they do not want to take a stance on this. This does not make them 'queen bees'; the women acknowledge the impact of their gendered context. The paper highlights how the gendered social order encourages differences between women.

Rindfleish, J. (2000) Senior Management Women in Australia: Diverse Perspectives, in *Women in Management Review,* Vol. 15, No. 4, pp. 172–180.

After analysis of interviews four broad categories were developed: 'conservatives', 'moderates', 'reluctant feminists' and 'definite feminists'. Two-thirds of respondents fell into categories representing women who did not hold views resembling those of 'queen bees'. The other one-third of the women were in the two categories that more closely resembled 'queen bees'.

Rindfleish, J. and Sheridan A. (2003) No Change from Within: Senior Women Managers' Response to Gendered Organizational Structures, in *Women in Management Review* Vol. 18, No. 6, pp. 299–310.

Research in Australia suggests that senior women see the need for change but have not used their role in senior management as a means of challenging gendered structures. Therefore it may be wrong to assume that change will come about simply through increasing numbers of women in management.

Warning, R. and Buchanan, F.R. (2009) An Exploration of Unspoken Bias: Women who Work for Women, in *Gender in Management: An International Journal,* Vol. 24, No. 2, pp. 131–149.

An exploratory study that seems to indicate that women do not like working for other women.

This annotated bibliography is based on an earlier version (Coleman, M. (2008a) *Annotated Bibliography: Support and Development of Women Senior Leaders at Work.* www.wlecentre.ac.uk/cms/files/projectreports/annotated_ bibliography_support_and_development_for_women_senior_leaders_at_ work.pdf. This was one of the outcomes of a research project funded by WLE (Work-based Learning for Education Professionals: A Centre for Excellence at the Institute of Education, University of London).

Index

Abramsky, Jenny, 119
advantages of being a woman, 43, 123–124, 127
affirmative action, 11, 14, 154, 200–202
see also positive discrimination
ageism, see under discrimination
agency, individual/personal, 47–53, 150
Alexander, Helen, 5
androgyny/ous, 9, 156–157
Ashridge Business School, 74

Bailey, Sly, 122
Boaden, Helen, 115–121
boards (of directors)/board membership, 3, 20–21, 24, 36, 42, 52, 70, 132, 149, 157, 159, 160
see also FTSE 100/250 companies/ FTSE listed
bullying, 15, 30, 145
business case for women on boards, 158–159

capital, gender, 42
human, 14, 52, 59
see also qualifications
social, 14, 59, 166
career model/plan, male, 99, 106–107, 127
of successful women, 99–101
Catalyst, 74
childcare, 96–99, 124–125, 134, 138, 144, 152–153, 154
City of London, 15, 72, 74
Livery Companies, 72
coaching, 63–65
see also mentoring, and coaching; role models
communication skills, 54
styles, 19
confidence, 47–48, 123
lack of, 39, 48, 116

Cranfield, Centre for Developing Women Business Leaders, 74
culture, long hours, 26, 103–104, 139
male/macho, 13, 20–23, 25–27, 33, 149, 159
and class, 142–143
managerial/ist, 22, 150
supportive, 58, 118

discrimination, 19, 27, 28, 95, 148
and age/ageism, 33–35, 117
and motherhood, 97
and pay/pay gap, 31–33, 120, 122, 203–204
Drew, Marisa, 115, 127–132

EHRC (Equality and Human Rights Commission), 3, 31
equal opportunities, 8, 157, 200–202
legislation, 6, 95, 140, 154
Equal Opportunities Commission, 11
Equal Pay Act (1970), see Equal Opportunities, legislation
ethnicity/ethnic minorities, 11, 35
European Work Directive, the, 134

Fawcett Society, the, 11, 74
femininity/competence bind, 37, 149
feminism
attitude to, including backlash, 47, 155–157, 213
cultural, 9, 156
first-wave, 8
post modern/post structural, 9, 10
second wave, 8–10, 76, 87
third wave, 9–10
feminist, 120
Fernandes, Helen, 115, 132–136
flexible working, 111–112, 139, 153, 161, 166–168
(Right to Request and Duty to Consider), 96, 154
see also scope creep

Fortune 500, 20
Forum UK, 75, 77, 165
FTSE 100/250 companies/FTSE listed,
    3, 13, 20, 22, 27, 61, 122, 159,
    160, 163
  Cross-Company Mentoring
    Programme, 61, 162
  see also boards (of directors)/board
    membership
Furse, Clara, 5

gatekeepers, 29, 160
gender barriers, 29, 205–213
  see also discrimination, glass
    ceiling, sexism
gender roles, 92
gender stereotypes, 13, 15, 18, 23,
    32, 35–38, 39, 93, 98, 116, 128,
    132, 149, 150
  and working differently, 39–42
  see also leadership, feminine/
    gendered leadership
glass ceiling, 10, 12, 13, 15, 18, 27–8,
    157, 158
  see also discrimination
glass cliff, 31, 46
Government Equalities Office, 74

Hanratty, Judith, 115, 140–146
Harman, Harriet, 5
Hunt, Jay, 120

identities, 107, 214–215
Institute of Practitioners in
    Advertising, 85
Intuition/trusting instincts, 117, 130

Kingsmill, Denise, 125
Koestler, Arthur, 7

labyrinth, 27
Lancaster University, Academy
    for Gender Diversity and
    Leadership, 74
Lane Fox, Martha, 5
leadership, 37
  feminine/gendered leadership, 40,
    42, 53–55, 56–57, 123, 150
  and values, 41–42, 56–57

legislation, *see* Equal Opportunities

male/macho culture, *see* culture
'marzipan layer', 61, 159, 162
maternity leave, 95, 96, 99–100,
    110–111, 125–126, 151–152, 162
mentoring, 59–62, 128, 129
  others, 65–66
  and coaching, 14, 16, 161–162,
    197–198, *see also* coaching, role
    models
micro-politics, 31
mobility, *see* travel
Morrissey, Helena, 5

networks/networking, 118, 142,
    163–166, 194–197
  expressive, 69
  informal, 88–90
  instrumental, 71–72
  male, 23–24, 27, 41, 72–73, 149
  'old boys'/ boys, 37, 72
  theories of, 80–81
  types of, 69
  see also support/supportive,
    networks, women only/
    all-women
networks, women only/all-women,
    73–88
  antipathy to, 85–87
  emergent/prescribed, 73
  exercising 'voice', 84–85
  offering professional development,
    see professional development
  in the USA, 87–88
New Zealand, 141, 142, 143, 144, 145
newspapers, attitudes to women, 4–6
non-executive directors (NEDs), 34,
    59, 159, 160, 163
Norway, 12, 20, 159

Opportunity Now, 66, 67, 74, 155, 162

part-time work, 101–103, 154, 166–168
  see also scope creep
pay gap, *see* discrimination
Peace, Carol, 115, 136–140
positive discrimination, 28
  see also affirmative action

preference theory, 13–14, 94
professional development, 59, 82–84

qualifications, importance of, 52–53,
129, 137
see also capital, gender, human
'queen bee', 157, 217

recommendations for employers,
173–174
for individual women, 171–173
representation of women at top levels,
2–5
role models, 39, 63, 113, 126, 131,
135, 161, 162–163
see also mentoring, coaching

Sapphire Partners, 167
'scope creep', 102, 167
see also flexible working, part-time
work
Segregation/differentiation of jobs,
horizontal, 22, 94, 95
vertical, 22, 93
Sex Discrimination Act (1975), *see*
equal opportunities legislation
sexism/ist, 13, 21, 28, 30, 136
new form of, 36, 149–150
see also discrimination, glass ceiling
sexual harassment, 121
Sloman, Anne, 120
Sotomayor, Sonia, 5
Spain, 159

Spring, Stevie, 115, 121–127
stereotypes, *see* gender stereotypes
support/supportive
emotional, 78
of family/partner, 107–110, 131, 138
instrumental, 80
see also culture, mentoring,
coaching, networks/networking
Sweden, 159
SWISS (Senior Women in Secondary
Schools), 75, 76, 138, 164

teams and gender, 42, 53–54, 158,
199–200
technology/information technology,
139, 144, 145, 161, 168–170
travel, 26, 104–105
TTGC (Through the Glass Ceiling),
75, 77, 164

values in leadership, *see* leadership

WACL (Women in Advertising and
Communications in London),
75, 76, 165
WinS (Women in Surgery-part of the
Royal College of Surgeons of
England), 75, 77, 132, 134, 164
women's lib, 11
see also feminism
work/family balance (work/life
balance), 110–113, 119, 124,
153, 154, 172–173, 215–216